THE
REENGINEERING
REVOLUTION

MICHAEL HAMMER IS THE COAUTHOR OF
REENGINEERING THE CORPORATION

THE REENGINEERING REVOLUTION

A Handbook

MICHAEL HAMMER
AND STEVEN A. STANTON

 HarperBusiness
A Division of HarperCollinsPublishers

HarperCollins books may be purchased for educational, business, or sales promotional use. For information please write: Special Markets Department, HarperCollins Publishers, Inc., 10 East 53rd Street, New York, NY 10022.

FIRST EDITION

Designed by Irving Perkins Associates

Library of Congress Cataloging-in-Publication Data

Hammer, Michael, 1948–
    The reengineering revolution / Michael Hammer and Steven Stanton. — 1st ed.
        p. cm.
    Includes index.
    ISBN 0-88730-736-1
    1. Organizational change—Management.   2. Industrial management.
    I. Stanton, Steven. II. Title.
    HD58.8.H355   1994
    658.4'06—dc20   95–73

95 96 97 98 99 ❖/RRD 10 9 8 7 6 5 4 3 2 1

To my students—past, present, and future
From the Talmud: Rabbi Judah said, I have
learned much from my teachers, more from my
colleagues, but most from my students

M.H.

To my wonderful wife, Patricia, for her constant love and
support, and to my extraordinary children Alec and
Graham, for teaching me the most important lessons

S.A.S.

Contents

Acknowledgments

No book is created solely by its authors, and a great many people have made important contributions to this one. Our first thanks must go to individuals who shared their reengineering experiences with us, even when they may not have been sure as to what we would do with them: Donald LaTorre and Stephen Pook of Engelhard, John Carl of Amoco, Therese Maloney and Gary Gregg of Liberty Mutual, Frank Everett of Vortex Industries, Everett Page of Matthew Thornton Health Care, Dick Chandler of Sunrise Medical, Tim Barnhart of Federal Management Partners, Jim Bernards of Facilitation Inc., E. Kane Casani of the Jet Propulsion Laboratory, Professor Marc Brettler of Brandeis University, Professor James Bruce of MIT, Bruce Marlow of Progressive Insurance, Mark Feighner of GTE, Fred Musone of Federal Mogul, Ron Compton of Aetna Life & Casualty, Janis Jesse of Texas Instruments, David Turner of Hitachi Data Systems, Reverend John Minogue of De Paul University, Chris Scott of Stanford University, Janis Del Sesto of the Boston Lyric Opera Company, Jill Vales of Certified Vacations, and Ted Ramstad of Scott Paper, as well as numerous others who prefer to remain nameless. Their experiences, both positive and painful, were the raw material for this book; they are the true architects of reengineering.

We also owe a debt of gratitude to our colleagues and coworkers who served as sounding boards for the early versions of our ideas and whose comments and critiques improved them greatly. Among them we especially want to mention Harry Bloom, Phil Bodrock, John Randolph, Bob Morison, Jim Hall, and Walter Popper.

Many people played important roles in this book's evolution from an outline to a completed manuscript. We want to thank Ellen Mary Carr, Bill Salamenta, Kathleen McQuaid, Denise Dillon, Kathleen Paggi, Linda Mellen, and Hannah Will of Hammer and Company, each of whom stepped into the breach at many a critical juncture. Our literary agent, Bob Barnett, was both an effective advocate and a wise counselor, while Adrian Zackheim and Jack McKeown of HarperCollins were true collaborators in this project from the beginning. Richard Lourie, Erik Hansen, George Feifer, and Donna Sammons Carpenter of Woodworks, Inc., provided outstanding editorial assistance in improving the coherence and readability of the manuscript throughout its development.

But our deepest note of gratitude is reserved for the attendees of our reengineering classes and seminars. Their questions and suggestions shaped and refined this material and helped us recognize what would be of greatest interest and value to our readers. They were our inspiration; we hope that this book is worthy of them.

A Guide to the Revolution

When *Reengineering the Corporation* was published in 1993, no one suspected how prophetic its subtitle would turn out to be. But by mid-1994, reengineering was in full cry around the world, and it seemed fair to say that the book was indeed *A Manifesto for Business Revolution*. In the year and a half after publication, more than 1.7 million copies were sold worldwide, including some three-quarters of a million in the United States and a quarter-million in Japan. The book has been translated into nineteen languages, including Finnish, Hebrew, and Thai.

But people have not just been reading about reengineering—they have also been *doing* it. Two of the "Big Six"—the major accounting and consultancy firms—conducted separate studies in 1994 and reached virtually identical conclusions: that between 75 and 80 percent of America's largest companies had already begun reengineering and would be increasing their commitment to it over the next few years. A leading market research firm has estimated that U.S. corporations would spend more than $7 billion on reengineering in 1994. This figure includes only expenditures for personnel and consulting services; if required technology investments are included, the figure balloons to over $30 billion. These figures are expected to grow by 20 percent per annum for the next three years.

These extraordinary numbers are mirrored in our own business, that of preparing people for the revolution through education and training. Over the last three years, we have trained more than 10,000 people from more than a thousand of the world's leading corporations in the techniques of reengineering.

Whether they are just reading about it or actually doing it, everyone seems to be talking about it. "Reengineering" has gone from being a neologism to a standard entry in the business lexicon. The term has become so prevalent that it's no longer enclosed in quotes; it is so established in our daily vocabulary that few authors who use it feel a need to define it. And use it they do.

It's nearly impossible to pick up a business publication without encountering an article on the subject. The number of articles with "reengineering" in the title increased from 10 in 1990 to well over 800 in 1994. The Lexis/Nexis electronic database of the daily press contains over 5,000 references to "reengineering" during a six-month period in 1994. Perhaps the most authoritative certification that a new phenomenon has become part of the culture is its appearance in comic strips. For this, the ultimate accolade, please see below.

DILBERT reprinted by permission of UFS, INC.

But neither reading nor talking nor even doing are the true measures of success. For that, we must turn to results; and the results have been remarkable. A few cases in point:

- American Express has reported reducing its annual costs by over $1 billion through reengineering.

- AT&T's Global Business Communications Systems unit turned a nine-figure loss into a nine-figure profit by reengineering its processes for manufacturing, servicing, and order fulfillment.
- Reengineering has enabled the Semiconductor Group of Texas Instruments to reduce the cycle time of its order fulfillment process for integrated circuits by more than half, which has thrust it from worst to first in customer satisfaction and helped it to achieve record financial results.
- Progressive Insurance reduced the cycle time of its claims process from weeks to days, dramatically improving customer satisfaction while considerably reducing costs, fraud, and litigation. Reengineering has helped the company increase its revenue per employee by over 70 percent.

These results are not isolated or atypical triumphs. Quite the contrary. The list of organizations that have already achieved major reengineering success includes Hewlett-Packard, Johnson & Johnson, PepsiCo, Chrysler, Ford, Shell Oil, EDS, Trane, American Standard, GTE, Agway, Hallmark, Engelhard, Amoco Oil, Liberty Mutual Insurance, Aetna Life & Casualty, Showtime Networks, MTV, Brooklyn Union Gas, the Social Security Administration, and many, many more.

We will review the experiences of some of these companies in later chapters. But reengineering hasn't stopped with the giants of American industry. More modest companies, some as small as fifty employees and a few million dollars in sales, have used reengineering to save themselves from disaster or to fuel further growth. Nor is reengineering a purely American phenomenon. People in Europe, Latin America, and Asia have also read the literature, attended our seminars, and begun to reengineer their companies' processes.

It is hard to think of a recent development in the world of

business that more deserves to be called a "revolution." Reengineering is clearly an idea whose time has come. That's the good news. The bad news is that reengineering has not been an unqualified success. There are numerous reports in the press of reengineering "failures." While many of these reports are misleading or even mistaken, it is nonetheless true that many companies have undertaken reengineering efforts, only to abandon them with little or no positive result. Even the concept of reengineering is widely misunderstood. Many have come to read it as a code word for layoffs and plant closings. Others dismiss it as merely the latest consultant's buzzword designed to confuse gullible management.

These failures are significant. They reflect a fundamental fact of reengineering: It is very, very difficult to do. As one early proponent of reengineering has put it, "Reengineering isn't mysterious. It's just hard." How could it be otherwise? Reengineering is an undertaking essentially unprecedented in modern business: the complete reinvention of how work is done and of all the attendant aspects of an organization (job designs, organizational structures, management systems, and the like). Few—if any—organizations have experience with such an ambitious endeavor. It is inevitable that many will stumble on this path. Merely setting off on the road to reengineering does not guarantee reaching the destination.

It is reengineering's failures that have led us to write this book.

For the last eight years—from the time when the term "reengineering" was known only to a handful of visionaries and seemed unlikely to become a household word—we've had the opportunity to observe and work with a great many companies attempting to put the concept into practice. Some have succeeded. Some have not. From each, we have learned important lessons. We have learned the ingredients of success and how to recognize the many snares for the unwary and the traps for the uninformed. We have learned to distinguish what works from what does not, to differentiate futile techniques from the promising and the proven.

This book is a distillation of what we have learned. Our aim is to give you, the reader, the benefit of the experiences of a great many companies without having to endure those experiences yourselves. This book is not about theory or concept; it is about practices, successful ones to emulate and unsuccessful ones to avoid. Our overarching goal is to help you succeed at reengineering.

Many readers of *Reengineering the Corporation* have told us that they were intrigued and excited by the concept of reengineering but were unsure how to make it a reality in their own organizations. This book is for them and for everyone else concerned with realizing the potential of this idea.

We wish we could provide an all-encompassing formula whose rote application would guarantee success, but alas, one does not exist. Perhaps such a methodology will be established one day, but that day is not nigh. Reengineering is not yet a science; but, fortunately, it is also no longer an art. It does not require genius, brilliance, or a rare degree of talent. Ability, stamina, and knowledge will suffice. It might be most accurate to call reengineering a *craft*. Although it requires the aptitude of an adept artisan, an artisan uses means and methods that can be studied, learned, adapted, and practiced.

And so, what we offer here is a guide to practical action. This book is a handbook, a tool kit, a compendium of techniques and tricks of the trade for addressing the key issues and problems that a reengineering effort will confront.

We are all still pioneers in the field of reengineering. Every one of you will encounter a unique problem, explore new territory, push the envelope of our collective knowledge. Moreover, each of you will be working in your company's unique environment. We cannot anticipate every situation that you will face or provide you with instructions for every contingency. Rather, we hope to provide a set of principles that will stand you in good stead no matter what you confront.

This book has three main parts. In the first, "The Elements of Success," we outline the basic requisites for embarking on the reengineering journey and indicate some of its major hazards. A self-assessment test helps you evaluate your own organization's readiness for this adventure.

The second part, "Making It Work," presents a number of specific techniques for solving key problems in reengineering implementation. These range from tools for generating out-of-the-box ideas to methods for counteracting individuals trying to derail your efforts.

The third part, "Tales from the Road," consists of a series of case studies and vignettes that explore in detail how reengineering has worked—or has not—at various companies. These reports from the front lines serve as a counterpoint to the prescriptive material in the first two parts.

A useful metaphor for this book is that it is a Swiss Army knife: a number of useful tools that share a housing. It is not necessary to read this book in a linear, front-to-back order. Feel free to jump around, concentrating on what will help you solve the problems you are facing today. We also hope that you will return to these tools repeatedly during the course of your journey.

A note on the cartoons: Scott Adams is a business philosopher whose medium is the comic strip. He also works for a major telecommunications company, where his daily experiences and observations provide his inspiration. We have anointed Adams as the poet laureate of reengineering. His nationally syndicated comic strip, *Dilbert,* is a daily reminder of the foibles of organizations and why they need to reengineer in the first place. One *Dilbert* strip contains more truth than a shelf of business-school case studies. We have selected a few of our favorites to illustrate these chapters, and we hope you enjoy them as much as we do.

PART I

The Elements of Success

CHAPTER 1

What You Need to Know to Read This Book

The purpose of this book is to help you succeed at reengineering. It presumes that you know what reengineering is. But just to be safe, let's have a quick refresher.

This is particularly important because over the past few years the term "reengineering" has been heavily overused, misused, and simply abused. So let's begin at the beginning—with the definition.

Reengineering: The Official Definition

The fundamental rethinking and *radical redesign* of business *processes* to bring about *dramatic* improvements in performance.

There are four key words in this definition. Let's start near the end, with the concept of "dramatic" improvement. Reengineering is not about making marginal improvements to your business. It is not about making things 5 percent or 10 percent better. It is about making quantum leaps in performance, achieving breakthroughs. Performance can be measured in various ways—reduced costs, increased speed, greater accuracy. The choice is yours, depending upon what is important to your business. The hallmark of reengineering is always a dramatic breakthrough in performance.

The second key word is "radical." Radical means going to the root of things. Reengineering is not about improving what already exists. Rather, it is about throwing it away and starting over; beginning with the proverbial clean slate and reinventing how you do your work. Some may find this notion extreme, even dangerous. But we are not alone in taking such a strong stance.

Listen to Edwin Artzt, the CEO of Procter & Gamble, the $30 billion manufacturer of consumer goods. When P&G launched a reengineering effort in 1993, Artzt kicked it off with the question: "If Procter & Gamble did not exist today, how would we create it?" This question is not what we are accustomed to hearing from senior executives. It would be more typical if he had stressed P&G's hundred years of success, its dominance of many product categories, its unparalleled growth, and its strength in marketing and advertising. Instead, he said: "We are going to take this place apart brick by brick and put it back together again." That's not a bad evocation of reengineering.

The third key word in the definition is "process." By a process, we mean a group of related tasks that together create value for a customer. For example, order fulfillment is a process, comprising a series of tasks: receiving the order, entering it into a computer, checking the customer's credit, allocating inventory from stock, picking the inventory out of the warehouse, packing it in a box, loading the box into the truck, and so on. Not one of these activities is of the slightest interest or value to the customer. The customer's only concern is with the end result—the delivered goods, created by the sum total of all these related activities.

In traditional organizations, processes are orphans. Fragmented across many organizational units, they are effectively invisible and essentially unmanaged. Yet processes are at the very heart of every enterprise. They are the means by which companies create value for their customers.

If filling a customer's order takes a long time, usually it is not because it takes a long time to perform the required tasks. Rather, it is the handoffs between the tasks that devour time and money. Reengineering says that such fragmentation lies at the heart of our performance problems and that the only way to achieve dramatic performance improvement is by holistically addressing our end-to-end processes.

The fourth key word in the definition is "redesign." Reengineering is about the design of how work is done. We often think of design as applying only to products. Yet, reengineering is based on the premise that the design of processes—how work is done—is of essential importance. Your employees may be smart and capable, well trained, highly motivated, and encouraged to perform by all manner of incentives. But if the work they are doing is poorly conceived and poorly designed, it will not be well executed. The starting point for organizational success is well-designed processes.

Reengineering the Corporation offered numerous examples of reengineered processes. We offer here two new examples— GTE and Federal Mogul—to illustrate how reengineering actually works.

THE GTE EXPERIENCE

GTE is the largest provider of local telephone service in the United States, with its main customer bases in California, Florida, and Texas. As of this writing, GTE is in the midst of a massive reengineering effort to reinvent nearly the entire company in response to new technology, a new regulatory environment, and to constantly changing—and tougher— competition.

One area in which reengineering has already made a significant impact is the maintenance and repair process. If you are a GTE customer and your phone isn't working, you call the company and report the problem. In the old days, you were connected to a repair clerk. The repair clerk took down your information, but didn't have the tools, training, or authority to do much more than that. The information was then passed off to someone called a line tester, who checked to see if there was a problem in GTE's central office switch or in its lines. If so, the line tester passed the information on to a central office technician or a dispatcher, who in turn assigned the case to a service technician who eventually arrived at your premises to repair the equipment.

From the customer's point of view, this process was very unsatisfactory because of its high degree of uncertainty. When your phone is out of order, the first thing you want to know is when service will be restored. The problem was that the repair clerk was able to make a commitment as to when phone service would be restored, but could take no further action. And, given the large number of handoffs, getting your phone working again would almost certainly take more time than you'd like.

GTE has reengineered this process. Now, maintenance and repair is handled from end to end by one person, known as a customer care advocate. When you call to report your problem, you speak to an advocate who has the ability and the tools to test the line, modify central office software, or locate the problem on the network—all while still talking with the customer. In many cases, it is possible for the advocate to diagnose and solve the problem while you are still on the phone. If it cannot be fixed at once, the advocate then acts as a dispatcher, checking the schedules of the service technicians and informing you when one will come to your home or office.

Performance has improved dramatically. Repairs that once

took hours now take minutes. Putting itself in the customer's place, GTE understood that a key measure of satisfaction was the percentage of problems fixed by the person the customer spoke to; under the old process, only one-half of 1 percent were. Under the new process, the advocate is now able to resolve over 40 percent of customer problems while the customer is still on the line. GTE expects to reach its goal of resolving 70 percent of customer problems on a "one-touch" basis by 1998.

This simple case illustrates all aspects of our definition. It is also worth noting that the reengineering was driven from a customer-first perspective, another of the key elements of reengineering. The company found out what the customer wanted and determined how the organization could best go about achieving it.

FEDERAL MOGUL

GTE is a service company. Let's look at a company that produces a product—Federal Mogul, a $1.8 billion manufacturer and distributor of auto parts. One of the company's key processes is sample development. It begins when an auto manufacturer gives Federal Mogul and its competitors the specifications of a component for a newly designed automobile. At that point, Federal Mogul and the competitors race to design and manufacture samples of this new design, which they must submit to the car company for evaluation and testing in order to win the contract to make it.

Under Federal Mogul's old process, the sales representative first visited the customer—the auto manufacturer—to acquire the specifications for the part. The specifications were then handed off to an engineer who designed the part. Then the design had to be manufactured. One of the company's plants was selected for manufacturing, based on available capacity; the design was sent there by U.S. mail. At the plant, the design first went to the "toolroom." There, the tools to manufacture the part were designed and produced. The tools next went to the manufacturing floor, where the metal was formed, the rubber was molded, and the part assembled; the finished part was then delivered to the customer.

This process typically took twenty weeks. Federal Mogul's worst competitor could do the same work in ten weeks; its best competitor could do it in six weeks. Auto companies give feedback on proposed designs shortly after receiving them; thus, the swiftest competitor had a chance at several revisions before Federal Mogul even came in with its first try. Needless to say, Federal Mogul was not winning many orders.

Enter reengineering. Once again, as at GTE, the entire process was rethought. As a result, a sales rep and an engineer now visit customers as a team. This avoids the ambiguities and misunderstandings that occurred when the sales rep handed off specifications to the engineer. The engineer then goes to work on the design. But now the engineer's work has been reorganized to take into account a very fundamental fact—that most designs are actually variations of existing parts.

Under the old approach, the engineer sat down and designed every part from scratch. Today, he or she first checks a computerized database to see if a part exists with the same shape. If so, the parameters of the new part are fed into the computer system, and the computer automatically reconfigures the existing part to meet the new specifications. To quote one Federal Mogul manager, "What used to take us three days, we now do in a minute."

Another change is that the company no longer uses the U.S. mail system. Rather, all units—sales, engineering, and manufacturing—are connected by an electronic workflow system, so that everyone is instantaneously aware of everyone else's activities and needs.

Tooling is done differently as well. Under the old process, even if a plant had manufacturing capacity available, the equipment in the toolroom was often tied up, resulting in significant delays. Today, the company no longer operates under the assumption that a sample must be tooled in the same plant where it will be manufactured. If a plant's toolroom is backed up, toolrooms at other plants are checked for availability. The tools are then made at one of these other plants and brought back to the original plant for use in making the sample. This may seem obvious, but in the past it was unthinkable.

Finally, everyone involved—sales, engineering, tooling, manufacturing—is measured and rewarded on a common basis: the performance of the end-to-end sample development process. This has eliminated the parochialism and incongruent goals of the old, fragmented organization.

The results of reengineering at Federal Mogul have been nothing short of astounding. The company has gone from a twenty-week to an eighteen-day cycle time. Its win rate on new proposals has gone up by a factor of four. This unit of the company has seen its profitability more than double.

The examples of GTE and Federal Mogul illustrate that reengineering is not a cookie cutter—no two processes look the same. Faced with different problems and needs, they assumed different shapes. In one case, the solution was to compress all the work into a single job (the customer care advocate); in the other, a disparate group of individuals were coalesced into a team by means of shared information and shared goals.

Yet in both cases, the focus was on improving total process performance, not task efficiency. In both cases, long-standing assumptions (about the need for specialization, about how tooling and design are done) were shattered, and the past abandoned. In both cases, the needs of the customer were the starting point for a complete reconsideration of how work was done. And in both cases, breakthroughs in performance were achieved.

WHAT REENGINEERING IS NOT

There are many widespread misconceptions about the nature of reengineering. Reengineering is not downsizing. Downsizing means getting rid of people and jobs to improve short-term financial results. Reengineering has nothing in common with that kind of superficial and reactive response to problems. Reengineering is about rethinking work from the ground up in order to eliminate work that is not necessary and to find better ways of doing work that is. Reengineering eliminates work, not jobs or people. It is true that in many cases, when you radically rethink your work, you may need fewer people to perform it. But that is not the essence or the intent of the undertaking.

Reengineering is also not "restructuring," usually a euphemism for moving boxes around an organizational chart or selling off some business units. Reengineering is centered on how work is done, not how an organization is structured. Reengineering is also not to be confused with automation. Even though technology plays an important role in reengineering, its role is to enable new process designs, not to provide new mechanisms for performing old ones.

Reengineering is also not a fad, not merely the latest in a long line of short-lived management panaceas, of ninety-day wonders, that promise the world but fail to deliver. Reengineering's distinctiveness has been established by the fact that it actually works, by the huge improvements that organizations around the world have achieved by applying its principles. Finally, reengineering is not more of the same. It is, in fact, a revolution, the most important one in business since the advent of the Industrial Revolution 150 years ago. Reengineering posits a radical new principle: that the design of work must be based not on hierarchical management and the specialization of labor but on end-to-end processes and the creation of value for the customer.

THE BUSINESS SYSTEM

While reengineering begins with process redesign, it does not end there. Radically changing processes inevitably has ripple effects on all other parts of the business. For example, at GTE, the redesigning of the service process entailed the creation of a new job—the customer care advocate. Different from any position that previously existed in the organization, it requires a person with a special background and a particular set of skills, and whose success is measured in terms of speed, customer satisfaction, and problem solving, rather than task efficiency and satisfying the boss.

Similarly, at Federal Mogul, the new sample development process has had dramatic impacts on how people are measured and rewarded, on their careers, on how they are organized, on the role of their managers, and on their basic value system.

These consequences are not accidental or coincidental; they are fundamental to reengineering. We see an organization as having four interrelated aspects. First are the processes, the mechanisms by which work is performed and value created. The design of business processes shapes the design of jobs and the kinds of people needed to perform them. These in turn give rise to an appropriate set of organizational structures and management systems for measuring, hiring, training, and developing these people. These systems in turn induce a set of attitudes, beliefs, and cultural norms about what is important; these support the performance of the process. Reengineering begins with process design, but inevitably moves through all facets of the organization. It leads to an organization that differs from the old one in all respects.

WHY REENGINEERING?

As one business leader has put it to us, "You don't reengineer unless you have to," and these days, almost everyone has to. In *Reengineering the Corporation*, the driving forces behind reengineering were characterized as the three Cs: customers, competition, and change. Customers have become much more sophisticated and demanding; they have a much greater range of alternatives, are much more knowledgeable about their own needs, and are exerting ever greater pressure on their suppliers. Competition, which at one time was local and relatively gentle, has become global and cutthroat. Whether in geopolitical realities, technology, or customer preferences, the pace of change is dizzying. What was unthinkable yesterday is routine today.

In a world of rapid flux, organizations must change their priorities from a traditional focus on planning, control, and managed growth, to emphasize speed, innovation, flexibility, quality, service, and cost. It is virtually impossible to retrofit organizations into this new reality. Reengineering is the only solution.

THE REENGINEERING CAST OF CHARACTERS

A variety of figures play important roles in reengineering. First and foremost is the reengineering leader, a senior individual who has both the authority and the commitment to launch an undertaking of this magnitude. Without committed leadership, efforts at such drastic change will quickly fizzle. Reengineering requires an understanding of processes in their entirety, a perspective not usually possessed by those at or near the front lines. The leader, whose role will be explored in more detail in chapter 3, does have that perspective. But the leader cannot do it alone.

The reengineering of a specific process is the responsibility of the process owner: a senior individual designated by the leader to have end-to-end responsibility for the process and its performance. In order to reengineer the process, the owner assembles a team comprising two sorts of individuals: insiders and outsiders. Insiders are people who work in the current process and bring knowledge, experience, and credibility to the team. They are counterbalanced by outsiders—people who know nothing about the existing process but can offer the creativity that flows from a fresh, objective perspective.

An organization seriously committed to reengineering will likely have a number of such process teams operating at the same time. It is the job of the reengineering czar to ensure that all these efforts are coordinated, facilitated, and supported. He or she provides guidance to each process owner and ensures that the various efforts are successful, not only individually but as a whole.

With this brief précis and these key terms in mind, let's begin our exploration of how to make reengineering succeed in your organization.

CHAPTER 2

The Top Ten Mistakes in Reengineering

The question we are most often asked about reengineering is this: What is the success rate? Pessimists prefer to phrase the question negatively, as: What is the failure rate? We find both versions troubling and misleading because of their use of the word "rate," which makes it sound as though the success or failure of reengineering were a matter of probability, like the yield of a chemical reaction. It suggests that if one began with 100 reengineering efforts, then a certain percent would inevitably succeed and the rest would inevitably fail. The implication is that reengineering success is largely a matter of luck, that it is out of the hands of those conducting the effort. This is dead wrong. Reengineering is deterministic, not probabilistic: The fate of every attempt is determined by the particular circumstances surrounding the specific effort, not by any set of aggregate statistics.

In *Reengineering the Corporation,* we estimated that between 50 and 70 percent of reengineering efforts were not successful in achieving the desired breakthrough performance. Unfortunately, this simple descriptive observation has been widely misinterpreted and transmogrified and distorted into a normative statement. In other words, many people think it means that 50 to 70 percent of all reengineering efforts *will* fail. Nothing could be further from the truth. There is no inherent success or failure rate for reengineering. The results depend entirely on the quality, intensity, and intelligence of the effort. Failure is not caused by cosmic rays, bad luck, or other factors outside of human control. Failure is caused by people who don't know what they're doing and who don't pursue reengineering the right way.

Success in reengineering does not require personal heroics, extraordinary talent or capability, or enormous amounts of good luck. The real key to reengineering success is staying focused and avoiding stupid mistakes. The overwhelming majority of reengineering failures can be traced to a very small number of underlying problems. Here, we must return to classical philosophy and distinguish between *proximate* and *underlying* causes. The proximate cause is the immediate source of a problem, while the underlying cause is the root source of the problem. If the proximate cause is the straw that breaks the camel's back, then the underlying cause is trying to load too much straw on the camel in the first place.

The proximate causes for reengineering failure are enormously diverse. Organizations have an amazing ability to find new ways of making mistakes. However, failure most often results from one underlying problem: The people engaged in the reengineering effort don't know what they are doing. They misconstrue or fail to comprehend the fundamental nature of reengineering. Their techniques are improvised or random, not based on practical experience. If you don't have a clear understanding of what reengineering is and how it works, you should hardly be surprised if your efforts end up in trouble.

Therefore, we have codified our secret to reengineering success into one short phrase: Don't fail. This is not as tautological as it sounds. This means that if you know what you are about and avoid the most common errors of reengineering, then there is every reason to expect you will succeed. The reengineering road runs through a minefield—but we can offer you a map of where most of the mines are located. What follows, then, is a review of the most commonly made mistakes in reengineering, a chart of the mines most frequently detonated by the unwary.

The first of these mistakes is to say you are reengineering without actually doing it. Many people complain to us: "You told us if we reengineered we'd achieve dramatic results, but we haven't achieved dramatic results." Upon examination it becomes clear they were never truly reengineering in the first place. They did something else and merely called it reengineering. Abraham Lincoln liked to pose the following riddle: If you call a horse's tail a leg, how many legs does the horse have? The answer is four; calling the tail a leg doesn't make it a leg. If you have not really committed to a reengineering effort, then saying you are reengineering won't make a dime's worth of difference. With the term suddenly fashionable, many people have simply taken last year's proposal that didn't make it through the budget cycle and slapped a reengineering label on it in order to get it approved.

Since the term "reengineering" is so accessible, a large number of unrelated ideas have been inappropriately labeled reengineering. Some are simply incremental quality improvements, some focus on functional rationalization, and others concern the implementation of new computer systems. Many of these ideas are valid and worthwhile, some are foolish and ill-advised, but none can achieve the dramatic breakthrough results that true reengineering produces.

Moral: Make sure that you know what reengineering really is before you attempt to do it—and then do it, not something else.

The second commonly made mistake is a variation of the first—trying to apply reengineering where it cannot fit.

People often tell us they are reengineering their sales department, or the accounting organization, or the Midwest Region. None of these statements have any meaning. You cannot reengineer an organization. The verb "to reengineer" takes as its object a business process and nothing else. We reengineer how work is done, how outputs are created from inputs. We cannot and do not reengineer organizational units. What could it mean to reengineer the sales department? The "sales department" is merely shorthand for a collection of people: Sally and Bill and Sue. What does it mean to reengineer Sally and Bill and Sue? It means nothing.

You cannot reengineer an organizational unit because an organizational unit is not responsible for a whole process. Typically, an organizational unit performs only a small set of tasks. If you limit your focus to the unit, you won't have the breadth of vision necessary to really make radical change, since you are confined on both ends. You are restricted by the demands of the people whose work precedes and follows yours, and so the scope for changing your own work is limited. Only if you are reengineering a whole process, where your sole constraint is your customer's needs, will you enjoy the flexibility to make truly radical changes in the way you work. The more narrow your focus, the more limited your ability to change.

Identifying your business processes is an indispensable part of reengineering, but it is one that people often skip entirely or do poorly. This is almost forgivable, because process identification is almost certainly the most intellectually challenging component of the entire reengineering enterprise. Identifying your processes requires that you *think* in terms of processes, and that is something with which few businesspeople have any experience. People are accustomed to thinking in terms of their activities, their departments, the managerial hierarchy above them. They are not given to thinking in terms of end-to-end cross-functional processes.

They think order entry, credit checking, inventory allocation, pick and pack, and traffic planning, not order fulfillment. The processes are there, and we perform them every day; but we are by and large unaware of them. One of us has a daughter, now eighteen, who would visit her father's office as a child. When asked what he did there, her reply was, "He talks on the phone and sharpens his pencils." It would be hard to say that she was wrong, but somehow this description fails to capture the finer nuances of our work. It is all a matter of perspective. Task-oriented thinking, like the young child's, focuses on the superficial. Process-oriented thinking concentrates on the objective and the final outcome. This shift in perspective is not easy, but it must be made. If people do not concentrate on their processes, they will end up trying to reengineer what cannot be reengineered.

Some people take the lazy way out. They use the term "process" without really understanding it and without making the effort to undergo the perspective shift understanding it requires. A common indication of this occurs when we ask someone to identify the organization's processes and the response is: "Sales, marketing, manufacturing, logistics, and finance." Simply calling your functions processes doesn't make them processes. Processes, by definition, are cross-functional and results oriented; they defy rather than respect organizational boundaries.

We offer the following rules of thumb to help you decide whether you are really talking and thinking about processes:

- You should be able to describe specific inputs and outputs for each one.
- Each process should cross a number of organizational boundaries; a rule of thumb is that if it doesn't make at least three people mad, it's not a process.
- There should be a focus on goals and ends rather than

actions and means. A process should answer the question "what?" not the question "how?"

- The processes, their inputs, and their outputs should be easily comprehensible by anyone in the organization. Complexity means artificiality, and is a very bad sign.
- All the processes relate to customers and their needs, either directly or as contributors to other processes.

Moral: Only processes can be reengineered. Before you can reengineer your processes, you must identify them.

The third, and perhaps the most, commonly made error in reengineering is to spend far too much time analyzing existing processes. Before organizations can create new designs, they do need to *understand* their current processes. However, too many people confuse *understanding* with conducting a full-scale *analysis*. What, exactly, is the difference between analysis and understanding? Our favorite answer is: about fourteen months.

Understanding means achieving a high-level, goal-oriented overview of an existing process, one that provides you with just enough information to begin with a clean sheet of paper. Analysis, on the other hand, involves the detailed documentation of virtually every aspect of the current process. The distinction here is one of mechanism and detail. Understanding focuses on the "what" and the "why" of the process; what it does, and why it tries to accomplish what it does. Understanding ignores the question of *how* a process works because the how is going to change anyway as a result of reengineering. Analysis in pursuit of completeness seeks to identify and document every aspect of how a process works.

There are two problems with conducting analysis in the

reengineering context. The first is that it is a profound waste of time. Through an analysis, you will create a huge, detailed description of how the existing process operates, which you will then proceed to throw away. Reengineering begins with the assumption that the extant mode of working is so far removed from what you need that you can't fix it, that your only option is to discard it and start over. Knowing this, what is the value of creating such exhaustive documentation? It's just going to be thrown away.

The second problem with analysis is that it can inhibit change. Too much time spent on analysis and documentation can cripple the imagination. You become so focused on the old way of doing things that you can no longer conceive of any other way. You lose sight of the forest for the trees. Eventually, after spending a long period studying the existing process, it begins to make sense to you; it doesn't look so bad. Your cognitive processes inevitably adapt to the business process you are analyzing. As a result, you lose your ability to think clearly and originally. Having become comfortable with the process, you will be incapable of proposing any radical change to it.

If analysis is obviously such a terrible waste of time, why then is it so common? Because it is safe, familiar, and comfortable. There are many valid precedents for conducting an analysis. Traditionally, we have automated rather than reengineered. In order to automate a process, you really do need to conduct a detailed analysis, since you need to know exactly how the process works so that you can tell your computer people exactly what their software should do. Similarly, if you are implementing total quality management—essentially an exercise in problem solving—then you must create a detailed analysis of the existing process, often called the as-is description. This description is necessary in order to isolate narrow problems with the process and fix them. Reengineering, however, is not about automation or

DILBERT reprinted by permission of UFS, INC.

problem solving; reengineering means reinventing the way you work. Detailed descriptions of the current state have no relevance. Still, the impulse to analyze is hard to resist; since we know how to do it, we tend to do it.

Analysis is also comfortable because it creates an illusion of progress. When we come to the office every day and conduct interviews and do studies and write reports and fill out forms, we feel that we are accomplishing something. But this feeling of false accomplishment is worse than merely comfortable; it is dangerous, because it is a substitute for action. The longer we analyze the current ways of operating, the further we fend off that awesome day when we will actually have to change something. Analysis thus becomes a defensive maneuver to avoid making fundamental change.

To avoid falling into the tar pit of analysis, you should always limit the amount of time that you will spend studying the existing process. The term for this approach is *time box*. You don't say that you will study an existing process until you are done, because your study could last forever. Rather, you specify at the outset how long it will take. Typically, four to six weeks is enough time to achieve the level of understanding necessary for reengineering. Just as you limit the amount of time that you spend studying the current state of affairs, you should also limit the amount of descriptive material that you produce. When you conduct an analysis, you can easily fill ten binders full with material. For understanding, ten *pages* is plenty. After all, what you need to know about the current process is what it does, how well (or poorly) it performs, and why it doesn't perform better. You certainly don't need to describe every mechanism it employs, since your goal is to create new mechanisms.

These ten pages should mainly consist of pictures and numbers. Those who say they can't fit what they know about a process into ten pages don't really understand it. If they complain that the process is too complicated and that they have too much information, then they haven't successfully conceptualized the process and are still stuck in the details. The French philosopher Blaise Pascal once said, "I didn't have time to write a short letter so I wrote a long one." The same phenomenon occurs here. Creating exhaustive documentation is in fact quite easy. It consists merely of collecting data and regurgitating it, and doesn't require much serious thinking. To create a concise overview, you must assimilate and internalize a wealth of information, and then find an effective means for communicating it. It is a much harder job, but absolutely essential to the success of any attempt to reengineer.

Moral: Understanding your processes is an essential first step in reengineering, but an analysis of those processes is a destructive waste of time. You must place strict limits, both on the time you take to develop this understanding and on the length of the description you create.

A fourth common mistake is to attempt reengineering without the requisite leadership. Strong, committed, executive leadership is the absolute sine qua non for reengineering. Only a senior executive who deeply believes in the reengineering cause can actually make it happen. People at lower levels of the organization, no matter how smart or well-intentioned, do not have the perspective needed to see whole processes and their shortcomings, nor the clout to institute the kinds of far-reaching changes that reengineering requires. Reengineering never proceeds bottom-up. It is a top-down phenomenon. And without top-down leadership, reengineering failure is a foregone conclusion. However, the failure may not occur right away. Undertaking reengineering without executive leadership can be a deceptive experience, since you may think you are making progress. You are dead, but you may not know it yet. You put together your team. You develop an understanding of your current process. You come up with breakthrough ideas. But you are living on borrowed time, because the instant you actually try to implement change you will be smashed to smithereens by all the vested interests committed to seeing reengineering fail.

Leadership is an absolute requirement when you try to turn a new process design concept into a reality, because that is when change affects people directly. When change bites people, they bite back. It is important that your leadership support you from the beginning, because if you don't start to get your leadership on board until you are near implementation, resistance will have already formed and will consequently be much more difficult to deal with. You need leadership from the beginning, not in order to overcome resistance but to preempt it.

Moral: If you proceed to reengineer without the proper leadership, you are making a fatal mistake. If your leadership is nominal rather than serious, and isn't prepared to make the required commitment, your efforts are doomed to failure.

The fifth mistake is timidity in redesign. Reengineering requires bold and imaginative thinking about process design and how work is done, and many people worry that coming up with these new ideas is the hardest part of reengineering.

Actually, we have never seen a reengineering effort fail because the organization lacked the ability to conjure up sufficiently imaginative ideas. In many organizations, there are numbers of breakthrough ideas already in circulation, part of the company's underground culture. The people with these ideas are only waiting for an officially proclaimed major change effort (i.e., reengineering) to surface and share their concepts. Even if there are no great concepts already in the air, it is not especially difficult for people to learn how to think creatively about process design. There are a number of very specific and concrete techniques for doing this kind of work, several of which we teach in our seminars; one of these is described in chapter 7. Innovative process design is a thinking skill that can be taught and learned. In the worst case, if you should happen to become really stuck, then you can always hire a consultant to help you come up with ideas. To repeat, no reengineering effort has ever failed because of an inability to generate breakthrough ideas.

Breakthrough ideas figure in reengineering failure in a more subtle way: not because of an inability to come up with them but because of a lack of will and nerve to see them through. The scenario is often as follows:

The reengineering team has developed a high-level overview of the existing process and has begun to design the new one. The team is seated around the table, when one member of the team looks up and cries, "Eureka! I've got it." Everybody expectantly looks at him, waiting for details. He then blinks, hangs his head, and mumbles, "Forget it. It's too radical. They'd never let us get away with it." People are full of bright and original and creative ideas. The problem is that in most corporate settings people have no faith that their ideas will even be given a fair hearing, never mind accepted, by the boss. When someone does have a break-through idea, he or she is very likely to take it out back behind the barn and drown it in a barrel of water. Self-censorship inevitably occurs when people are skeptical of management's seriousness and are afraid to share their ideas.

The leaders of the reengineering effort must therefore create an environment in which people feel that not only is it safe to have breakthrough ideas but it is required. One insurance company took a dual approach to the problem: When people proposed incremental changes, they were chastised and told to try again; at the same time, senior management offered a cash prize to anybody who came up with an idea that the executive management said was too radical. In other words, at this company, if you have a great new idea, there are two possible outcomes: Management will either adopt your idea or they will give you money. It's hard to see the downside here. People have become unafraid to share their ideas because they have nothing to lose and everything to gain.

Many people who have been successful at reengineering have told us that if they could do it again, they would have been even more ambitious. They say that they placed unnecessary limits on themselves and could probably have gone even farther than they did if they had been less timid in their redesign. And mind you, this comes from people who have achieved breakthrough performance improvement.

Moral: Reengineering requires radical, breakthrough ideas about process design. Reengineering leaders must encourage people to pursue stretch goals and to think out of the box; to this end, leadership must reward creative thinking and be willing to consider any new idea.

Mistake number six occurs when you attempt to go from a new process design directly into implementation. No matter how smart you are, or how much experience you may have had with reengineering, there is no way that the design that you create is going to be identical to the design that you implement. It is impossible to invent a new process design that will work effectively and achieve the performance breakthroughs that you need without some trial and error. No matter how clever your idea is, something will go amiss. The situation is always more complex than you realize at first. The technology does not live up to expectations. The reaction of the organization is different from what you anticipate. There is always something.

For instance, a reengineering team at a manufacturing company envisioned a new process for equipment maintenance that involved presenting all service representatives with a standardized and prepackaged set of tools. However, it developed that service reps did not want anyone else selecting their tools for them; picking the right tool for their personal styles of working was very important to their self-image and self-esteem. The team only learned this when they tried the process out on a small scale. It proved possible to modify the new process design to accommodate this human need, but it would have been very expensive to do so after all the standardized tool packages had been purchased and assembled. Similarly, a consumer products firm decided to reengineer its sales process in order to differentiate between large and small accounts, handling the latter through outbound telemarketing. The initial notion was to have this new sales work performed by customer service personnel who were handling customer inquiries. It turned out, however, that a very different style was required for initiating calls as opposed to receiving them. The company was fortunate to learn this before it installed the new process and antagonized its customers.

To proceed from a conceptual design directly to real implementation is a terrible idea. If the two companies just cited had done so, they would have made serious, expensive mistakes. The alternative is to go through a series of intermediate steps. *R*eengineers should act like *real* engineers. A real engineer with a design for a new product or system does not immediately go to full-scale manufacturing, but first develops a laboratory prototype: a mock-up version of the new idea that can be tested in a safe environment. In the laboratory, the product concept can be tried, validated, and improved. Only then will it proceed to implementation. The same principle applies to new process designs.

Let's imagine that you are reengineering an order fulfillment process. You take a room and set it up the way you envision the actual workplace. You train a group of people in the new process, providing them with all the necessary tools. You then create fictitious orders and let these test workers process them. In this sheltered workshop, you can observe how the process operates, where it succeeds and where it fails. The laboratory can be made real enough so that those involved forget it is an artificial environment. And because the whole exercise is "make-believe," it doesn't cost very much, especially compared to actually implementing a process only to discover that it functions poorly.

In this way, no real customers are exposed to the shortcomings of a rough or imperfect process. Moreover, through a series of iterations, the initial concept can be refined and improved repeatedly before the first real implementation is attempted. The laboratory is an inexpensive crucible for learning. In fact, the two companies mentioned above actually discovered the flaws in their new process designs in laboratories and were able to correct them before proceeding to full-scale implementation.

Moral: Before implementing a process in the real world, create a laboratory version in order to test whether your idea works. You will inevitably discover shortcomings and mistakes in your design, which you can then repair. Proceeding directly from idea to real-world implementation is a recipe for disaster.

Another blunder, the seventh on our list, is not reengineering quickly enough. From the time that you start thinking about a process until you have some concrete business benefits to show for it should never be more than twelve months. This time constraint doesn't mean that the whole new process will be fully implemented within a year. Nor does it mean that the process has to have been rolled out throughout the organization. It simply means that enough of the process is operating at a higher performance level so that you can point to it as proof that the new design will actually work in the real world.

This means that within twelve months, you have to develop an understanding of the old process, come up with your breakthrough ideas, test the new process design in a laboratory, and implement some of it in the real business. In other words, you must do an amazing amount of work in a very short period of time. However, the alternative is sure and certain failure. If you let a reengineering effort drag on for more than a year, it will die. Executive management will lose faith and begin to withdraw its funding, since alternative programs are competing for these resources. The naysayers, who have been carping and criticizing from the beginning, will say that nothing has happened, that reengineering is just a lot of baloney. The resisters will have more time to dig in their heels. And workers most directly affected will collapse from nervous exhaustion, anxiously waiting for the other shoe to drop, to learn what their fates will be.

Reengineering is not a stately procession; think of it as stumbling forward. You're never fully in control, but you are moving quickly. There is no choice; you must be able to deliver real value within twelve months.

A major reason that reengineering efforts stretch out longer than they should is that reengineers allow themselves to lose focus. Reengineering entails a constant tension between what is desirable and what is achievable. The overwhelming need of a successful reengineering effort is to deliver significant results quickly. Yet the realities of human nature and organizational dynamics conspire to keep this from happening. As soon as the prospect of significant progress starts to rear its head, you will be immediately set upon by hordes of people who want you to expand the scope of your effort. Broadening the process definition, extending it to cover more work activities, adding features to the design—there are innumerable ways in which any redesigned process can be augmented and "improved." Some of those beseeching you are well-intentioned; they sincerely believe that making the changes they suggest will turn a good effort into a great one. Some have private agendas; they want to leech onto the reengineering effort in order to promote some vested interest of their own. And some are malicious. They recognize that the larger the scope of the project, the less likely its success. The only response is to say "No!" loud and repeatedly. We tell reengineers that their minimum quota is to say no at least ten times every day. But even taking such a strong stance may not be enough. It is sometimes necessary to go further and cut back on the previously agreed-upon scope of the effort in the interest of getting results. One electronics manufacturer threw out fully half of the features of its new process design six months into its implementation when it became clear that adhering to the original design would take them past the twelve-month deadline.

Moral: You must reengineer quickly. If you can't show some tangible results within a year, you will lose the support and momentum necessary to make the effort successful. To this end, "scope creep" must be avoided at all costs. Stay focused and narrow the scope if necessary in order to get results fast.

Mistake eight occurs when you limit the range of the reengineering effort, placing parts of the organization off-limits. If you radically redesign your processes but refuse to change the compensation plan, the structure of the organization, or job titles, then you will certainly fail. It is inevitable. Whenever you change a process, you change the nature of the work that people do, requiring them to learn new skills. The way people are measured, paid, and offered incentives must also change; people working in new ways must be managed in new ways. Yet some organizations try to avoid the inevitable. They shy away from making the necessary organizational changes. The compensation system is often the test of sincerity and commitment because it is so sensitive and so central. Many companies have refused to cross this Rubicon, with fatal consequences for their reengineering efforts.

If you think that you can change a process without changing everything else related to the process, you are fooling yourself. You are in fact guaranteeing that reengineering won't work. When a new process tries to compete with old systems, the old systems win, for the simple reason that they encourage people to revert to their old ways of working.

Moral: You cannot reengineer a process in isolation. Everything must be on the table. Any attempt to set limits, to preserve a piece of the old system, will doom your efforts to failure.

The ninth route to failure is to adopt the wrong style of implementation. Many companies feel that they have to get all their ducks neatly lined up in a row before they begin a reengineering effort. They charter and develop a reengineering staff group; they formulate careful and detailed plans; they develop precise milestones for every stage of the upcoming journey; they work out complete and rigorous cost-benefit analyses; they try to ensure that everyone in the organization is solidly behind the effort. These companies are doomed to failure. They are pursuing an illusory dream and applying a style of implementation where it does not belong. These activities, while ostensibly rational, are in fact absurd. Reengineering cannot be carefully planned like a traditional project. Reengineering begins with a vision, a mandate, a concept, not with detailed specifications. The shape of the outcome does not emerge until one is well into it. Reengineering is a venture into the (at least partially) unknown. Attempting to achieve a high degree of precision and completeness before beginning is at best a waste of time and at worst disastrous. The cost-benefit analyses can only be estimates; the milestones are, in fact, guesses; the plans must be written in pencil. Nor will everyone get on board before the effort gets under way; some will never get on board. Companies that do not recognize this will spend forever getting ready for reengineering and will never get around to doing it. The way to reengineer is to *do* it, not think about it, plan it, or discuss it.

Moral: Reengineering needs its own style of implementation: fast, improvisational, and iterative.

The final common mistake is failing to attend to the concerns of the people in the organization. Reengineers can behave too much like real engineers, and that behavior can have serious consequences for reengineering implementation. There is an aesthetic in engineering just as there is in art, and the highest accolade that engineers use to describe their work is "elegant." Engineers are creative people, and they often have great emotional investments in their designs. Reengineers are also creative people and have similar feelings. They can naively expect that the elegance of a new process design will automatically cause everyone to wholeheartedly embrace it. In reality, however, it doesn't matter how elegant, efficient, and original the process design may be; the first (and only) question most people will ask is: What's in it for me? If you concentrate exclusively on the logical and design issues without considering the personal concerns of the people who actually do the work, the reengineering effort will inevitably sink under the weight of individual self-interest.

Moral: Any successful reengineering effort must take into account the personal needs of the individuals it will affect. The new process must offer some benefit to the people who are, after all, being asked to embrace enormous change, and the transition from the old process to the new one must be made with great sensitivity to their feelings.

You have been forewarned and forearmed. There is no excuse for making these popular mistakes—you will have to invent your own.

The Top Ten Ways to Fail at Reengineering

1. Don't reengineer but say that you are.
2. Don't focus on processes.
3. Spend a lot of time analyzing the current situation.
4. Proceed without strong executive leadership.
5. Be timid in redesign.
6. Go directly from conceptual design to implementation.
7. Reengineer slowly.
8. Place some aspects of the business off-limits.
9. Adopt a conventional implementation style.
10. Ignore the concerns of your people.

CHAPTER 3

The Primary Ingredient: Leadership

It is an unalterable axiom of reengineering that it only succeeds when driven from the topmost levels of an organization. No matter how hard they try, people on or near the front lines are in no position to launch and sustain such a major venture. First, they lack the breadth of perspective needed to see entire processes from start to finish rather than from their own narrow expertise and purview. For example, a pharmaceutical company employee who analyzes data from physician-conducted clinical trials may know how to make marginal improvements to data analysis, but is unlikely to know how the protocol for the study was developed in the first place—how patients and physicians are recruited or how the results of the analysis are communicated to the FDA so that they can determine the efficacy of the drug. As a consequence, he is not positioned to recognize and understand the systemic difficulties of the process as a whole or to develop new ideas about it.

His position constricts him in other ways as well. Because they are located in different parts of the organization, he and his process colleagues cannot easily exchange ideas and explore problems. He is in data analysis; someone else is in physician recruitment; another is in the protocol design department; still others are in the FDA submissions department. They are all separated from one another by the high walls of functional departments and specialization, across

DILBERT reprinted by permission of UFS, INC.

which communication is cumbersome and indirect. If by chance they stumble into one another in the halls and start to discuss their collective concerns, they may come up with some creative ways of performing the process as a whole, but their attempt at innovation will not last long. They will very quickly recognize that they can do nothing without the engagement of the middle managers, who control resources and translate policy into practice.

We refer to this managerial hierarchy in the corporation as the Death Zone of reengineering. Middle managers have the most invested in the status quo and stand to lose the most in reengineering. They have risen up through the ranks and have achieved their positions of authority, responsibility, and higher income and status by mastering the current system. If the processes are radically changed, then the structure—and the roles and responsibilities of the managers—will face fundamental review. In the resulting game of musical chairs, some people will be left without a seat. Consequently, the instinctual reaction of most middle managers is to attempt to forestall or freeze any reengineering effort.

Such people can be astoundingly inventive at finding reasons to reengineer, and at discovering mechanisms for thwarting it. They rarely behave in a consciously Machiavellian way; they are not *deliberately* resisting change. Subconsciously, however, they have so closely identified their personal agendas with the current state of the organization that they sincerely believe that fundamental change would not just be bad for them personally, but in fact be a disaster for the company as a whole.

Such resistance to change is not limited to the lower levels of the organizational hierarchy. The higher people rise in the organization, the more they have to lose; the greater their investment in the current structure, the greater their risk of not finding an equivalent position in the new order. Consequently, without relentless pressure from the very top, middle management will inevitably smother a reengineering effort.

In our experience, the quality of an organization's leadership is an absolute predictor of its reengineering success. Companies with strong leadership will succeed because they will do what it takes to ensure that all the other necessary components of reengineering are in place. Without such determined leadership, the effort will fail.

What kind of person does it take to lead a reengineering effort? Does it have to be the CEO? No. Put most simply, a leader is someone in a position to compel the compliance of all parties involved in reengineering. At the end of the day, if all else fails, the leader can simply demand that people contribute to the reengineering effort, that they subordinate their own domains to the needs of the new processes.

A leader must therefore have authority over the entire end-to-end processes that are to be reengineered. He or she must also have sufficient stature to demand that supporting staff organizations, such as human resources and information systems, also adapt their operations to meet the needs of the new process. The most common title associated with the reengineering leader is chief operating officer. The chief executive officer might seem the most likely person to lead the reengineering effort, but in a large company, the CEO is typically Mr. or Ms. Outside, while the COO is Mr. or Ms. Inside. The CEO is primarily concerned with issues that affect external constituencies—Wall Street analysts, major investors, the government, large customers, and industry associations—while leaving internal operating issues to the COO.

We should observe, however, that without at least the support and acquiescence of the CEO, the COO will get nowhere. We once witnessed how the absence of this support crippled the reengineering effort at a major retailer. The COO, who also had the title of president, had decided to launch a major program of reengineering. He convened a major management meeting to kick off the effort, but he had failed to enlist the support of his boss, the CEO. This CEO was relatively new to the company, and financially rather than operationally oriented. He was not terribly sensitive to the problems that the COO was trying to address. Nonetheless, the CEO gave the luncheon address at this kickoff meeting, but during it downplayed the significance of the reengineering effort. In effect, he cut the COO off at the knees. The effort went nowhere, since managers who felt threatened realized they could defy the COO with impunity. The lesson here is that if the reengineering leader isn't the top dog, you have to make sure that the top dog is not biting the leader in the leg.

Another candidate for the role of reengineering leader is a divisional general manager who heads a business unit, or an executive VP with responsibility over a broad area of the organization. Here, too, the leader will have end-to-end control over processes and the people who perform them. Divisional leaders will not be in a position to reengineer the entire company, but only those parts under their jurisdiction. There is nothing inherently problematic about this. It is far better to reengineer some business unit processes well than to do nothing at all. Success in a given business unit can then spur action and progress in others.

On the other hand, staff executives, such as CFOs and CIOs, rarely become reengineering leaders because they don't have line responsibility and full control over major processes. Similarly, senior functional heads, such as the senior VP of manufacturing or the senior VP of sales, are also unlikely to be effective reengineering leaders because they just preside over one of the stovepipes of the organization. They will not have the leverage needed to compel the participation of their peers.

Where does the decision to reengineer originate? As a rule, it is with the leader. Leaders are basically self-anointed. No one tells the leader what to do. Ideally, the urge to reengineer wells up from within the leader, based on his or her personal experience, intuition, and wisdom. The decision to reengineer is not a dispassionate one, based on cool analysis of indisputable numbers. Business realities are complex, replete with ambiguity, uncertainty, and confusion. The decision to reengineer is often the result of an epiphany, a fundamental insight on the leader's part that the old ways will no longer do and something dramatic must be done. John Martin, CEO of Taco Bell, puts it this way: "We were working awfully, awfully hard, a lot of good people working awfully hard to get just mediocre kinds of results. It didn't feel right. We ran faster, we tried harder, but we weren't getting anywhere. After a while we began to say, are we even on the right road here?" Ron Compton of Aetna phrases it like this: "If you're sixty years old and you've been in the business for thirty-nine years, then you have the right to use your instinct. And when you think you're right, you've just got to do it. I ran Aetna branches and I ran an Aetna SBU and I ran Aetna departments, and it was too tough, so I decided we had to make it easier, and that was it."

Leadership is not merely a matter of having the right title; any warm body with a prestigious position and large office is not enough. In order to discharge the responsibilities of leadership, the leader must possess certain personal characteristics. The first of these is passion. No one will follow a leader anywhere unless that leader is absolutely committed to the journey and its destination. Passion is expressed in various ways. It can of course be communicated by what one says. The leader must talk about reengineering in terms that convey the intensity of his or her feeling and the critical nature of the undertaking. If it is discussed like any other corporate program, then it will be received and treated like any other corporate program: with disdain, cynicism, and boredom. Peter Lewis, CEO of Progressive Insurance, describes how he expressed his sense of urgency about the reengineering of the company's claims process: "I was relentless in pursuit of the idea because I really believed in it, and I began hammering away. At one point, I made a statement I am wont to make when I am desperate. I said, 'Look, damn it, this is important. I really know it's important and I don't care what it costs. Spend whatever it costs.'" That's passion.

To paraphrase Forrest Gump, however, passion is as passion does. What really convinces an organization of the leader's seriousness of purpose is his or her actions. For instance, one company had a history of halfhearted change programs, none of which had gotten anywhere because a key audit process had always been declared off-limits. When the leader of reengineering explicitly put the audit process on the reengineering agenda, and followed through on this commitment, the skeptics were convinced. At another company, the top 120 managers of the corporation were gathered together for a special meeting to kick off the reengineering effort. This by itself was nothing special, except for two facts: First, this was the very first time in the company's history that these people were ever brought together for a meeting. Second, the meeting itself lasted four days: Thursday, Friday, Saturday, Sunday. The message went out loud and clear: This is not a typical program. This is for real.

Nothing, however, speaks louder than dealing sternly with those who impede a reengineering effort. Leniency toward those who refuse to cooperate with the reengineering effort gives the lie to the leader's pronouncements about reengineering's critical importance. Sometimes acting on your beliefs can be painful indeed. One reengineering leader we know was faced with a terrible dilemma. His oldest colleague in the company, a close personal friend, was not supporting the reengineering effort and was in fact actively impeding it. Repeated conversations produced no results. At last, the leader had to take an extremely difficult step: He dismissed his friend. Personally wrenching though it was, this act had profound repercussions throughout the company; the universal conclusion was—this guy is serious.

We are sometimes accused of bloodthirstiness, of advocating violence and intimidation. We reject this claim. The regrettable reality is that some people will not get on board the reengineering train, and the leader cannot afford to keep the train in the station waiting for them to board. Extreme measures are sometimes the only way to overcome entrenched opposition. Such measures are not taken with glee, but with regret. As one CEO we know tells newly hired managers, "If you can't dismiss people, don't aspire to hold my position. And if you enjoy dismissing people, also don't." A leader who is not prepared to take the ultimate step in dealing with those compromising the success of the reengineering effort has no fire in his or her belly, no passion; his or her weakness and insincerity will be all too apparent to everyone.

Passion is the most critical personal characteristic for leadership, but it is not the only one. The ability to inspire trust and confidence is also of great importance. For the people in the organization, after all, reengineering is a terrifying leap into the unknown. When the journey begins, the destination is not even in sight. The only certainty is that everything familiar is being left behind. In such circumstances, people will inevitably look to the leader as a source of comfort and calm. No matter what confusions or uncertainties the leader may be experiencing, he or she must project the sense of being fully in control. To illustrate, imagine you are on an airplane flight and the weather has gotten dicey. The skies are filled with thunderstorms, the plane is bouncing up and down, and it seems to be circling endlessly. Your knuckles are white and your nerves are on edge. At last, the pilot comes on the intercom. What do you want to hear? "Well, folks, I'm sure you've noticed it's a little bouncy up here, but there's absolutely nothing to worry about. We're just waiting for some clearance. I've been through this a thousand times, and everything is just fine." What do you not want to hear? "Uhh, gee, I'm not really sure what's happening right now . . . oops, gotta go!"

The leader must also exhibit an unusual combination of impatience and patience. On the one hand, he or she must be possessed by a restlessness, an inability to accept the status quo, an urgency to get things done quickly. At the same time, the leader must persevere and not lose heart despite obstacles and setbacks. If there is a single word that captures an effective leader's style, it is relentlessness. A single-minded drive to make things happen, no matter what, is what distinguishes a truly committed leader from just another empty suit parroting the latest faddish buzzwords.

A reengineering leader in many ways is a living contradiction. On the one hand, this individual will have achieved a high degree of success in the old business, having ascended to the lofty level from which reengineering leadership can be exercised. On the other, he or she must be sufficiently disenchanted with the old system to want to destroy it. In short, a reengineering leader must be prepared to lead a revolution against himself or herself and the very system that created him or her. Such individuals will have strong personalities, a powerful sense of what their companies need, and the charisma to enlist others in their quest. For a person like this, "leader" is indeed the most appropriate and most descriptive title.

In some cases, making the decision to reengineer is easy. If your company is losing millions of dollars a day and on the verge of collapse, it doesn't take a lot of deep thinking to recognize that you have to do things differently. It takes greater foresight and vision and far greater powers of persuasion to lead an organization into reengineering in the face of apparent success. Jim Schultz, head of Trane's Commercial Systems business, a leading manufacturer of commercial HVAC systems, was one who had what it takes. Although many in the organization thought it was doing well, Schultz recognized in the early 1990s that its success was directly correlated, on a lagging basis, with the number of new construction starts in commercial real estate. He understood that tax law changes, combined with a glut in office space, had sent construction starts into a nosedive, and so it would only be a matter of time before the good times would be over.

Schultz realized that he had to initiate radical changes in the way he did business. To survive, he would have to focus not on selling new systems for new construction but on maintaining and upgrading systems in existing buildings. Unfortunately, his processes were not set up to support this strategy. A process as simple as finding a spare part could take hours, since spares are relatively unimportant when you are selling new products all the time. Schultz recognized this and demonstrated strong and visionary leadership by making the commitment, while in the midst of apparent success, to undertake the radical change necessary to keep his business from falling apart in the future.

Progressive Insurance offers a similar example. In the early 1990s, although current financial results seemed fine, Progressive undertook a large-scale reengineering effort. Peter Lewis, the CEO, and Bruce Marlow, the COO, foresaw that encroachment by larger competitors on their niche of high-risk drivers, combined with a growing consumer revolt as exemplified by Proposition 103 in California, would threaten their heretofore profitable business. Rather than wait to be steamrollered, they had the foresight to change their processes, concentrating initially on claims, in order to compete in a new environment.

True leaders always have a vision of the future, of what their organization can become, that fuels their enthusiasm for change. The decision to make radical change almost invariably arises from the emotional right brain rather than from the purely analytical left. Of course such decisions are never made on a whim, or without careful exploration and ample supporting data. Ultimately, however, after all the other factors have been considered, the personal commitment necessary to generate and sustain change can only spring from an organic recognition that runs deeper than reason.

If the leader's first responsibility is to make the decision to reengineer, the second is to make reengineering succeed.

But reengineering is never a one-person show; the leader cannot "do" it alone. The leader cannot expect to devote all his or her time—or even a major share of it—to reengineering; after all, there is a business to be run. But the reengineering "monkey" stays on the leader's back—he or she is responsible for seeing the project through. To this end, the leader appoints process owners, each of whom is responsible for the reengineering of a specific process, and provides them with the resources they need. The leader also works with them to establish standards of performance that they must achieve. The process owners cannot have even a scintilla of doubt that their compensation and career will be heavily impacted by the success or failure of their efforts. If it currently takes six months to fill an order, but customers want it done in three weeks, then that's what's gonna be. No excuses accepted.

While the leader will enlist many others—process owners, team members, staff assistants—in the reengineering enterprise, this is not to be confused with delegation. In most other areas, senior managers are accustomed to assigning responsibility to others, with their own role limited to oversight and evaluation. Reengineering, in contrast, is the leader's personal crusade, in which many others will be enlisted, but in which no other can serve as a substitute. Ongoing and visible participation is necessary in order for a leader to live up to the demands of the role. This is one of the most difficult personal adjustments that executives must make in adapting to the style of reengineering.

A third responsibility of a leader is to create the environment in which reengineering can succeed.

By environment we mean the organization's climate of opinion, the temper of its times, the mind-set and attitudes of its people. If, for instance, the company environment is characterized by fear, suspicion, cynicism, complacency, or defensiveness, then reengineering will face an uphill struggle. Participation will be grudging and episodic; promises will be made and not kept; commitment will be halfhearted; the reengineering cup will be universally regarded as half-empty; creativity and enthusiasm will be absent. It is the leader's role to transform this climate, to reshape the organization's attitudes and feelings about reengineering.

Complacency and arrogance kill the impetus for change.

If "I'm all right, Jack" is the prevailing mood, then people cannot feel a need for reengineering at a visceral level, and their engagement will be superficial at best. In contrast, an environment conducive to reengineering is characterized by ambition, striving, and humility. There is a quote of uncertain provenance that we like very much: "The hallmark of the truly successful organization is its willingness to abandon what has long been successful." Pride and satisfaction in one's prior accomplishments should not cause you to conclude that all is well for the future. As the saying goes, "That was then and this is now." In a constantly changing world, there is no permanent answer; there is only the answer of the moment. What sufficed yesterday will probably be wrong tomorrow. The winning organization never confuses temporary success with intrinsic virtue.

Similarly, a willingness to fail is a prerequisite for significant success. A policy of avoiding failure at all costs dooms an organization to incremental improvements at best. People need to be encouraged to experiment fearlessly with new ideas.

A comment made at Progressive Insurance captures the style and environment that reengineering leadership must create. When Progressive's executive management introduced the ideas of the reengineered claims process to the organization, there was, not surprisingly, a good deal of consternation. Objectors discovered a number of ostensible flaws in the proposed design. The leadership listened carefully, considered the critiques, and came back with a revised design. Additional problems were then discovered. Management responded as before. But when objections continued to be raised, the leadership responded with a powerful statement: "Trust us. If it doesn't work, we'll try something else." This phrase deserves careful explication. "If it doesn't work": This is an admission of fallibility. We are not claiming perfection and omniscience, but rather are admitting the possibility that things might go awry. "We'll try something else": We do not say that if it doesn't work, we will execute all involved. Risk is acceptable and to be tolerated. On the other hand, we *will* try something else. There is no standing still. The only option ruled out is maintaining the status quo.

We have assigned the reengineering leader a variety of duties. The leader is the instigator of reengineering, the person who decides that it must be done and takes it upon himself or herself to see that it is accomplished. The leader is the motivator, the cheerleader, the spiritual adviser of the reengineering program. He or she appoints process owners, sets their goals, and gives them the authority, the resources, and the incentives they need in order to succeed; he or she ensures the compliance of all who might impede the program. The leader also creates an environment that will permit reengineering to flourish. But how does the leader discharge these various responsibilities? We submit that there is nothing mysterious about it. Reengineering leadership makes use of three key instruments in a very deliberate fashion. We call them the three *S*s: signals, symbols, and systems.

The Tools of Reengineering Leadership

Signals	Explicit Communications
Symbols	Personal Behavior
Systems	Measurements and Rewards

Signals are what one says. They are the explicit communications that the leader shares with the organization about reengineering. We will have considerably more to say about this in later chapters. For the time being, let us simply summarize the key characteristics of an effective communications program:

- Communication must be relentless. When it comes to reengineering, there is no such thing as overcommunication. Virtually every reengineering leader we know has told us that they seriously underestimated the amount of communication required. And communication does not cease when implementation begins. The messages must continue to be sent; stopping them could be interpreted as the end of executive commitment.
- Communication must be simple. Basic concepts must not be wrapped in fancy jargon. The motivation for reengineering must be expressed in terms accessible to everyone in the organization.
- Communication must be dramatic. An exciting message communicated in a pedestrian way becomes pedestrian. Given the life-or-death quality of reengineering, suitable means must be found to make people feel its urgency, to experience it on an emotional rather than an intellectual plane.

The second S is symbols, what one shows by doing: the personal symbolic acts that the leader performs. Talk is cheap. If behavior supports the talk, then it is believed; otherwise, it is dismissed. If you say reengineering is important but don't devote any of your own time to it, then why should anyone else believe that you really think it is important? There are many ways in which the leader can demonstrate the criticality of reengineering. The key to understanding symbolic behavior is to see it as another form of speech, the proverbial actions that speak louder than words. Its content matters less than its form. For instance, one reengineering leader gave his home phone number to every reengineering team member. He told them to call him if they ever had a problem, day or night, and he would take care of it. Another leader wanted to authorize rule breaking in an organization that had always played by the rules. Of course, he told everyone that such activity was permitted, even required. He then waited until someone actually took him up on it and broke some rules, and publicly praised this individual as a hero. A third took it upon himself to review all the key milestones in all the reengineering projects in the company. He actually had useful suggestions to offer, but more importantly he demonstrated the depth of his own personal commitment to the effort.

The third *S* is systems, the scales by which people are measured and rewarded in the organization. It is absolutely necessary that these systems support the messages being conveyed through signals and symbols. If, for instance, you say that reengineering is the most important thing in the company but don't offer members of reengineering teams opportunities for reward and advancement at least as good as those offered their peers, then you will have a very hard time staffing your teams. If you tell your process owners that they have to reengineer their processes, but then you hold them accountable for process performance by old metrics during the transition, you put them in an untenable bind. You will get either slipshod reengineering, highly creative accounting, or schizophrenic process owners. The way to people's hearts and minds is not through their ears but through their wallets. The systems you use to measure and pay people are important shapers of attitude and behavior.

In summary, an effective reengineering leader must be one part visionary, one part communicator, and one part leg-breaker. Individuals who hold the title of reengineering leader but who don't fulfill these roles will doom their venture to failure. Even companies that understand reengineering both as concept and practice will fail if they lack strong leadership.

Weak leadership has many manifestations. One is skimping on resources. If management is truly serious about reengineering, they will insist that their very best people commit themselves to it. Failing to do so indicates insincerity and weakness.

Another sign of weak leadership is burying reengineering in the middle of the corporate agenda. Reengineering can't be number five on a list of ten; it must be number one on a list of one. Reengineering means the complete reinvention of how you operate; the resultant changes percolate into every nook and cranny of your business, from job design to corporate culture. Reengineering is a mammoth undertaking that can't take a backseat to anything else.

Another symptom of inadequate leadership is quitting too early. This takes two forms. Sometimes leadership gives up before getting any payoff because it lacks the intestinal fortitude to weather (the inevitable) difficulties. Such leaders will push forward until they hit the first patch of slipups and then simply fall apart under the stress. It is easy to be a reengineering leader when everything is going very well and you are receiving enormous amounts of positive feedback. But what happens when it turns out that one of your ideas wasn't so great? Or that resistance is stronger than you expected? Or that costs are going to be higher? To paraphrase Kipling, the true test of leadership is keeping your head when all those around you are losing theirs.

The second form of quitting too early is giving up as soon as some positive result has been achieved, even if it is less than the initial goal. "Leaders" who are tentative and unserious rush for the exit at the first sign of success, grateful to have made it through alive. They had been so uncertain of success that they consider it to be any result other than abject failure. In reengineering, however, real success comes not from settling for half measures or preliminary results but by pushing ahead to attain dramatic, breakthrough improvements.

In Aetna's personal lines business, one reengineering goal was to reduce costs by $40 million annually. The reengineering design team assumed the challenge but then concluded that saving $40 million was not feasible. However, they did come up with a design that promised a clear $17 million in savings. This presented the company's management with a true test of their leadership. Their response was to insist that $17 million—hardly an insignificant sum—was not nearly good enough. They had asked for $40 million and would not settle for anything less. The team went back to the drawing board and eventually came up with $50 million in savings. They achieved their breakthrough results because the leadership had the strength of character not to accept a very good second best.

Another sign of weakness is slapping people's wrists instead of breaking their legs. Often, as a reengineered process is implemented, some key senior manager will perceive it as an intrusion on his domain. By various means, explicit or covert, he resists the change. If, instead of confronting this individual harshly, the executive leadership cozens him and gently urges him to reconsider his opposition, the game is lost. This kind of response to resistance rarely changes the behavior; in fact, it encourages it. Moreover, it undercuts the leadership's messages to the rest of the organization.

Rising to this challenge is doubly difficult, and doubly significant, when the people who must be dealt with in this way are longtime associates or even mentors of the reengineering leaders. Fred Musone, president of Worldwide Manufacturing at Federal Mogul, recalls: "Some of the people that I had worked for many years ago and who were key in my personal development were some of the people who were unable to adjust to the change. They were good people, fine folks, and it was heart-wrenching."

Then we are agreed: Passionate, committed, engaged executive leadership is an absolute prerequisite for reengineering. But what do you do if your organization doesn't have it? How do you go about recruiting a leader?

Imagine that you are working in an organization and you recognize the need for your company to reengineer, either because it is in trouble, or because you see change looming, or because you see the opportunity to gain an important competitive advantage. Your top executives, however, are not making it happen. Under these circumstances you should ask yourself a simple question: Why *aren't* they leading? Why *don't* they see the need to change, when you do? Or, if they do see the need, why won't they act? The answer to that question will determine how you proceed.

In some cases, a senior management team is incapable of undertaking change because they lack the moral fiber and strength to break with the past. They are administrators rather than entrepreneurs. Fundamentally, they have grown accustomed to doing an easy job and don't want a harder one. One senior executive has put it this way: People work hard to become senior executives so that they don't have to work hard anymore. In reference to his own job, he said, "As a leader of our reengineering effort, I am working harder now than I ever have in my life." Some people simply don't want to be burdened with such major responsibility. If that sort of attitude is endemic to the leadership of your organization, then they aren't going to reengineer in the foreseeable future. And your future lies elsewhere.

In most cases, however, lack of leadership is not the result of any fundamental shortcomings in senior management. Rather, leadership isn't leading because it is *ignorant*. Many executive managers tend to suffer from a very real occupational hazard: They are insulated from reality and consequently don't know what the hell is going on. Typically, the information that reaches them is summary instead of detailed, financial instead of operational, historical instead of current. This sort of information can convey what happened—the company made money or lost money—but doesn't explain *why*. What is it about the way we manufacture that makes our work-in-process inventory levels so high? Why are customers deserting us? What is it about how we develop products that makes us noncompetitive? Financial figures can only show results; they cannot explain or describe the factors that contributed to those results.

As a result of receiving information so aggregated and processed that all the flavor and insight has been cooked out of it, many senior managers make business decisions based on an outdated model of how the business operates, since their understanding of the business derives from those long-ago days when they were much closer to the action. Many aspects of the business will have changed enormously since then; even worse, some executives may have never been close enough to the action to really know how the business functions at the operational level.

If the underlying problem is ignorance, the cure is information. To catalyze potential leaders, you must get them to experience the reality of today's business, to appreciate the need for reengineering, and to recognize its potential. To accomplish this you must play on the two most basic human emotions: fear and greed. You must frighten them by demonstrating the serious shortcomings of the current processes, spelling out just how drastically these defective processes are hurting the organization. In order to do this, you must make them aware of the existence of these processes in the first place. Until senior managers recognize a process *as* a process, they cannot be convinced of how poorly it operates.

Fear can be used in many different ways as a catalyst for

change. At one large airline, a group of operating managers examined a very simple process that had never been considered as a process before: getting an airplane off the ground. This does not refer to the aerodynamics of flight but to all the activities required to get into the air, such as collecting the tickets, boarding the passengers, loading the baggage, computing takeoff speed, and so on. These managers diagrammed all these activities and produced a picture so intricate it became known as the "Rat's Nest Diagram." The process was so complex that the fact that it operated at all was a miracle. Demonstrating this complexity and inefficiency was the first step in convincing the airline's executive management that something fundamental had to be done about it.

To convince executive leadership of the need to reengineer, you must make them bitterly aware of process shortcomings. You will have to conduct detailed analytic studies to document the excessive complexity and cost of current processes, and the consequent customer dissatisfaction. For example, some people at Texas Instruments recognized that the company's order fulfillment process was in deep trouble. They created diagrams that graphically illustrated the operation of this process, which until then had not been recognized as a process, and so, of course, had never been managed as such.

One diagram mapping the steps from the receipt of a customer's order until the start of manufacturing demonstrated that only 18 percent of the effort was useful work. Another documented the steps from the start of manufacturing until the delivery of the product to the customer, and showed that only 11 percent of those steps actually involved value-adding work. These diagrams revealed that every product that TI manufactured went on six plane rides, eight truck rides, and through countless handoffs. When executive management saw these graphs, their hearts stopped. The panic necessary to make the leadership realize that there was a problem with this process—and with others—had been effectively induced.

Benchmarking can also help to create a sense of fear and urgency. Identifying far superior process performance by other firms can goad leadership to action. Although it is important to see what other people are doing, benchmarking should be used cautiously, since it can be a real creativity killer. If you merely seek to imitate others, then the best you can hope for is to eventually catch up with the lead sheep in the pack. The value of benchmarking is as an *incentive* to action, not as a *guide* to action. Benchmarking should prompt people to think: "Oh, my God, these people are so much better than we are; we'd better get cracking." The goal is not, "Let's do what they have done," but, "Let's be even better than they are."

Greed can also be an important catalyst for leadership. By communicating the promise and potential benefits of reengineering, you offer management the prospect not only of surviving but of thriving. To that end, you will need to conduct a crash course in reengineering. Have those you are trying to persuade read documented case histories. Have them visit peers at other companies that have reengineered successfully. Take them to a seminar. Do whatever it takes to turn them into believers.

If you undertake these activities, you are in effect playing what we call the role of the catalyst: an individual or small group that incites a senior manager to assume the mantle of reengineering leadership. Clearly, the role of catalyst cannot be played by just anyone. It requires access to senior management so that they will hear your story; respect and credibility so that they will believe it; and persistence so that they cannot avoid the truth it holds no matter how they try. A high degree of self-effacement is also needed, since the leader must always believe that the decision to reengineer is his own; no executive wants to believe that he has been manipulated into a decision. But before you embark on becoming a catalyst, be forewarned: The person who is standing there when the senior manager is seized with the inspiration to begin reengineering is likely to get roped into the effort. We know many people who were surprised to find that a selfless attempt to get reengineering off the ground changed their careers forever.

CHAPTER 4

The Second Ingredient: The Reengineering Team

Leadership is the key ingredient for reengineering success. But while it may be necessary, strong leadership is far from sufficient to guarantee a positive outcome. There is a great amount of work to be done in reengineering, and it is far from a one-person show.

If reengineering sits at the top of the company's agenda, then it follows that the company's best and brightest must be assigned to it. But what exactly does that term mean? What kinds of talents and capabilities are required of members of a reengineering team? What kinds of backgrounds and experiences make for a good reengineer? And how can a group of high-caliber individuals be fashioned into a high-caliber collective, an effective reengineering team?

Clearly, the kinds of people needed for the reengineering program must reflect the nature of the endeavor itself. This book describes in some detail the work performed by reengineers, but let us summarize it here in terms of its content, its context, and its style.

The *content* of reengineering work can be expressed as follows:

- *Understanding* the old process and customer requirements, so as to recognize the weaknesses of the existing process and the performance demanded of the new one.

- *Inventing* a new process design that shatters long-held assumptions.
- *Constructing* the new process, including fleshing out the full details of its operation, developing its implications for all aspects of the organization, training people, building requisite information systems, and so on.
- *Selling* the new way of working and living to the organization as a whole.

By the *context* of a reengineering effort, we mean the environment in which this work will be done. Reengineering as a rule is conducted in conditions of:

- *Uncertainty*. When reengineering begins, we know little other than that the old process is inadequate and that we need something far better. This uncertainty is not eliminated quickly, but only gradually, over the lifetime of the project.
- *Experimentation*. Reengineering is an iterative experience. It is impossible to design a new way of working on paper; it must be tried in reality. And this inevitably means that mistakes will be made.
- *Pressure*. An organization never undertakes reengineering unless it needs the results yesterday. Since reengineering must proceed at a headlong pace, reengineers always operate under conditions of great urgency and intensity.

Reengineering's *style* differs from that of traditional business projects. Those generally start with well-defined goals and a clear project plan. Reengineering does not. It is about exploration and discovery rather than analysis and knowing. It is a journey into the unknown. The reengineer lives in a stream of options, alternatives, possibilities. Ideas must be formulated before all the facts are in, tested before the environment is stable, and evaluated before the results are conclusive. Reengineering is conducted in a state of uncertainty and ambiguity, but moves quickly nonetheless. We sometimes characterize it as "stumbling forward." The direction of motion is right, but one is not fully in control along the way.

An operative definition of a good candidate for a reengineer is someone who will be capable and comfortable working in the reengineering context and style. Fortunately, it is not necessary to rely on such a tautological formulation. Rather, we suggest that the following traits characterize the kind of person who is most likely to make a good reengineer:

- A process-oriented and holistic cognitive style: a facility for seeing the big picture, for distinguishing trees from forests, for understanding how tasks fit together to form a process, and how process designs and organizational designs fit together to form a business.
- Design skills: the facility both to envision a new way of doing things and then to flesh it out, turning it from a concept into something that can actually be implemented.
- An inclination toward change that borders on restlessness: a congenital inability to accept things as they are, and a determination to find what lies over the rainbow.
- Enthusiasm and optimism: the internal fortitude to keep going despite the slings and arrows of outraged constituencies, and despite the fact that it often seems as though the light at the end of the tunnel is an oncoming train.
- Persistence and tact: the ability to keep pushing despite the fact that people are pushing back at you, and eventually to wear them down and convert them to your point of view.
- Interpersonal, teamwork, and communication skills: the

ability to work as part of a tightly woven team, the patience to listen to the needs, fears, and concerns of everyone who will be affected by reengineering, and the talent to craft messages that will induce them to accept unpalatable truths and their consequences.

The Profile of a Reengineer

Process-orientation	Optimism
Holistic perspective	Persistence
Creativity	Tact
Restlessness	Team player
Enthusiasm	Communication skills

But how do we go about identifying people with these characteristics? Surprisingly, it is not necessary to conduct complex psychological profiles. In fact, the desired qualities of a reengineer correlate surprisingly well with information contained in that most basic of hiring tools—the résumé.

For openers, it's not that hard to find someone with good design skills whose thinking style is centered on processes. You just need to find an engineer. Reengineering is, in fact, a branch of engineering; its domain is organizations and work rather than structures or electronic devices. At a fundamental level, all engineers—electrical, mechanical, civil, software, industrial—have much in common. Their thinking styles can be readily adapted from one domain to another. An engineer's natural inclination is toward design, toward synthesis and invention rather than analysis. Scientists may be concerned with understanding what *is;* engineers are focused on what can be *made.* All engineers know how to cope with complexity. Engineers do not have the luxury of simplifying the world, of carving out a narrow corner in which to operate. Their creations must operate in the real world, with all its complexity and multidimensionality. Engineers are holistic problem solvers. Moreover, process is what reengineers live and breathe. The terminology may vary from field to field (some use the term "system," for example), but big-picture thinking is intrinsic to all engineering disciplines.

Engineers will also have had experience with the practical components of successful design: creativity—inventing something entirely new; trade-off evaluation—fashioning designs that must satisfy competing criteria; performance analysis—determining quickly and intuitively whether a design concept is merely appealing or whether it promises to deliver the performance required; troubleshooting—finding and coping with inevitable design flaws.

The desirable quality of restlessness is also easily identifiable on a résumé. Potential reengineers often exhibit a tendency to change jobs. Their inclination is to come into a situation, learn it fast, and make improvements to it. But eventually, they are susceptible to boredom and frustration, either because there are no more mountains to climb or because the rest of the organization is unwilling to continue striving. And so they move on in search of the next cause to which they can devote their energies. Frequent job change not only demonstrates restlessness, it also gives a person diversity and breadth, very valuable attributes in a cross-functional context. Needless to say, it is important to distinguish between people with a mission and people who can't hold a job, whose career shifts are the result of incompetence.

The requisite traits of enthusiasm, optimism, and persistence are usually found in people who have served some time in a sales department. Salespeople are constantly putting themselves on the line; their egos can be shattered and their self-confidence demolished on a daily basis. To survive, they have to develop a strong belief in themselves and in what they are doing. Salespeople are terminal optimists. If the design component of reengineering is fundamentally an engineering task, implementation is a sales job. Reengineers must "sell" a new concept to a group of reluctant customers—company employees who are often suspicious of change—and who is better equipped for that than a former sales rep?

When it comes to teamwork and interpersonal skills, we have found one easily identified attribute with which these are highly correlated: being female. We do not want to be accused of sexism, reverse or otherwise. Nor do we wish to hurt the feelings of those who might be described, in the language of political correctness, as "estrogen challenged." But it is observable that, on the average, women exhibit a greater capacity than men for communicating. The reasons are unknown. Some attribute it to women's being socialized to be supportive rather than competitive. Others theorize that since women have only been admitted relatively recently into the corporate ranks, they have less vested interest in the existing structure and can be more flexible. Still others suggest a biological basis. Obviously, this is not the place to speculate on the issue of "nature versus nurture." However, we do have one bit of anecdotal data that would support this folk wisdom: namely, that women are represented in the ranks of first-rate reengineers well out of proportion to their representation in the corporate workforce. This observation has been substantiated by reengineering leaders in many industries.

To wrap it up—albeit a little simplistically—the perfect reengineer would be a female engineer who has changed jobs frequently and has a background in sales.

Obviously, it is unlikely in the extreme that all of your reengineers will pass this rather stringent qualification. But they don't need to. Reengineers, as we have said, do not work alone, but as teams. The team as a whole, rather than each of its members, must possess the desired attributes. It is to the team, rather than its members, that we now turn our attention.

"Team" is a much overused term of late. To us, a team is a group of people working toward a common set of goals.

In reengineering, all members of the team must share a dedication to three things: the process that is being reengineered, the needs of the customer of that process, and the team itself. Collective identification and goals are the secrets of team success.

To that end, the team must transcend the constituencies that it represents. The needs of the reengineering effort must take precedence over the needs of home departments and former bosses. To this end, team members should not expect to return to their home departments when the reengineering assignment is over. That would be likely to bias their thinking and distort their priorities. Similarly, the measurement and reward systems used in managing the team must foster a sense of cohesion and unity. If home department managers are reviewing team member performance, these members will at best be subject to divided loyalties. Rewards must reflect the progress of the team as a whole toward the reengineering goal.

But a group of individuals does not turn into a team overnight—it usually takes at least a week of serious effort. Many organizations contend that they don't have the time for team building. They beg off, saying they are buried in work, racing tight deadlines. They fail to shape their teams at the outset, and as a result the teams never function as well as they should. It takes time to build trust, develop a set of working principles, clarify objectives, get to know each other professionally and personally. Teams that take that time may lose a week up front, but they more than make up for it later on when their unity allows them to speed through problems and crises. We call the principle "slow trigger, fast bullet."

Successful team building should be fun and should involve discovery of oneself and of other team members. But above all it must build trust. To use a term from physics, trust is

DILBERT reprinted by permission of UFS, INC.

the "strong force" that binds the atoms of the team. The members are going to have to rely on each other in moments of stress and confusion. Like a trapeze artist sailing off a swing, they need to know that there will be someone to grab them at the other end.

Team building is not a one-time event; it begins in the first week and must be reinforced throughout the life of a team. A sense of solidarity and camaraderie requires frequent rejuvenation, especially since most people have little prior experience with it in the workplace. People must be constantly reminded of the nature of a team, of their role in it, and of its rules of engagement. This process of reinforcement must run parallel with the entire reengineering process.

One organization we know has defined three characteristics it seeks to instill in its reengineering teams—caring, daring, and sharing.

Caring means having an environment that allows open and honest communication. People must feel free to support or attack an idea without threatening the person who first proposed it. Caring involves mutual support. You don't have to be enamored of everyone on your team, but you must identify and be concerned with them.

Daring means encouraging everyone on the team to be innovative and adventurous, and to ask the hard questions. But the quest for innovation cannot turn into a competition; all brilliant ideas must be marked as team property. A team should remember Newton's dictum: "If I have seen further, it is because I stood on the shoulders of giants."

Sharing means that a team has a common objective; as the saying goes, "There are no winners on a losing team." Sharing also requires a clear sense of how everyone fits into the team. If there is a team leader, he or she must be acknowledged as such. Explicit operating procedures are needed; everyone on the team must be familiar with what is expected and acceptable, and what is not.

An important part of team building is making everyone aware of commonplace dysfunctional behaviors, so that they can try to avoid them:

- Not listening. Nothing is more distressing than to be sharing an exciting idea—or just an interesting observation—only to look around and see that half your teammates are asleep while the rest are writing notes or reading their mail. Listening is not just common courtesy—it is the heart of teamwork.
- Idea killing. All too often a team member will propose an unconventional idea, only to have the rest of the group attack it as stupid and unworkable. Of course, it is important to think critically and to analyze ideas rigorously; at the same time, it is a mistake to kill ideas too fast. Even outlandish proposals sometimes contain nuggets of gold.
- Personal attacks. Criticizing an idea must never extend to the person who conceived it. A hostile environment causes defenses to be thrown up and debate to shut down.
- Silence. A team member who doesn't participate in discussions deprives the team of input and perspective. In addition, the rest of the team can grow to resent or even fear their silent partner.

- Oversharing. On the other hand, there are people who simply don't know when to stop talking. They will beat anything into the ground or share personal details much better kept private.

Team members must be alert to these behaviors, both in themselves and in others. In extreme cases, intervention by the process owner may be necessary.

Other traps await the team as a whole rather than members individually. For instance, democracy can easily degenerate into anarchy. While an informal, freewheeling style is appropriate for reengineering, the danger is that the team will waste energy trying to figure out how to operate. Similarly, some teams can't stop talking. They circle an issue endlessly, never arriving at a decision. Others fall into a "beat-the-clock" situation, where so much time is spent on the first agenda item that all others get short shrift.

To avoid such problems, many successful reengineering teams employ such commonsense techniques as time boxing (establishing fixed time slots for resolving an issue); using a facilitator to keep discussions moving; designating a scope monitor who assures that discussions do not digress from their stated purpose; assigning a scribe to capture everything, so note taking does not interfere with thinking; establishing explicit agendas; and ensuring that team meetings start and end promptly (and penalizing latecomers).

Teams also need careful management guidance to help them overcome the often entirely unpredictable challenges that invariably arise during reengineering. It is the job of the reengineering czar to address issues like the following:

Career paths. Since people leave their jobs to join a team, they often worry what will happen to them once reengineering is over. We've already noted that it is generally inadvisable for individuals to return to their home departments because it can bias their attitude toward reengineering. For that reason, it is important for organizations to craft alternative career paths for people upon completion of their reengineering assignment. Promotions for reengineering alumni send the message that reengineering is not just good for the company but good for individual careers, too.

Compensation. Many programs develop a bonus program for reengineers based on the success of the reengineering effort, to be paid in addition to salary and organization-wide performance bonuses. This is another good way of making reengineering a desirable assignment.

Celebration. Reengineering is intense and unrelenting. Fun—in the form of parties, karaoke nights, ball games—relieves tension while reinvigorating *esprit de corps*.

Communications. Because a great many people can be involved in reengineering, the czar must put in place communication mechanisms so that the left hand knows what the right is doing. Many reengineering programs publish their own internal newsletters or hold town meetings to facilitate the rapid and dependable flow of information.

Care and compassion. Reengineering is so intense and stressful that it can affect the reengineer's private life as well. The leaders of reengineering must protect their people from themselves. For example, one team we know included a male employee who was commuting from a remote location. His wife was about to have a baby. A month before the baby was to be born, the czar grounded him. The czar knew that this man was so absorbed in the project that he would continue working virtually up to the moment his wife entered the delivery room; instead, he forced him to do the right thing.

For all its complexities and unique challenges, we can find precedents for the reengineering experience if we only know where to look. Reengineering is quite unlike traditional business improvement programs, with their deliberate pace, formal cost-benefit analyses, and meticulous project timetables. The role model for reengineering is not finance, but R&D. Just as a company's researchers live in a constant state of uncertainty as they try to push the envelope on product and technology, so too do reengineers inhabit a space characterized by confusion and ambiguity as they seek to innovate in the domain of process. Wise reengineering leaders will seek guidance from their peers in R&D as to how to lead and manage people in such states of uncertainty.

Many reengineers have confided in us that reengineering has been the most difficult, intense, demanding, and exhausting experience of their professional lives—but also the most exciting, rewarding, significant, and fun. Most of them tell us that they cannot imagine ever going back to a "real" job again. The sense of contribution, the freedom, the flexibility, and the opportunity to make a real difference makes reengineering a heady experience.

Actually, our reengineer friends will not have to go back to a real job—nor, in a sense, will anybody else. The reason for this is that reengineering is a harbinger of its aftermath. The ways in which people work on a reengineering team give us a powerful preview of how people will work on any kind of reengineered process: in teams, under pressure, with autonomy, with a lot riding on the outcome. We had all better become more familiar with the reengineering lifestyle, for we shall all be living it soon.

CHAPTER 5

Do You Need Help?

Businesspeople don't all share the same feelings about consultants: Some hate them, while others hate them a lot. While it's easy to resent consultants for their exorbitant fees and not infrequent arrogance, they're very prevalent in reengineering. The novelty, difficulty, scale, and pace of reengineering make even many organizations that pride themselves on handling things on their own wonder whether they should get some help with *this* novel venture.

There's no doubt that reengineering has been very good for the consulting business. Market research firms estimate the 1994 market for reengineering consulting services at anywhere from $1.4 to $2.6 billion. One of the ten largest consulting firms has estimated that at least 20 percent of its 1994 revenues came from reengineering projects. The use of consultants is on the rise. In 1992, one-third of corporate expenditures on reengineering went for consultants; by 1996, it is expected to approach two-thirds.

We should stress that we have no vested interest in the question of using consultants. We're not in the consulting business—although one of us used to be—and have no allegiance to any consulting firm. Nor do we receive any royalties or commissions on consulting revenues (more's the pity). Our sole interest is seeing that reengineering is done well and successfully—with or without consultants.

With that said, let's get to the essentials—the four basic

issues that organizations considering whether to use a consultant should address:

1. What do reengineering consultants do?
2. What are the pros and cons of hiring one?
3. If you decide you need a consultant, how should you select one?
4. How do you manage your consultant?

WHAT DO CONSULTANTS DO?

There's no such thing as a prototypical reengineering consultant. There are at least four distinct types of consulting firms plying their wares in the reengineering marketplace. First are the large general management consulting organizations, with anywhere from hundreds to thousands of consultants. In response to client demand, these firms now include help with reengineering in their broad array of services. The second group consists of firms that specialize entirely in reengineering, focusing either on the full life cycle or on one aspect, such as change management or training.

The third group is that of information-technology-oriented firms, several of which are arms of hardware or software vendors. They concentrate on—but are not restricted to—reengineering's technical side, including systems development and infrastructure construction.

Finally, a growing number of small advisory firms, typically with from one to twenty-five professionals, are being formed by alumni of corporate reengineering programs who have decided to market their experience and knowledge.

Whatever the type of firm, we often characterize a consultant's contribution in terms of heads, hearts, or hands.

First, consultants can bring knowledge and brain power to their engagements. For most companies, reengineering is terra incognita, a journey into an unknown land. Consultants live on the cutting edge of business change. It is their responsibility to chart new frontiers of business thinking. A percolating brew of new and exciting concepts is an important part of what a consultant offers his or her clients. Moreover, people who gravitate toward consulting tend to be intellectually and conceptually oriented (although this is often counterbalanced by short attention spans and minimal interest in implementation). Thus, consultants can be particularly helpful in reengineering's more conceptual aspects: clarifying its nature; fashioning a vision of the future; developing a process model of the business; diagnosing the existing process; creating breakthrough concepts; designing communications and marketing programs.

Consultants can also serve as the heart, the emotional core, of a reengineering program. Their dedication to the reengineering ideal and lack of investment in a company's old ways of operating can make them ardent advocates of change. Their commitment can reinforce a client's resolve when things look bleak, and can help sway a skeptical organization. "Heart" work includes counseling leaders and czars, participating in communications efforts, supporting reengineering teams, and helping pilot sites navigate the rapids of transition. The unyielding optimism of one consultant we know, an individual with the ability to exude absolute confidence even in the face of serious adversity, was potently contagious in several of his clients' organizations. It helped sustain their reengineering programs through early setbacks. Without the motivation supplied by his personal enthusiasm, the clients would likely have folded their tents and gone home instead of pushing on to ultimate success.

Finally, the hands. Some organizations, after downsizing, or rightsizing, or whatever, simply do not have enough people to spare for reengineering. In such situations, hired hands must be brought in to staff design teams, to serve as program managers, to develop information systems. Reengineering programs also often require specific skills, notably change management, that most companies have never had occasion to develop.

Each of these kinds of consultants offers advantages and disadvantages. In the realm of the "head," it's often the general management consulting firms who take the lead in creating design concepts and in linking reengineering to an organization's strategic direction. These are able to attract—and afford—the best talent. However, many of their clients have difficulty installing these consultants' grand designs because they find that design was emphasized over the nitty-gritty of implementation. In addition, these firms usually have the highest fees and most overbearing manners; for many of them, reengineering is not the most desirable, glamorous assignment and so you may not get their best and brightest. The firms that specialize in reengineering can also provide significant value in the "head" sphere by offering clients prepackaged design solutions developed through extensive experience and research.

For "heart"-oriented assistance, high value is often provided by smaller advisory firms. These boutiques are usually populated by senior consultants who have years of experience in counseling reengineering leaders. Reengineering specialists tend to be the most wholeheartedly committed to the cause (since it is their sole livelihood), and their enthusiasm is often contagious. But they may also operate from a particular ideological stance on reengineering, which may limit their flexibility. The scale of "heart" work is generally less attractive to the larger general management and I/T-oriented firms.

"Hand" work requires large-scale support. Here, firms with an I/T capability may have an advantage, since they are the only ones positioned to assist in this critical aspect of implementation. The risk, however, is that these firms may be so focused on the technological dimension that their effectiveness in other areas is limited.

But of course, when you hire a head, a heart, or hands, the rest of the body comes with it. Many reengineering consultants are accustomed to working twelve-hour days, living on airplanes, and throwing themselves into the fray with abandon because their rates—and, frequently, their degree of dedication—are so high.

THE PROS AND CONS

We have no bias either for or against consultants. Our basic answer to the question of whether a company should use one is *"It depends"* (which, by the way, is the classic consultant response to almost every question). It's not a simple issue. We've seen companies succeed at reengineering with no outside help as well as companies where consultant involvement was absolutely critical to success. However, we've boiled down the key advantages and disadvantages to relatively few. It's important to weigh them carefully and to base your decision on clear analysis of the pros and cons rather than on pride and prejudice.

Perhaps the most common reason companies hire consultants is that they have a great deal more reengineering experience than the client does. Good consultants enable their clients to leverage other companies' experiences and avoid their mistakes. (You'll still have ample opportunity to make your own mistakes, but consider that as part of the learning process.) An effective consultant should help you avert the potholes and hairpin turns on the reengineering road. (This book can also help, but there's a limit to what will fit in a few hundred pages.)

Avoiding the pitfalls will accelerate your program, propelling you more quickly to payoff. Most unguided roads lead nowhere. As the Cheshire Cat told Alice, "If you don't know where you're going, any road will take you there." To put it another way, those who attempt a Himalayan climb for the first time usually hire an experienced Sherpa guide.

Consultants can also suggest the best path to your destination, with all the helpful shortcuts. Having traveled the road before, they usually have a clear picture of the journey—and a reliable map, that is, a reengineering methodology. Obviously, reengineering is not a free-form set of activities. Recurring phases and activities must be performed as you move from today to tomorrow.

Any responsible consulting firm will have such a methodology, an overview of the flow of work that must be accomplished. This methodology should identify major work activities and related tasks; time frames and resource requirements for each task; and key milestones, management reviews, and decision points for each stage of the journey. The methodology should also address critical supporting requirements such as I/T and HR, the management of change, and the integration of all the elements of reengineering into a coherent program.

While leveraging a consultant's experience can be beneficial, there's a danger in outsourcing a capability vital to your organization's long-term health. It's likely that you will want to reengineer many of your processes, possibly more than once. Eventually, you'll either develop self-sufficiency in this or become a major source of a consultant's annuity. In other words, even if consultants facilitate your first reengineering success, you'll want to avoid developing a debilitating dependency on them.

Another advantage of consultants is their range of reengineering skills. For example, many in-house redesign teams are hard-pressed to get "out of the box" on their own. The power of the prevailing paradigm—the context in which the team has always operated—often blocks their way.

Consultants are good at smashing the box and assisting the team in envisioning breakthrough ideas. They do this by using creativity tools that stimulate the client's imagination.

In information technology, too, even large organizations are not likely to have enough staff to support reengineering and ongoing business simultaneously. That was the case at Pepsi-Cola, where an overwhelming demand for programmers, database administrators, and technology trainers dwarfed its internal capacity and forced the company to seek outside resources. Consultants' specialized skills in a particular technology can be invaluable. Having no previous internal experience or expertise in point-of-sale devices, Hallmark used consultants to support its use of that technology.

Some companies also retain consultants in order to gain their expertise in accelerated systems development. You know by now that reengineering implementation must be conducted at breakneck speed, typically in two to three years. Reengineering will be imperiled if an internal MIS shop takes two years—which would actually be remarkably fast in many companies—just to develop the first version of new process-supporting software. At Liberty Mutual Insurance, external I/T consultants were used because they had experience with innovative development techniques, such as rapid prototyping and object-oriented programming. Enabling the system development activity to keep pace with the rest of the program was a key element in Liberty Mutual's success.

As we've repeatedly noted, change management lies at the heart of all reengineering programs. Few organizations possess the combination of skills, attitudes, and experience needed for navigating a complex change through a maze of constituencies. Not many in-house reengineers have designed and executed a full-fledged communications program. Broad, vision-based marketing campaigns are rare, except in the consumer products industry—and even there, selling soap powder is very different from selling organizational change.

Many consulting firms have great analytic strength, but this can be a double-edged sword. Rigorous data collection and analysis—on which consulting firms have a near monopoly—can be very important in making an effective business case for reengineering. On the other hand, we've described how tempting, and dangerous, it is to slip from process diagnosis into exhaustive analysis, as people of analytic temperament are inclined to do. A very fine line must be trod here, especially since some consulting firms have a penchant for collecting and processing vast amounts of data only to prove what everyone already knew.

Reengineering success also requires strong program management capabilities. Imagine a company that is reengineering three processes, all of which are in the implementation phase. Eight to ten teams might well be at work on various aspects of each process. This collection of twenty to thirty teams must be coordinated; their project plans must be integrated, their interdependencies identified, their timelines harmonized, and their change management activities synchronized. Aerospace firms, defense contractors, major construction firms, and others with large-scale project management experience may be skilled at managing such complexity. Few other organizations are, and here again consultants can be of help.

At a very considerable cost, however. Skilled advisers are expensive. At top-tier consulting firms, even newly minted MBAs can cost up to $2,000 to $3,000 a day: a lot of money to pay for rookies in the reengineering game who may be getting their first field experience on your nickel. The beginners are of course managed by more senior consultants—who, however, charge even more. It's not uncommon for a single project team at a large company to employ three to ten consultants for three to eight months or longer. The arithmetic can yield astounding numbers. Some clients pay well over $500,000 *a month* in consulting fees.

Obviously, the cost must be measured against the potential benefit. For one large chemical company with a reengineering business case promising $250 million in annual benefits, the $10 million consulting fee was easy to swallow, particularly because the company leadership had little confidence they could achieve the benefits on their own. The company calculated that if the consultants accelerated the benefit realization by even one month over the course of the two-year program, they would receive an excellent return on their consulting investment.

Even if the size of the benefit may make the use of consultants seem attractive, the timing of the investment and the uncertainty of the return make the decision somewhat more problematic. Reengineering benefits conform to the Protestant ethic: Pay now, and enjoy the payoff later. This front-end loading can present cash flow and capital allocation problems. Companies' cash flow and tolerance for investing in uncertainty play large roles in shaping their decisions on whether or not to use consultants.

These factors are relevant to small and large companies alike. Obviously, small companies can't afford anything like the fees we cited—but they don't have to, since their use of consultants is at a much lower scale. Still, costs relative to revenues can be high, and they may outweigh the benefits.

A third virtue of consultants is the *objectivity* most bring to the effort. Everyone inside a company has a political stake in reengineering, some turf or job to protect, some position to covet. Since power is a zero-sum game and change virtually always disturbs power relationships, everyone on the inside can probably be seen as having a vested interest or a hidden agenda in reengineering. Their behavior recalls Byzantine palace intrigues, where statements of principles masked purely personal agendas. As an outsider with nothing to protect, and no ulterior motives, a consultant can help cut through this political labyrinth. The truth is that it's very difficult for people inside an organization to be objective, to cast off the biases, filters, and prejudices that distort vision and blind them to new possibilities. The outside view is often far clearer.

The flip side of objectivity is *responsibility*. Consultants may be objective, but they're also ultimately not accountable for a reengineering project's success or failure. At the end of the day, they leave, the employees stay, and the client must live with the result. To a consultant, a failure may mean refunding some fees at worst. For the internal reengineering team, however, the differences between success and failure are enormous: promotions, opportunities, career fulfillment, and perhaps company survival.

Relying too heavily on a consulting firm's expertise led to failure at one Chicago bank. To support its reengineering initiative, the bank hired a major general management consulting firm. During the six-month design phase, the consultants positioned themselves as the leaders and owners of the reengineering program. They, not the internal reengineering team leaders, went to senior management review meetings. They, not the reengineering teams, received comments on the process designs. And they, not the internal staff, set the schedules and organized the implementation plan. By the time the

DILBERT reprinted by permission of UFS, INC.

bank discovered that the consultants were using their control over information flow to hide a host of problems, it was too late. Six valuable months had elapsed, the design and implementation plans didn't make any sense, and the bank had to start over.

The Pros and Cons of Using Consultants

Pros

The ability to leverage other companies' experiences
Getting access to essential skills
Third-party objectivity

Cons

The risk of outsourcing an important capability
Incurring significant expense
Diffuse accountability

To answer the ultimate question of whether to use a consultant to support your reengineering efforts, we suggest structuring your decision in terms of the pros and cons we've just explored. If you're new to reengineering, if you lack strength in the areas—out-of-the-box thinking, change management, program management—where consultants typically bolster their clients, if you can fund the required investment and wait patiently for the benefits, if your environment is so politicized that clarity and truth telling are rare, you may well want to retain a consultant. Be sure, however, that you understand why. And define what you're seeking in the way of help. As we'll see in a moment, your evaluation of consultant candidates should be based on the same sort of analysis that led to your decision to hire one in the first place.

One additional factor should be considered before taking the plunge: your organization's ability to make effective use of consultants. Some companies have had such bad experiences with consultants in the past that they may be unable to get full value from new ones. Sometimes these problems can be attributed to the consultants, but often the flaw lies in the companies themselves: their arrogance, their not-invented-here syndrome, their xenophobia. Some companies simply cannot work effectively with outsiders. The worst of all worlds is spending the money on consultants and not getting the benefit.

HOW TO SELECT A CONSULTANT

We offer the following criteria for evaluating consultants, once you've decided to hire one.

First and foremost, you must be sure that the consultant has previously participated in actual, successful reengineering and has solid references to prove it. Many consultants will assure you that they've been doing reengineering for years—that they invented it, in fact—when all they're doing is using a fashionable new label for one of their standard practices. Check references very carefully. Were the projects they cite true reengineering? Were they process focused? Did they center on radical redesigns? Did they achieve dramatic results? Were all aspects of the business system affected?

Confirm the results. Were they as advertised? Precisely what role did the consultants play in achieving the results? Was the client satisfied at the end of their engagement? Would they hire them again? And check the firm's expertise. Do they have a methodology that's both flexible enough to be tailored to your precise needs and rigorous enough to incorporate previous client experiences? Do they invest in training all their personnel in reengineering concepts and techniques? Do they maintain an advanced research capability that keeps them abreast of developments in this fast-changing field? Do they have a broad base of knowledge of the best practices and other companies' experiences? Beyond general reengineering capability, it's very helpful for a consultant to have experience in your industry and the specific processes you want to reengineer.

Second, be sure that the consultant's capabilities match your needs. A small firm, no matter how wise its principals, is unlikely to be able to support you in large-scale project work; conversely, large firms are focused on deploying massive teams and will not be interested in playing a smaller-scale, advisory role. Some firms are stronger at mobilization and planning, others at change management, still others at project implementation. Know your own needs, your strengths and weaknesses, before you start evaluating consultants. Be especially sure to avoid a consultant whose strengths duplicate, rather than complement, your own. This is an easy trap to fall into, because we are all attracted to those whose world-views mirror our own. As the seventeenth-century French epigrammatist, the Duc de La Rochefoucauld, observed, "We rarely find that people have good sense unless they agree with us." By the way, be sure that you avoid being taken in by the soft soap; La Rochefoucauld also said, "We also like those who admire us."

Make certain you distinguish between a consulting firm's selling skills and its ability to deliver. There are some notorious gaps here. Many firms can put on a great show to market themselves, trotting out articulate senior "thought leaders." What you want to know, however, is *who will actually do the work?* Demand the names of the proposed staff, then check their references. Have they personally reengineered before? To what outcome? Find out from their last few clients.

You must also know how long this staff will be assigned to your project, and not only to avoid a "bait-and-switch" ploy. It's important to know with whom you'll be forming long-term relationships. Consulting firms generally dislike all this. They want the latitude to staff each assignment based on what's best for them. Insistence on an explicit staff list will irritate some consulting firms. Tough. The customer has the right to know.

Selecting consultants who will share their reengineering knowledge with you is vital. They must reengineer *with* you, not *to* you. Your people must not be bystanders, and the consultants must have mechanisms to ensure they won't be. This should include an explicit training and education plan for your own reengineers. The consultant must be ready to leave you better prepared for the future.

Price is a very complex factor in consultant evaluation. Surely you can't buy on price alone, as with a fungible commodity. On the contrary, with consultants, you generally—but not always—get what you pay for. To further complicate matters, it's often hard to compare the prices quoted by various firms. Some practically give away up-front planning and design work in the hope of capturing the much more lucrative implementation and change management phases. Our advice is to rank the candidates on your evaluation of their capability and fit, and then pick the highest name on the list that you can afford.

Since working with a reengineering consultant means establishing a close, extended relationship, you must make certain of your compatibility with your potential partners. Do you have similar working styles, comparable world-views, consonant standards and principles? Do you trust them? Have confidence in their judgment and discretion? Factors like these often determine a project's ultimate success or failure. It's wise to begin by hiring a consultant for a minor piece of work that will throw you together for a

getting-to-know-you period, during which you can assess
work quality as well as compatibility.

Some companies attempt to short-circuit the process we've
just outlined. At one insurance firm, the reengineering czar
rounded up five likely candidates whose reputations impressed
him and whose promotional materials had caught his attention. He invited the five to deliver two-hour sales presentations—all on the same day—to him and a cross-functional
consultant selection committee. Management believed it
would be inconvenient and time-consuming to ask the candidates to visit the company in advance to interview management or collect data. Thus, the consultant would be selected
solely on the basis of its performance in the daylong "dog
and pony show."

On the fateful day, each set of consultants staged a generic
sales pitch, hoping their personal chemistry would jibe with
that of the decision makers. The selection committee made
its choice based on its "comfort level" with each of the five.
Six months later, the winning firm was fired. Its aggressive
approach clashed with the client's restrained culture—and
factors in the client environment of which they'd been
unaware made the consultants' promised outcomes unattain-
able. Six critical months and a lot of money were lost
because of a haphazard decision.

"Hire a consultant in haste, repent at leisure" is our version of an old aphorism. A lot rides on digesting its wisdom.

MANAGING CONSULTANTS

Having selected your consultant, you need to ensure that
your working relationship will be a success. This will depend
largely on how well you manage the consultant. Start by
drafting a contract that specifies each party's roles, relationships, and responsibilities; identifies mechanisms for quality

control, performance measurement, and conflict resolution; and clarifies how success will be determined. Consider the contract less a legal document than a means for making certain that important issues are explicitly addressed. The key is anticipating problems and structuring the relationship to avoid them.

You and your consultant should also agree on measures and mechanisms for assessing progress. Establish key milestones and deliverables and stay on top of them from the very start. But don't assume that these will be sufficient; you must also listen to the grapevine. If the consultants are providing good value, your people's buzz will be positive. But beware of excessive enthusiasm. Consultants are paid to express unpopular truths, remove comfort zones, tread on sacred rules, speak the unspeakable. Good ones serve as lightning rods in the client organization—a valuable role that will not, however, win them popularity contests. Consultants about whom you hear *only* good things may not be demanding enough of your organization. A certain amount of pushback is par for the course; too little as well as too much signals a problem.

It must never be forgotten that the client, not the consultant, owns the project. Consultants are advisers, not managers. They can recommend and suggest but not hire or fire, pay salaries, or give orders. Consultants use persuasion and influence rather than power to make things happen. If they try otherwise, they are likely to provoke resentment on the part of the client's people, which will limit their effectiveness. Making certain that your employees as well as the consultants understand this will help you avoid a host of problems.

Above all, be a smart client. The more you know about reengineering and the consultant's work, the more you'll be able to contribute to the effort and the greater the chances of its success. An intelligent, resourceful client brings out the best in a consultant. Have the firm's senior consultants educate you on their process. Ask them to give you five articles to read, five seminars to attend, five other clients to talk to. Then do your homework. The investment in time and energy will more than pay for itself.

Finally, recognize that your agenda and the consultant's are similar but not identical. You want reengineering success, as big and as quick as possible. Consultants do too, but for different reasons: They want references and a positive story to tell. They also want to be paid, and possibly extend their current engagement by selling you follow-up work. Understanding each other's needs and perspectives will increase the chances that you'll both be winners. In fact, this absolutely has to be a win-win. The client will not succeed unless the consultant does, and of what value is a consultant whose client fails?

CHAPTER 6

Are You Ready for Reengineering? A Self-Assessment Diagnostic

Grab a pencil before you start this chapter. You will be quizzed on your knowledge of your own organization and tested on your ability to assess its capabilities. The only right answer is the truth.

This diagnostic, designed to help you determine your company's strengths and weaknesses at reengineering, consists of twenty statements that characterize an organization that is well positioned for successful reengineering. These statements are organized around three major themes.

You should ask yourself how true each statement is of your organization. The answer scale runs from 1 to 5, with 1 representing strong disagreement (i.e., the statement is not at all true of your organization) and 5 representing strong agreement (i.e., the statement is very true of your organization).

After you complete the diagnostic, use the next section, Evaluating Your Scores, to do precisely that. Minimum scores are given for each statement, for each section, and for the diagnostic as a whole. While there are obviously no passing or failing grades, these base scores are intended to help you identify problem areas. The chapter concludes with advice on how to go about improving scores for each of the twenty statements.

And now it's time for the test. No peeking.

The Self-Assessment Diagnostic

REENGINEERING LEADERSHIP

1. The leader of reengineering is a senior executive who is strongly committed to reengineering and who possesses the title and authority necessary to institute fundamental change. *Score:* _____

2. The reengineering leader truly understands the nature of reengineering and the magnitude of the change—organizational change in particular—that it entails. *Score:* _____

3. The reengineering leader has a vision of the kind of organization he or she wishes to create and is able to express that vision clearly and simply in operational terms. *Score:* _____

4. The reengineering leader is ready and able to exercise leadership—through communications, personal behavior, and systems of measurement and reward—in order to make reengineering succeed. *Score:* _____

5. The reengineering leader is prepared to commit both the organizational resources and personal attention that reengineering requires. *Score:* _____

6. The entire senior management team shares the leader's enthusiasm for reengineering. *Score:* _____

ORGANIZATIONAL READINESS

7. The organization as a whole recognizes the need for reengineering and fundamental change.
   Score: _____

8. The organization understands the nature of reengineering, including the fact that it results in multidimensional change that impacts processes, jobs, organizational structure, management responsibilities, etc. *Score:* _____

9. The organization believes that the reengineering leader and the senior management team are truly committed to reengineering, and that this commitment will be long-lasting. Score: _____

10. The organization has none of the complacency and arrogance that often follow a sustained period of success. Score: _____

11. The organization is free of the skepticism, mistrust, and ambivalence that often follow a program of downsizing or restructuring. *Score:* _____

12. The organization has the financial and human resources needed to implement reengineering.
    Score: _____

13. Key staff organizations—human resources, finance, and information systems—are positive about the prospect of reengineering and capable of innovative response to its demands. *Score:* _____

14. The organization's experience with total quality management (TQM) has created an environment that is receptive to reengineering.
    Score: _____

15. The organization places a high value on serving customers and has a solid understanding of customer needs. *Score:* _____

STYLE OF IMPLEMENTATION

16. The organization is comfortable with the way in which reengineering proceeds, through risk taking, learning, and ambiguity. *Score:* _____

17. The members of reengineering teams will feel empowered to "break the rules" and to challenge long-standing assumptions. *Score:* _____

18. The reengineering effort is directed at key business processes rather than organizational units. *Score:* _____

19. Managers have been given end-to-end responsibility for the processes to be reengineered and are motivated to assure that the processes are successfully reengineered. *Score:* _____

20. Measurement systems and performance goals have been established to chart the progress of reengineering. *Score:* _____

EVALUATING YOUR SCORES

The following list indicates the minimum numbers we believe an organization should score before tackling reengineering—that is, prior to launching the effort. Some issues are more vital than others, and hence have a higher minimum score. If your score on a statement is lower than the indicated minimum, you should take steps (such as those suggested later in this chapter) to raise it. While there is no precise mathematical formula for success, a higher score obviously means you are better positioned to achieve it. Scoring above the minimum does not absolve you of further effort, however. You may be ready to begin, but you should strive to raise each number as high as possible to further improve your position.

Although we recommend minimum scores for each statement, each section, and the diagnostic as a whole, your primary focus should be on the individual statements themselves, since strength in one area does not really compensate for weakness in another. Note, too, that the minimum recommended section score is larger than the sum of the minimum statement scores. Why? Because mere adequacy in each category is not enough to guarantee success; overall strength is what is needed.

Minimum Scores

REENGINEERING LEADERSHIP

Statement 1: 4
Statement 2: 3
Statement 3: 4
Statement 4: 4
Statement 5: 4
Statement 6: 3
Minimum score for section: 24

ORGANIZATIONAL READINESS

Statement 7: 3
Statement 8: 2
Statement 9: 4
Statement 10: 2
Statement 11: 2
Statement 12: 3
Statement 13: 2
Statement 14: 3
Statement 15: 3
Minimum score for section: 28

STYLE OF IMPLEMENTATION

Statement 16: 3
Statement 17: 4
Statement 18: 4
Statement 19: 3
Statement 20: 3
Minimum score for section: 18
Minimum score for diagnostic as a whole: 75

These minimum scores, as we said, are what you need before you start. Once implementation is under way, however, required minimum scores go up—sometimes way up. In particular, scores for statements 1, 5, 9, 12, 18, and 19 must be 5 (or better!). The rest should consistently grade out at 4 or 5. As implementation progresses, intensity increases—meaning that leadership, resources, and focus, already strong, must get stronger. So don't just take this test once and then forget it; use it again and again. During implementation, the diagnostic can help you monitor your progress and identify areas requiring further attention and improvement.

If you think these minimum scores are somewhat high and even intimidating, you are right. We never said it would be easy. The entrance requirements for reengineering are stiff.

IMPROVING YOUR SCORES

The following comments explain the significance of each of the twenty statements that make up the diagnostic and offer recommendations for improving low scores.

Reengineering Leadership

1: The leader of reengineering must be a senior executive who is passionate about reengineering and has a strong commitment to it. Passion and commitment are not enough, though. He or she must also have the authority to implement the changes needed to support major process redesign.

If the nominal reengineering leader is not demonstrating passion and commitment, he or she must be made to understand the complexities of reengineering and why dynamic leadership is so important. Reviewing case histories (successful and unsuccessful) and meeting with counterparts at other firms can help provide a model of what is required—and an appreciation for why it is so vital.

If no one naturally fills the role of leader, a leader must be recruited. Potential leaders within the company should be targeted and educated about reengineering, its mechanisms and its potential.

To demonstrate the need for reengineering, you should document the costs and consequences of existing processes. Customer testimony about process inadequacies can be particularly persuasive in convincing potential leaders that they need to act. So are financial data that demonstrate the costs of your processes and benchmarking information that documents competitor superiority.

2: Unfortunately, many senior managers try to reengineer without really understanding what it means. They use the term because it is fashionable, without appreciating its consequences. Overlaying a new process on an old organization is a recipe for disaster. Unless the leader really understands and pushes radical change, reengineering will not succeed.

The leader must understand where reengineering is headed, or the effort will be abandoned in midstream. To assist a prospective leader in developing this understanding, you should dramatize as vividly as possible the changes that reengineering will likely bring to the company's structure, personnel, compensation system, and other areas.

3: The leader needs to develop and communicate a vision of the destination of the reengineering journey around which people can rally. Clarity and simplicity are critical. They reduce the terrors of the unknown for employees and allow them to proceed with confidence. For example, at one insurance company, the vision was expressed as "one and done," meaning that any customer request would be handled by one person, and one person alone. By making the final destination clear, real, and attractive, the leader makes it easier for people to begin the long march.

The vision must not only be communicated but infused with enthusiasm. If the leader is unable to combine passion and logic, resources should be allocated to help him or her do so.

4: Personal commitment is not enough; the leader must *actively* exercise leadership. A gap between words and deeds causes employees to become cynical and disillusioned. Communications, personal behavior, and measurement and compensation systems are the levers of leadership. The leader must aggressively and consistently use all three levers or face an inevitable crisis of confidence.

5: Reengineering requires energy and hard work. The leader must commit his or her own time to it. The leader cannot afford to delegate responsibility; a lower-level manager will not possess the authority to overcome resistance and to make necessary changes. In addition, some of the company's best people must be drafted onto the reengineering team, as both a valuable talent pool *and* a signal of serious intent.

6: Even the most committed leader cannot make reengineering happen alone. The entire executive team must contribute. Noncompliance by a single key executive can derail the entire program, by withholding resources, failing to meet commitments, or malicious rumormongering.

If senior management as a whole does not share the leader's enthusiasm, their support must be enlisted through a combination of persuasion and coercion. Over time, communication and commitment usually overcome initial reluctance. If support is not forthcoming, however, the leader has no choice but to replace those who do not embrace the vision. Do not put off this step. The longer a high-level resister is allowed to remain, the greater the likelihood of trouble. Even companies that have succeeded at reengineering tell us that, in retrospect, they should have removed highly placed resisters earlier.

Organizational Readiness

7: Reengineering inspires fear and resistance. So if people don't see what's at stake, they have no incentive to change. Why should they? Change is painful. Only an organization that recognizes the need for change will be receptive to the reengineering message.

There are many reasons to reengineer. The reason may be defensive—a reaction to financial or competitive pressures or customer concerns. It may be anticipatory—for instance, when impending market changes or new technologies may put your company at a sudden disadvantage. Or it may be proactive, to help your company gain a competitive edge. Bottom line: If employees are to believe in reengineering, they need to know why it's being done.

They must also know that "business as usual" will absolutely not work. The best way to deliver this message is by making what we call a Case for Action, which lays out the business climate in simple, understandable terms and shows why the company must change. Again, this argument must be clearly presented *and* passionately argued.

8: Employees who do not understand reengineering almost always assume the worst. They assume it is a euphemism for "downsizing," a synonym for total quality management (TQM), or just another management fad. The less they know, the more they dream up scenarios that pit them against the reengineering effort. At best, they will become reluctant participants. At worst, they will be active antagonists. The antidote for this situation is communication: universal, hard-hitting, and repetitive.

The reengineering leader must continually talk up the program, recognizing that the message may not get through completely the first or second or even fifth time. It is always better to risk repetition than to assume a level of understanding (or commitment) that is not there. Reengineering leaders consistently tell us that they underestimated the amount of communication effort that reengineering would demand of them.

9: When it comes to management's own commitment, perception *is* reality. Even when the reengineering leader and the management team are serious about reengineering, that sincerity is useless unless the employees perceive and believe it. And usually employees would prefer not to. After all, that's easier than accepting the prospect of massive disruptive changes. Unfortunately, such skepticism is often warranted. In many companies, senior management has a history of talking "change" while maintaining the status quo. Employees grow understandably cynical when they hear the word "change" again. Cynicism stifles enthusiasm, and defeat becomes a self-fulfilling prophecy.

How to combat this cynicism? Thoughtful and nonstop communication; assigning high-profile resources to the reengineering effort; and taking irrevocable actions (e.g., a reorganization or a major realignment of resources) that will only work out if reengineering becomes a reality.

10: Successful organizations are the hardest to reengineer. People point to the signs of success and ask, "If it ain't broke, why fix it?" They brush off recent difficulties or dismiss looming problems because it's more comfortable to believe these are temporary setbacks rather than permanent threats to the organization's health. Such complacency—or worse, the arrogance into which it often evolves—is a serious impediment to reengineering.

The reengineering leader and his or her team must get the organization to look to the future. While past accomplishments need not be diminished, it must be made clear that they are no guarantee of future success. It is also important to discourage, publicly and explicitly, any behavior and attitudes that reflect this sort of complacency. Again, do not assume such attitudes will simply evaporate on their own.

11: After painful layoffs or other realignment measures, employees are naturally even more resistant to change. Stressed and pained, survivors tend to crave a period of stability. Cynicism may predominate if recent changes have failed to produce the promised results.

In such situations, management must recognize the realities of human nature. It is important to respect employees' feelings and address their concerns. Where appropriate, senior managers should admit past mistakes and distinguish them from current efforts. Above all, management must make achieving quick results their top priority. That is the best way to show that reengineering is not just empty talk.

12: Reengineering requires a dedicated team of talented, imaginative people who are unafraid to break rules, who can work together in a multifunctional, multidisciplinary manner, and who put customer needs above organizational turf battles. It is essential that team members devote full time and energy to reengineering. By not tapping the best people or by limiting their involvement, management sends a message, however unwittingly, that reengineering is not of prime importance.

Any organization lacking experienced reengineers faces three choices: develop them through special training programs, import them from other organizations, or make use of consultants. If it appears impossible to place first-rate people on the reengineering effort, management should take stock of all company activities and eliminate or reduce those not vital to day-to-day operations so that valuable resources can be redeployed to reengineering. This will further underscore its high priority.

13: Reengineering usually focuses on value-adding operational processes like product development and order fulfillment. Changes in these areas, however, require the involvement of key staff units such as MIS, HR, and finance. These must help create the infrastructure to support the new processes. In so doing, these units will be forced to violate many of their long-standing norms. New financial measurements will be required, assumptions about personnel will be broken, information systems will need to be developed in nontraditional ways. If the leaders of staff units lack the vision or will to make these changes, reengineering is in trouble. If staff units themselves are unable to rise to the reengineering challenge, they may need new leadership. In extreme situations, it may be necessary to outsource the staff work to a vendor less invested in the ways of the past.

14: Most companies undertaking reengineering today have some experience with total quality management. This can be helpful, or it can be a problem. TQM and reengineering share many characteristics, including a focus on customers, orientation toward processes, and commitment to improved performance. There are, however, important differences between the two. TQM stresses incremental improvement through structured problem solving, whereas reengineering is about radical improvement through total process redesign. TQM assumes the underlying process is sound and looks to improve it; reengineering assumes it is not and seeks to replace it. Reengineering is best seen as the next step after TQM. Success with TQM can position an organization to take that next step. On the other hand, organizations that have fared poorly with TQM may reject reengineering as just another passing fad. Moreover, some who confuse the accoutrements of TQM with its essence may dismiss reengineering for not fitting the quality mold.

Management must clarify the nature of customer-focused quality and explain how TQM relates to reengineering. It may be wise to reinforce this relationship by integrating the units responsible for the two approaches.

15: To reengineer means, fundamentally, to rebuild the company on the customer's behalf. This requires a deep appreciation of customer needs; without that, reengineering will be mistargeted from the outset. To overhaul the wrong processes or to reinvent the right processes with the wrong objectives is worse than useless.

The reengineering leader must orient the company toward the customer through explicit communications, targeted reward systems, and by getting everyone to talk to customers. Direct customer contact helps people develop a renewed sense of the value of their own work as well as a sharper sense of the customer's overriding importance to the company.

Style of Implementation

16: Reengineering is not a traditional implementation exercise that begins with a highly defined goal and a precise blueprint for achieving it. Rather, it is a collective voyage of discovery, which begins with only a rough outline of the destination and races toward it at breakneck speed. Some cultures are naturally comfortable with this style. Those that are not must learn to adjust.

It is the leader's responsibility to help the organization make this adjustment. This can be done by personally exhibiting the implementation style required, rewarding others who exhibit it, and, above all, by pushing projects forward rapidly to completion in order to demonstrate that the new style is indeed the one required.

17: All too often, people who have bold ideas are afraid to act on them. They may remember what happened to the last guy who stuck his neck out with a creative concept. Or they may simply assume that, public pronouncements to the contrary, senior management will automatically reject anything that is truly innovative. To counteract these attitudes, rule breakers must be publicly applauded, and all timid suggestions must be summarily rejected.

18: Many companies claim to be reengineering while actually continuing to work within the confines of the old organizational chart. Inevitably, they accomplish little beyond incremental functional improvements. Real reengineering is always directed at cross-functional processes, not organizational units. Management must begin a reengineering effort by identifying and mapping the company's processes, and then be certain that reengineering efforts are focused exclusively on these processes.

19: In most companies, process responsibility is fragmented. No one has end-to-end accountability for a process. It is virtually impossible to reengineer in such an environment, since no one has the perspective or the motive to make sweeping changes.

Therefore, a process owner must be designated for each of the processes to be reengineered. The process owner must have the authority and the personal clout to get all departments involved in the process to make necessary changes. To keep the process owner personally motivated, his or her own performance must be keyed to improvement in the performance of the process itself.

20: Without clear process performance measures, an organization cannot establish where it is or where it wants to go. The first step in establishing such measures is to have customers identify the aspects of process performance they care about most (e.g., cycle time, accuracy, cost). The second is to establish baselines: how your processes currently perform in terms of these measures. Next, through competitive benchmarking, customer input, and self-assessment, establish "stretch goals" for each process. These goals should be high enough to rule out doing business as usual without being so high as to be intimidating. Above all, they must be challenging enough to have a major—and transformative—impact on overall company performance.

Do not be discouraged by the rigor of this test or by the high passing grades we demand. This test is not a classroom exercise; it is what reengineering will demand of you as you proceed. We would much rather have you delay your efforts at reengineering than begin them only to see them fail. Most of all, we want you to succeed at reengineering by using this diagnostic to find your weak spots and do something about them before you begin.

PART II

Making It Work

CHAPTER 7

Assumption Busting for Fun and Profit

"Writing is the act of staring at a blank sheet of paper until beads of blood form on your forehead." So said Ernest Hemingway about the stress and terror of the creative act. Hemingway's words, we believe, could equally well describe what all too many people feel when faced with the need to invent a new process design. Creativity is daunting. It requires the ability to see what isn't there yet, to perceive the invisible, to produce what never existed before. This is not what is taught in business schools.

Neither is our Rule of Whacko. We often describe the demands of reengineering by invoking this rule. It reads: Any valuable new process design will at first appear to be whacko. That is, if someone approaches you with a proposal for a new process design that strikes you as interesting and plausible, our advice is: Throw it away. That the notion appeals to you means that it fits your preexisting models of how the process should work—that it is only a modest variation on the existing theme and not a radical innovation at all. If, on the other hand, you initially feel a new idea is ridiculous, absurd, and out of the question, our advice is: Look at it again, for it holds at least the potential of being important. That it appears whacko means that it departs sharply from the existing process, and so at least satisfies the criterion of being radical.

Naturally, not every whacko idea is a good one. Some

whacko ideas are merely whacko. However, an idea that does not initially seem somewhat whacko has no potential at all. As Linus Pauling, the Nobel-winning chemist, once said, "The way to have lots of good ideas is to have lots of ideas and throw away the bad ones."

But breakthrough ideas don't come easily. Most people aren't trained in out-of-the-box thinking. In conventional organizations, people are encouraged to find and fix the problems in front of them, to enhance what they have inherited. Few people get training in how to kick over the table and start anew.

Yet the essence of reengineering is creation—and this can be very frightening and intimidating. Imagine that you're on a reengineering team that's about to get down to business. You've created a high-level description of the old process, which, with great decorum, you and other team members ceremonially shred and dump in the wastebasket. Well stocked with coffee, you lock yourselves in a conference room whose walls are covered with blank white boards whose unblemished purity will soon seem as threatening as Arctic snow.

Everyone rolls up his or her sleeves, ready to work. All the conditions are ripe for producing a brilliant new idea. And what happens next is: nothing. Everyone is trying to be creative, but no one knows how. Eventually, someone cracks under the mounting pressure, jumps up, and makes a beeline for the wastebasket. Reassembling the shredded copy of the old process design, this person announces the real solution lies in modification of the old. The flash of insight has led only as far as the wastebasket. Imagination has failed.

Several techniques can help break this deadlock of creativity. Breakthrough thinking is not an inborn talent possessed by only those with artistic temperaments. It is a skill that can be taught and learned. In our reengineering seminars, we teach a variety of ways for people to develop whacko ideas in a systematic fashion. One of them is called *breaking assumptions*.

Remember that the definition of reengineering contained the phrase "fundamental rethinking." One route to discovering new process designs is by surfacing and questioning the underpinnings of the old process, the reasons why it was designed to work the way it did. When these are exposed to the light of day, it often becomes crystal clear why the old design is no longer the right one, and what the centerpiece of a superior one would be.

In general, reengineering is called for when an old process no longer produces adequate results and a new one must be created. We can ask the simple question: Why didn't we use this new process from the beginning? Why did we have the old process in the first place? Consider, for instance, one of the classics of reengineering, the story of accounts payable at Ford. In the old days Ford had a department called accounts payable, which would get a purchase order from purchasing, a receiving document from the receiving dock, and an invoice from the vendor. It would then compare them and, if they matched, issue a check.

This process was replaced by one much simpler and less labor-intensive. Now, the person on the receiving dock takes possession of the goods, checks to see if they match against an order, and if so, authorizes payment; if they don't match, the shipment is not accepted. So why wasn't that done all along?

There are three answers to this question. One is that in some cases the old process was never actually designed, it just happened. People blundered about, making ad hoc decisions about specific situations. The old "design" was simply an accretion of decisions that had coalesced into policy.

Second, in some cases the old process could not have been replaced any earlier because the requisite technology had yet to be invented. Without a computer screen glowing on the receiving dock, there was no way of quickly reconciling order and delivery.

But these answers are of purely historical interest. From the point of view of future action, all that matters are the forces that are presently preventing a process from undergoing redesign. It's the third answer that addresses this. In nearly all cases, no matter how it developed, the old design was based on some assumption about the way in which the world works. Perhaps that assumption was once valid. But, like everything else in creation, assumptions are rooted in time and can become as dated as last week's newspaper.

The assumption at Ford was that accounts payable had to be a complicated, slow, bureaucratic process because the people at the receiving dock were not in a position to match invoice and order. But the advent of on-line computer systems made that assumption obsolete. As at other companies, the mere fact that the assumption was no longer valid didn't mean that it ceased influencing the way work was done. Quite the contrary: At Ford and elsewhere, assumptions remain firmly fixed in mentality and process precisely because they remain as invisible as the air we breathe. The first step in the brand of creativity we call assumption busting is making those assumptions visible. When Ford recognized it had limited itself by the assumption that people at the receiving dock were unable to authorize payment, it took the first step toward operating in a different way.

Each of the cases we examine in this book revolves around a similar constraining assumption, whose eventual rejection paved the way for the breakthrough design. At GTE, the limiting assumption was that one individual could not master all the skills needed to deal with customers, test the lines, and dispatch service technicians. At Federal Mogul, it was that every design was unique, that engineers couldn't interact with customers, and that a part had to be tooled in the same plant where it was to be made.

Some assumptions become outmoded over time; others are false from the outset. The case of IBM Credit Corporation, known to many from its description in *Reengineering the Corporation,* provides an example of the latter.

Recall that IBM Credit's old credit approval process went through four steps. One person checked the applicant's credit rating; another decided what interest rate to charge; a third person put together the lease agreement; and a fourth prepared the response to the customer.

What is the underlying assumption here? What would have been IBM Credit's response if, five or ten years ago, it had been advised to do what it eventually did—have one person handle the entire transaction? The company's response would have been that this was a crazy idea (even, maybe, "whacko") and utterly impossible. Why? It would have said the work was too complicated for one person to do. Why? Because requests for credit were very complex, each requiring the sophistication of a legal expert, the analytic capability of the financial specialist, and the cynicism of a specialist credit checker. It would clearly have been impossible for one generalist to do all that.

In other words, the assumption is that all deals are complex. The only problem is that this assumption was wrong. Upon examination, it became clear that only a small fraction of the deals were truly complex. The great majority were very straightforward and eminently doable by one person. The new concept—one person does the entire job—is perfectly viable once you discard the old, and mistaken, assumption.

Such revelations—that work processes are based on faulty assumptions—crop up time and again during reengineering. Reengineering means identifying these underlying assumptions, questioning them, and discarding them. This is the act of destruction that has to precede creation. Once people assemble, brew their coffee, and grab a notebook, the quest for assumptions begins. Two interesting things then happen. First, people can't start, and then they can't stop.

We once undertook an assumption-busting exercise with an electronics firm. We asked a management group to identify the assumptions that were limiting the performance of their order fulfillment process. The initial response was one of thunderous silence. Everyone in the room looked at one another blankly, struggling to identify those pesky assumptions. This wasn't so surprising, since, after all, these assumptions lie deeply buried in people's working consciousness. No one is even aware of them. Asking people to bring them to the surface is not unlike asking people to identify their own psychological hang-ups; it requires more perspective and distance than most of us have. After a time, however, with some gentle prodding, a few members of the group gradually began to explore some assumptions: Our customers know what they want; it is best to sell through sales representatives; a major technology advance occurs about every five years.

Before long we were drowning in a sea of long-suppressed assumptions. Given the chance, people were eager to put on the table every possible notion that they thought had been taken for granted. Eventually, we called the exercise off because it was clear we were getting nowhere. While the flood of assumptions may have had a cathartic effect on the

DILBERT reprinted by permission of UFS, INC.

participants' psyches, it was contributing little to the reengineering effort. The problem was twofold: Most of these assumptions were still in fact entirely valid, and virtually all of them were irrelevant to the poor performance of the order fulfillment process.

We've said that assumptions are what give processes their specific shape, and old assumptions must be destroyed if new ones are to take their place. But the faulty assumptions are lost in a sea of valid ones. What is needed is a more disciplined discipline for dealing with assumptions. To explain, we need to define three terms. The first is "problem." The second is "rule." And the third is "assumption."

What's a *problem*? A problem is the specific performance shortcoming that you want to improve. The problem at IBM Credit was that credit approval was too slow. At Ford, it was that accounts payable was too labor-intensive.

What's a *rule*? A rule is the particular aspect of a process design that gives rise to the problem in question. IBM Credit's problem was that the process was too slow, while the rule that generated the problem was that each task was done by a different specialist—specialist credit checkers to check credit; specialist pricers to do the pricing; specialist issuers to do the issuing. That was the particular aspect of the process design responsible for the performance shortcoming. Because IBM had specialists, it had handoffs between them, and therefore, the process was slow.

At Ford, the problem was that people in accounts payable spent vast amounts of time checking and reconciling different documents. The rule that caused this problem was that the company paid when it received the invoice, then checked it against all the other documents.

An *assumption* is something that we take for granted about the world and that causes the rule in the design. The rule is the functional consequence of the assumption. An assumption is an idea about the environment in which the work is performed that we take so for granted that it is invisible to us. At IBM Credit, the rule was we need specialists to do the work. The assumption that led to that rule was that credit approval is very complicated work. Very complicated work requires specialists. At Ford the rule was we can't pay until we get the invoice. Why? Because we assumed that the person on the receiving dock had no information about what has been ordered.

Problem, Rule, and Assumption	
Problem	A specific performance short-coming of the process Example: Slow cycle time
Rule	A specific aspect of the process design that causes the problem Example: We must have a specialist for each task
Assumption	A belief about the environment that gives rise to the rule Example: The work is complex

Let's consider another example. A consumer goods maker distributed its products to retailers through a network of route drivers. A driver would come to a store, see what was missing from the shelf, go back to the van to pull inventory, bring it into the store, fill out a manifest for the store manager's signature, and then send the form to headquarters for processing and billing. Clearly, this was an inefficient, time-consuming process—and it depended heavily on the inventory floating around in the back of the truck. That inventory was expensive to finance, complex to manage, and had an annoying way of falling off the back of the truck and into the hands of the driver's friends. Even worse, because of market changes, the company needed to broaden its product line. This was going to mean larger inventories and larger trucks.

Assumption breaking provides an angle of attack on this situation. The *problem* is that the company is carrying lots of inventory on the trucks. The *rule* behind the problem is that drivers decide what to put on the shelves only when they get to the store. The *assumption* that gives rise to this rule is that the company doesn't know what's missing from the shelf until the driver gets there. Upon reflection, the company realized that its assumption could be rejected. If, for example, it used historical data to project consumption patterns, it could predict what would be missing from the store's shelves before loading the truck at the depot. This would enable the company to make up a package of just what would be missing from a particular store's shelves; these packages would then be loaded into the truck in the same order in which the stores would be visited. The driver then would merely have to wheel the prepared package into the store, break the shrink-wrap, put the goods on the shelf, and leave behind the preprinted invoice. By taking this approach, the company improved productivity and pulled a large amount of inventory out of the system. It also did not have to buy a fleet of new trucks.

In summary, there is a method to the madness of finding faulty assumptions. Step one, find your problem. That's not so hard. The problem is probably biting you in the leg. Step two, trace backwards to find the rule. Isolate the particular piece of the process design that is the flaw, the cause of the problem. Step three, determine the assumption that underlies that flawed design.

As another illustration, consider the plight of a chain of retail stores. This retailer, like many, had trouble matching the goods at each store with the needs of the local market.

The company couldn't get the right goods to the right store because of the rule that goods-allocation decisions be made at headquarters. (Since headquarters, of course, didn't know what one store sold versus another, goods got allocated poorly.) The assumption behind this rule was that the people in the stores were not very competent; all the smart people were assumed to be in headquarters.

Having identified the assumption, the next step is to question it. Whether it was true or not in the past doesn't matter. What matters is if it's true today. IBM Credit proceeded from the assumption that all deals are complex and designed its process to reflect that assumption. Questioning the assumption, we ask if all deals really are complex. Close examination proves the assumption dead wrong. The overwhelming majority of deals are simple. A process design for complex deals was in fact being employed in deals that were anything but complex.

Once an assumption has proven untrue, the rule that constrained the process can be eliminated. Locating the operative assumption also provides a means for destroying it. Once the assumption that all deals are complex has been destroyed, the question becomes how to design a process for simple deals. Clearly, all the specialists are no longer needed—one person can handle a simple transaction from start to finish.

Finding and subduing all bad assumptions, however, may not be so easy. Often, you trace a problem back through the rule to the operative assumption, but as bad luck would have it, the assumption proves to be true. For the sake of argument, let's say that people in retail stores were in fact none too competent. Now a different question entirely must be asked. Can this true assumption be *made* false?

Up to now, we have implied that the only way to get rid of assumptions is to reveal them as untrue. In the harsh light of scrutiny, they then simply wither and blow away. But you can rid yourself of bad assumptions in another way—through intervention. After all, human beings are creatures that shape their environments. Even if people in the stores have limited capabilities today, they need not remain that way. For example, training could make store employees capable enough to handle the allocation of inventory. New hires could replace current employees. Or the company could give current employees more information or support, by connecting them to headquarters, for example, for advice on product selection.

Ford used just this kind of thinking when it reengineered purchasing. The assumption underlying the rule underlying the problem at Ford was that the fellow at the receiving dock didn't know what had been ordered. And that assumption was true. The real question was whether Ford could change the environment so that the employee would know what had been ordered. The answer to this was yes. Ford saw that if it created a database of everything that had been ordered and put a computer terminal on the receiving dock, then the dock worker could check invoices against orders. The original assumption thus became untrue.

One last problem—what if the assumption proves true and cannot be made false? In this case, we have to try again: Find another assumption behind the rule, or try another rule altogether.

But we are not done yet. While our methodology based on the problem/rule/assumption triad is easy enough to describe, it is not so easy to apply. In particular, it turns out that step two—going from problem to rule—can be quite tricky. The problem is usually all too obvious, and once the rule is identified, the assumption behind it is usually quite clear. It can be difficult, however, to go from a performance problem associated with the process as a whole (such as it's too slow or that it requires too much inventory) to identifying a specific aspect of the process design (the rule) that is the culprit. We offer a simple technique to help you over this hump. It consists of a series of starter questions that you can use to identify possible rules responsible for your process problem.

We have found that a small family of questions can point to the great majority of rules behind process problems. For instance, one of these is the "who" question. That is, one kind of rule is expressed in terms of *who* does the work of a process. At IBM Credit, for example, it was a "who rule"—specialists do all the work—that was responsible for the slow process. We would uncover this rule by asking the who question: Was a who-type rule responsible for the delay? There are also *whether, when,* and *where* rules.

A "whether rule" relates to the conditions under which the work is done. To use a humorous but true example, most auto insurance companies require applicants to fill out a form indicating any previous accidents. This form is then checked with the state Department of Motor Vehicles, never the swiftest of institutions. One insurance company faced a dilemma. It wanted to turn applications around quickly to keep potential customers from shopping elsewhere, but how could it do so if it had to always conduct a DMV check?

The insurance company realized that the "rule" creating the problem was that all applicants had to be checked with the DMV. This rule was uncovered by asking the "whether" question—that is, under what circumstances the applications had to be checked. The assumption, of course, was that *everyone* is a liar. On examination, the company, to its amazement, learned this is untrue. When it comes to driving records, females over the age of thirty-five *never* lie, and so their applications do not have to be verified. On the other hand, males under the age of twenty-one nearly always lie. Having found a "whether rule," the insurance company was able to redesign its process appropriately.

It was a "when rule" that helped solve Ford's problem of accounts payable. They asked about the timing rules of their process. In this case, it was that they paid *when* they got the invoice. That was the point of impasse, the real flaw in the design. Finding it led back to the operative assumption that had generated it.

Similarly, the consumer goods manufacturer we discussed could have found its rule through a *when* question: Restocking decisions were made *when* the driver got to the store.

In the example of the retail chain that had the wrong goods in the stores, it was not so much a "when" problem or a "who" problem as a "where" problem. Decisions about inventory were not made at the store but at headquarters.

The use of these questions provides a structure and a way of isolating the rule that is then traced to the assumption. "Who, where, when, whether" all reveal specific aspects of the design process.

To summarize our method of unearthing assumptions: Start with your problem, and use these rule types to stimulate your thinking and help you discover the rule responsible for the problem; then trace the rule back to the assumption. Is it false? If it is, destroy the assumption and discard the rule; that opens the space for creating a new process. If, however, on close examination, the assumption still holds true, ask how you can intervene to *make* it false. Lastly, if the assumption is neither false nor falsifiable, then the entire procedure should be repeated until an assumption that can be broken is finally revealed.

When asked what advice he would give aspiring writers, Hemingway joked that they should go hang themselves—if they failed, they'd at least have something to write about.

What he meant, of course, was that no one can perform the creative act for someone else. Still, as this chapter has shown, we can provide tips on jump-starting the brain to generate creative electricity—and that's an essential beginning for the "fundamental rethinking" that is vital to reengineering.

CHAPTER 8

The Hardest Part of Reengineering

Ron Compton, the CEO of Aetna Life & Casualty, describes reengineering as "agonizingly, heartbreakingly tough." Virtually everyone who has lived through the experience would describe it in similar terms. But why? What is so difficult and painful about reengineering? At first, it would seem that the most daunting part would be creating a radical, out-of-the-box model for a new process. But as we have seen in chapter 7, it isn't especially arduous to come up with breakthrough process ideas; even if it were, that would not seem to warrant the emotion-laden terms we have quoted. So what's the real problem here?

The answer, in short, is living through change: getting people to let go of their old ways and embrace new ones. We have said it before, but it bears repeating: Reengineering changes all aspects of a business. When a process changes, perforce so do the jobs of the people who work in that process. But more than jobs and skill requirements change. People's styles—the ways in which they think and behave—and their attitudes—what they believe is important about their work—must also be realigned to fit the new process. In effect, a new process requires new people. They may have the same Social Security numbers and inhabit the same bodies, but make no mistake about it: These are new people.

Those who think the purpose of their work is to please the boss, or to perform the same task over and over again, have little in common with those whose first concern is creating value for the customer and taking responsibility for the performance of an entire process.

New people in new jobs also need to be managed and measured in new ways. If you measure and reward people in the same old way, your behavior fits a remark by the writer Rita Mae Brown: "A good definition of insanity is doing the same old stuff in the same old way and expecting different results." New people working in new ways also need to be organized differently. The traditional emphasis on hierarchical, functional departments is replaced by an emphasis on process teams. These changes create a ripple effect as career paths, management roles, interpersonal relationships, and value systems all undergo profound transformations in order to support a very different way of working.

When a major insurance company introduced a new process for handling insurance applications, people's jobs changed. Gone were a multitude of narrow, specialized jobs; in their place was the new generalist role of customer account manager. The old departmental hierarchy was replaced by a flattened, team-oriented structure. The compensation system was adapted to recognize and encourage personal performance and customer focus. The roles of managers were redefined from control-oriented supervisors to supportive facilitators. At Engelhard, the responsibility for the selling process was coalesced around a multidisciplinary team with responsibility for long-term customer relationships. Team members needed to learn new skills for working together, to unlearn traditional hierarchical behavior styles, to adopt new measures that emphasized customer acquisition and retention rather than transactions, and to develop a new set of attitudes about cooperation and mutual respect. At GTE, several traditional jobs have been compressed into the customer care advocate, who is measured not on how many calls are "handled" in an hour but on how many customer problems are resolved on the first customer contact.

In each of these cases, the transition from the old process to the new was a painful experience for everyone involved. It should come as no surprise that people regard such a transition with much trepidation and anxiety, and that they find the experience itself to be unsettling and dislocating.

In our experience with companies struggling to implement reengineering, the number one source of their difficulties has been in this area of coping with the reactions of the people in the organization to the enormity of the change. These difficulties take a vast array of forms, some predictable, others quite surprising:

- A key senior executive, head of a major business unit of an insurance firm, was concerned that the reengineering of a process on a cross-business-unit basis would erode his authority and independence. His response was to try to kill the project from within by passive aggression. He would promise to provide people and resources to the effort but never actually delivered, always citing other pressures, unexpected emergencies, and the like. He also managed to "forget" to share critical information with his people, all the while swearing eternal fealty and devotion to the effort.

- Shortly after the reengineering program was announced at a financial services company, rumors started running rampant: Reengineering was merely a euphemism for downsizing and massive layoffs; the company was on the brink of bankruptcy; workloads would be dramatically increased. These rumors seemed to spring from nowhere, but were nonetheless omnipresent.

• The union leadership of a major manufacturer felt that a proposed reengineering effort would undermine the job categories and work rules that they had won over the years, and that the spirit of management-worker cooperation that might ensue would erode their own position. They persuaded their membership to vote for a strike.

• One of the senior managers of a manufacturing company was uncomfortable with power sharing and the pushing of decision making down into the ranks. He resigned to start a new competing firm.

• The designer of the old process at a service company was appointed to the review team assigned to evaluate the new process design. He impeded the effort for four months by nit-picking, by claiming that the old process already included many of the proposed new features (it didn't), and by suggesting that the new design was based on faulty premises (it wasn't). His emotional attachment to the old process turned him into a foe of the new one.

• Many of the frontline workers at a telecommunications company refused to shoulder the new responsibilities that a reengineered process placed on them. They continued to operate in the old "disempowered" way, claiming that they lacked adequate training or information to perform as the new process required. They constantly sought direction from their (now far fewer) supervisors, effectively causing the process to grind to a halt.

We could go on forever. Generally, these behaviors are called "resistance to change," although that is an overly simple term to describe a very complex phenomenon. It is this resistance that reengineers find the most perplexing, annoying, distressing, and confusing part of their job. The vagaries

DILBERT reprinted by permission of UFS, INC.

of human behavior seem infinitely more intricate than even the most complex processes. For the well-prepared reengineer, however, resistance to change need not be overwhelming or intimidating. If you understand the root causes of the phenomenon and follow a simple set of principles and techniques for dealing with it, then it will not derail your reengineering effort.

The first principle is that resistance to change is natural and inevitable. To think that it won't occur, or to view those who exhibit its symptoms as difficult or retrograde, is a fatal mistake. We have little patience with those who complain to us, often with surprise, that their reengineering efforts failed because people resisted change. The real cause of reengineering failure is not the resistance itself but management's failure to deal with it.

In fact, resistance to reengineering change is a sign that something significant is happening; we become very nervous if we observe no resistance, because that suggests that the change being undertaken is incremental at most. Machiavelli, writing in *The Prince*, recognized this truth in the fifteenth century: "There is no undertaking more hazardous nor more uncertain of its success than the introduction of a new order of things, because the innovator has as fierce opponents all those who profit from the existing system and only lukewarm defenders in those who might profit from the new one." In short, reengineering has no constituency in the organization. Its process orientation means it crosses organizational boundaries; the scale and breadth of the changes it brings means that almost everyone is affected. Indeed, since reengineering is change on an unprecedented scale, it inevitably provokes resistance on an unprecedented scale.

The second principle is that resistance does not always show its face. The naive expectation is that resistance will be manifested as sabotage. Would that it were so! Explicit resistance has the virtue of being on the surface, open to view and response. Unfortunately, resistance is often expressed in a much more subtle and indirect fashion. Don't be misled by surface calm and rationality; it masks distress and dissent.

If you go into an organization and bring the people who work there the glad tidings that you are going to change what they do, how they do it, who they do it with, how they are measured, how they are paid, how they are organized, and even what goes on inside their heads, their response is likely to be utter panic. Outwardly, their reactions may be polite and reasonable, but inwardly they are in a state of sheer terror.

Resistance wears many masks and takes many forms. The first is simple denial. You tell people that reengineering will solve a terrible problem facing the business, and often their reply will be, "What problem?" The company may be on the verge of Chapter 11 and people will still tell you there is no problem. The human ability to deny the existence of problems is astounding. Upton Sinclair said, "It is very difficult to get someone to believe something when his salary depends on his not believing it." John Kenneth Galbraith also has a trenchant observation on the subject: "Faced with the alternative between changing one's mind and proving it is unnecessary, just about everybody gets busy on the proof."

We encountered an example of this phenomenon at a very

prestigious electronics company. One of its processes—informing customers about new products—was in deep trouble. We knew it. Everybody who dealt with the company knew it. When we talked to people at the company about it, they replied, "We beg your pardon. Everything is just fine." We said, "But your customers hate the way they're informed about your new products." They denied this and insisted that their customers were in fact satisfied; as proof, they cited a survey that showed an 80 percent satisfaction rate with this process. We asked to see the survey instrument, and indeed it asked: How satisfied are you with the way we inform you of new products? The catch was that customers were given a choice of only three answers: (1) extremely satisfied, (2) very satisfied, or (3) satisfied. Not only is this a true story, but we later encountered the identical situation at another company!

What happens when you get past denial, after you prove that there really is a problem and demonstrate the necessary solution? You'll be told that they tried it already. "We tried that years ago—we put in that new process. It was a terrible failure. They shot everybody involved. In fact, even today they shoot anybody who even mentions it, so I wouldn't say anything if I were you."

If you persist, and they realize that you're serious, then their tactics shift. They say, "Your idea is terrific, and we support it 100 percent. However, we are terribly busy right now. We are about to introduce a new product, and then comes the holiday season, and then we have budgets to do, and then the strategic plan, and then we have the road show, and then a major industry conference. Why don't you come back two years from Thursday? It is a great idea, but just not right now." Or, "This is a very great idea, but it is so important that we have to proceed slowly and carefully. Let's study and evaluate it for a few years." The point of all this, of course, is to stall any attempt at change; what these people are really thinking is, "Let's be sure not to do anything."

When people realize that stalling isn't going to work, then they switch to what we call the Kiss of Yes. Everyone vows, "Yes, yes, yes, we are fully with you. We are going to do it." But they don't do it. They lie. Managers promise to give you their best people, but don't give you anyone. Or they give you their worst people. Or they assure you that everyone in the organization will be informed of the effort, and then they keep it a secret.

Even the most dedicated reengineers can get worn down by such relentless, disguised resistance. The lesson is never to give up. Always be on the lookout for resistance, never be taken in by its false fronts, and keep up the good fight.

The third principle is that resistance is manifested not only among people who will "lose" because of reengineering. The human psyche is much more complex than that, and even ostensible "winners" can turn out to be implacable foes. It is necessary to understand the variety of motivations behind resistance to reengineering. To illustrate this point, we will describe a situation that we have encountered in almost identical form in four different contexts: a plastics manufacturer, an insurance company, a maker of electrical components, and a major office equipment company. The details varied, but the key factors were the same. The process in question in each case was order acquisition and fulfillment—from the time the customer says, "I'm interested," to the time the order is delivered.

In the old process, the sales rep would push new products at the customer until eventually the customer expressed interest in buying. But when the customer asked the cost of a product, the sales rep couldn't answer. He or she did have a price list, but it was a mere formality. Customers were always given discounts, the size of which depended on a host of factors. The sales rep had to fill out an SPR, a Special

Pricing Request, which included information on the customer, the deal, the volume, the competitive situation, and
so forth.

After filling out this form, the sales rep would send it back
to the pricing department at headquarters. It would typically
take them two weeks to come back with an approved price.
The customer would then ask, "When can I get delivery?"
The sales rep now had a choice—tell the truth or keep the
sale. Needless to say, the sales rep would promise any delivery date the customer wanted just to get the order. Having
"satisfied" the customer on the issue, the sales rep would
scoop up the order, disappear in a puff of smoke, and drop
the paperwork at the nearest plant. The plant manager and
his or her staff of production schedulers would then determine when the order would actually be filled. Should the
customer begin to get anxious about the unfilled order or
want to inquire as to its status, he or she had to call the customer service department at the plant, since the sales rep
could not be reached. The job description of the customer
service reps boiled down to answering the phone and saying,
"I don't know." They lacked any real information about the
order status and could do little for the customer.

Other than being glacially slow and almost completely
unreliable, this process was a real winner.

In the reengineered process, when customers ask about
product cost, the sales rep takes out a brand-new laptop
computer and activates a pricing software module. More
than 95 percent of the time, this software gives the rep an
appropriate price right on the spot, simply because the vast
majority of the requests are very straightforward. When the
customer asks about delivery dates, the sales rep connects to
a database and checks inventory as well as production and
delivery schedules; he or she can then promise a date that is
rock solid. A new-order-dispatching group picks the right
plant to make the product and schedules its manufacture.

Should the customer have any questions, he or she calls a new centralized customer service unit, which has access to every plant's production plans and can provide accurate and current information.

For the customer, the new process is an impressive improvement over the old. Our concern, however, is with the people in the organization. The two important questions here are: Who is affected by the new process, and who's in favor of it? The answers are everybody and nobody.

It is not surprising that the pricing department hates the change. Except for a few special cases, the bulk of all pricing decisions are now made by the sales rep on the computer. And nearly all the pricers have suddenly been rendered redundant. Similarly, the plant managers hate the new system because their power has been usurped by the centralized order-scheduling unit. And customer service reps will hate it for reasons of their own—they have to relocate to corporate headquarters.

What about the sales reps? "Logically," they should be in favor of the new process. They will have happier customers, more control, more sales, and bigger commissions. But in fact the sales reps hate the new process more intensely than anyone else.

Why? First, because they are now accountable. The sales reps now have the responsibility for assuring that the orders are delivered as promised. They can't lie anymore. Once a sales rep makes a commitment that the product is going to arrive, he or she has no excuses left. Telling the truth and taking responsibility are more arduous and demanding than blaming others. To those accustomed to passing the buck, this shift can be very uncomfortable.

Second, in the new process, the sales rep will have to utter the most hated word in his or her vocabulary, a word he or she has assiduously avoided ever saying to customers— "No." In the old days, if the customer insisted he or she needed something tomorrow, the sales rep's stock answer was, "No problem."

This is not a trivial issue. Dealing differently with customers represents a fundamental change for sales reps; it requires that they behave in an unfamiliar way that makes them feel awkward and uncomfortable.

Third, the sales rep's sense of who he or she is, of his or her very identity, is under threat. The rep will no longer be selling on a smile and a shoe shine. He or she now has to do an analysis of distribution, scheduling alternatives, inventory allocation. Those who have always thought of themselves as being people persons now have to become technical analysts. They worry that they won't be able to do the analysis, and that they will hate it if they can.

Too many people who are responsible for implementing reengineering take an entirely rational, analytical approach, which does not acknowledge complex emotional realities. In this case, they would operate on the assumption that there won't be any snags because the sales reps are likely to make more money. But when we met with the sales reps and outlined what the new process would mean, they said something that we thought we would never hear: "We have enough money." From their point of view, the money was worth less to them than what they were being asked to give up. They would have to operate in new ways, become very different people, and, if they did, they still weren't sure they would succeed. And, even if they did succeed, that success didn't necessarily fit their mental model of what they wanted to do or who they wanted to be.

In short, the reasons for resistance to change are not limited to ostensibly "rational" ones. Ultimately, it is how people *feel* about a new situation that determines how they will respond to it. If they feel frightened, or threatened, or uncomfortable, or uncertain, then their reaction is likely to be a negative one.

Our fourth principle for dealing with resistance is to treat the disease rather than the symptoms. In the case at hand, no sales rep is going to break down and say, "I am frightened and feel threatened and insecure about this new way of doing things." Instead, the rep projects his or her fear and doubt onto something else. "This computer is no good. It's hard to use and takes forever to learn." It would be a mistake to take this response at face value and to deal with it by trying to improve the computer system. The ostensible issue is masking the real problem.

One of our favorite aphorisms is this: Never try to teach a pig how to sing; it wastes your time, and annoys the pig. Along the same lines, never try arguing logic with someone in a state of total inner panic. You can't debate process design with a person experiencing abject terror.

The fifth principle is that there is no single way for dealing with resistance to reengineering-based change; to use the vernacular, there are "different strokes for different folks." You need to consider the specific reasons why individuals are resisting and the ways in which their resistance is being manifested before deciding how exactly to handle it.

Principles for Overcoming Resistance to Change

Resistance is natural and inevitable: Expect it
Resistance doesn't always show its face: Find it
Resistance has many motivations: Understand it
Deal with people's concerns rather than their
    arguments: Confront it
There's no one way to deal with resistance: Manage it

However, there is a standard repertoire of techniques to be used in addressing resistance. We call them the five *Is*: incentives, information, intervention, indoctrination, and involvement.

Incentives are inducements, both positive and negative, to get people to behave as required by the reengineering effort. They include, but are not limited to, financial incentives. Continued employment is also a powerful incentive, and one that can be effective; confronting resisters and making it clear that termination is the consequence of their behavior is a very valid technique. But there are other forms of incentive as well: sharing in the psychic rewards from a successful effort, having new career opportunities, working in a more fulfilling job.

While incentives are the first change-management technique that most people think of, and while they can be effective, there are limits to their use. For instance, you can only use the threat of termination with people that you can actually afford to lose. More subtly, incentives are only truly effective when you use them on people whose resistance is motivated by a perception of tangible loss. If someone is losing authority or income, there are ways of making that up to him. But attempting to bribe someone who is fearful of a new environment, or whose self-image is undergoing a drastic shift, is like trying to reason with a snowstorm.

Information means supplying people with the details of what is happening and will happen. Knowledge reduces uncertainty. In many cases, people resist reengineering out of ignorance. Not exactly sure what is going on, they assume the worst. (This is hardly a rash assumption in the corporate world.) Information, however, does not blow away all resistance. In some cases, people who *think* they are opposed to reengineering will, after receiving more complete information, decide that they *know* they are opposed. However, reducing confusion and uncertainty is always a good thing. General anxiety is the most difficult thing to deal with because it is so amorphous and nebulous. When people are clear about what is happening, it becomes easier to deal with them, even when they are in opposition. It is easier to cope with facts, even unpleasant ones, than with specters.

Intervention means dealing with people one-on-one, to offer them support and reassurance so that they can overcome their discomfort and fear of a new situation. This is a form of hand-to-hand combat. It requires listening (sometimes endlessly) to people's concerns; digging past their stated objections to help them articulate what is really bothering them; counseling them; standing by them in new and difficult circumstances. It might mean giving sales reps a pep talk about their ability to handle the new process; going out with them on their first few sales calls under the new regimen, to make sure nothing goes awry; taking phone calls from them in the middle of the night when they are having trouble remembering how to use the computer; and so on. This is a form of corporate psychotherapy. You have to work closely with each individual to exorcise whatever private demons stand in the way of reengineering success. Clearly, this is time-consuming and laborious work and should be reserved for those who need it the most.

Indoctrination means convincing people that reengineering change is absolutely inevitable—not an option, but a necessity. The message must be sent out loud and clear that there is no choice. This can eviscerate the basis of resistance. One union local president was kept fully informed about the motivation and progress of a reengineering effort. At one point, he confronted the business unit head and said, with considerable force, "I know what this reengineering is, and I don't like it." But then in a resigned tone, he added, "But I do understand that it must be done." When people see the purpose and necessity of a reengineering effort, it is far harder for them to reject, demonize it, or misconstrue it.

Involvement means co-opting people into the reengineering effort so that they are criticizing from the inside rather than resisting from the outside. To bowdlerize a saying of

Lyndon Johnson's, it is better to have people in the tent "looking" out than to have them outside the tent "looking" in. Participation creates a feeling of control; instead of "them" doing it to "you," we are all doing it together. It also builds self-interest in the outcome, since we all share in the payoff.

Participation provides a catharsis for negative feelings; they can be directed toward improving the design rather than carping about it. It also soaks up a lot of energy that might otherwise be mischievously deployed.

The Key Mechanisms for Overcoming Resistance

Incentives—positive and negative
Information—dispel uncertainty and fear
Intervention—one-on-one connections
Indoctrination—make change seem inevitable
Involvement—make people part of the effort

We have used a variety of contemporary examples to illustrate the five principles of change management, but additional lessons can be drawn from a classical source, namely, the Bible. We refer here to the story of the Exodus, as recounted in the Books of Exodus and Numbers; we might call it "The Case of the Road to the Promised Land." Despite its antiquity, this story is one of the most insightful and compelling cases of change management we have ever encountered, and it is entirely relevant to reengineering.

This case has a before and an after: Before is slavery in Egypt, and after is freedom in the Promised Land. By any measure, this is a dramatic improvement. But a desert lies between the old and the new. Similarly, reengineering can lead you to a promised land of its own, but the road to get there is a perilous one.

There are six very useful lessons to be learned from this biblical story. The first lesson concerns what it takes to get started. Beginning any process of change is very difficult. People are terrified of what lies outside the boundaries of the familiar; they hate uncertainty. They may agree it is pretty unpleasant where they are, but they worry that it is even worse elsewhere. In a company, even if life seems bad now, people assume that reengineering will make it even worse.

Why, then, did the Israelites agree to follow Moses out of Egypt? Imagine them all standing at the border. Moses tells them that they are going to the Land of Milk and Honey, but all they see is endless sand. Moses says, "Don't worry. This will only take forty years. Let's go." The situation hardly looked promising, but still they agreed to flee Egypt. There were two reasons behind their decision: the wedge and the magnet. The wedge is something that causes you to let go of the past; in this case it was Pharaoh's Army.

Fear of destruction is a powerful incentive to change, but it is not enough in itself because it doesn't tell you where to go. In addition to a wedge, you need a magnet, which draws you toward some goal. The wedge repels, the magnet attracts.

The magnet is often a vision, and Moses had one. What did he do with his vision? The most important thing was what he didn't do—he didn't confine it to a confidential strategy document. He worked hard to turn *his* vision into the *people's* vision, and when that happened, the people arose and followed.

The second lesson is taught by the events at the Red Sea. Moses says, "We are going to march into the Red Sea and the waters will part." The children of Israel looked at the Red Sea, looked at Moses, and said, "You first." The very important and very simple lesson here is that there is no substitute for personal exemplary behavior on the part of the leader. It is not enough to talk the talk—you have to walk the walk. If you want people to behave in new ways, you can't just tell them—you have to show them. You also have to take some risks. Leaders must have a personal stake in the outcome so that others feel inspired to stick their necks out as well.

The third lesson is illustrated by the battle with the Amalekites, a pagan tribe. During this hard-fought battle, Moses went to the top of the nearest mountain and raised his hands. The Bible says that when his hands were up, the tide of battle turned in favor of the Israelites; but when his hands grew tired, the Amalekites began to prevail. So, Moses enlisted his brother Aaron and his nephew Hur to help him hold up his hands, and the Israelites emerged triumphant.

The lesson is that you absolutely must have executive consensus, because no one person, even a Moses, can keep his arms up all the time. If the rest of the executive team isn't behind the effort, failure is almost certain. The flip side of this lesson is that if the people around you aren't assisting, replace them with people who will.

In recent conversations with a number of successful reengineering executives, we asked how they would have reengineered differently if they had it to do over again. They all agreed that they would have gotten rid of their naysayers more quickly. They had to get rid of them in the end anyway. Keeping the naysayers on didn't do them any good, and it certainly didn't do the companies any good. Achieving executive alignment is extremely important, and the earlier, the better.

Next we come to the story of the golden calf. Moses leaves his people to ascend Mount Sinai and receive the Ten Commandments. But as soon as he is gone from view, they slip into orgy and debauchery. The lesson is that constant vigilance and visibility are necessary. People are always looking for opportunities to backslide, for excuses to revert to inappropriate behavior. Change requires leaders who are relentlessly committed and practice absolute vigilance.

Now the Israelites are traveling through the desert, and they begin to panic because there is nothing to eat. The Lord gives them manna, the miracle food, but after a while they come to Moses and complain that they are tired of manna. "We remember the fleshpots of Egypt, the fish, the melons, the onions," they say. What exactly are they remembering? The good old days. What are they forgetting? That they were in slavery—the taste of the whip.

The lesson here is that all change is loss. Even when change is for the better, there is still loss. The old life always had some redeeming aspects; no matter how bad it was, isolated aspects of it were good. Moreover, whenever people change, they leave a piece of themselves behind. Change management is about helping people cope with this loss.

At last, the Israelites approach the Promised Land, and the people send scouts ahead to check out the new terrain. The people want to know if the Promised Land is as wonderful as Moses promised. When the scouts return, they confirm that it is indeed a land flowing with milk and honey. But they also tell the people they cannot enter: "There are giants in that land, and we were as grasshoppers in our eyes." Note that the scouts were referring to their *own* eyes; they described how they saw themselves, not any real threat posed by the so-called giants. When everybody came to believe that they were as grasshoppers, the Lord decided that that generation would die in the desert. Only the next generation could enter the Promised Land. The essential lesson here is that if you believe that you can't change, then you won't change. Leadership has to instill in people the belief and conviction that they can survive and thrive in the new Promised Land.

Change Management Lessons from the Bible

A wedge and a magnet are needed to get started
Leadership must demonstrate commitment
Executive consensus is a requirement
Constant vigilance must be maintained
All change is loss
If you believe you can't change, you won't

These, then, are our principles for overcoming resistance to change. If you anticipate it, understand it, and manage it as a normal part of the reengineering journey, you can overcome it every step of the way and enter the promised land, an outcome that, on the whole, is preferable to dying in the desert.

CHAPTER 9

The Art of Selling Change

Over and above all their other challenges—the striving for innovative process designs, reinventing all aspects of a business, achieving breakthrough benefits on an accelerated schedule—a reengineering team faces one overwhelming obstacle: They are trying to sell something to a group of people who don't want to buy. The commodity they are selling is change, and the reluctant buyers are the people in the company.

As we've already said, nobody likes change—it's frightening, unsettling, messy, and uncomfortable. The bigger the change, the less people like it—and change doesn't come much bigger than reengineering. No wonder people's first reaction is, "No thanks, I'll pass." But if people don't buy into the change—if they don't accept it and begin working in the ways that the new process requires—then the reengineering effort will be nothing more than a paper exercise. While reengineering is one part engineering—the reconfiguration of an entire business system—it is also one part sales—the unabashed promotion and merchandising of a new way of working. And, at its heart, sales is communication: sending the message to people so that they respond positively. Just as reengineers must "get out of the box" when designing processes, they must also be extraordinarily innovative when communicating, creatively crafting a message and adroitly utilizing media so that people both understand and embrace reengineering.

In this venture, reengineers must confront and surmount a specific set of communications challenges.

Impediments to Communications

Disbelief
False familiarity
Fear of layoffs
The rumor mill
Sloppy execution: incomprehensibility, abstraction,
    complexity, and clichés

First, in most organizations, people put little stock in anything senior management says, and for good reason. Too many senior managers have a history of issuing extravagant pronouncements that bear no relation to what people experience on a day-to-day basis. One company we know, despite quarter after quarter of operating losses, kept assuring employees that "all is well, we're just witnessing a brief dip in the market." The employees knew better. They heard complaints from customers, they saw competitors' products outperforming their own, and they knew that their costs were way too high. But all they heard from senior management was denial and alibis. Of course this organization was riddled with cynicism and mistrust. You can't blame the employees for wondering, "If management is not telling us the truth about our position in the market, what else are they lying about?"

Unfortunately, situations like this are the norm rather than the exception. Consequently, management communications are usually taken with a large grain of salt, if at all. The blame lies squarely with senior managers who treat their employees as slow children who can't be trusted with bad news, confusing news, or adult news. And so information is diluted, filtered, and distorted until its meaning and value are lost.

Hypocrisy may have even more pernicious effects than sugarcoating reality. In one large telecommunications company, senior managers were talking up empowerment while behaving autocratically. They were all in favor of autonomy until someone disagreed with them.

The CEO in particular was notorious for cutting dissenting managers off at their knees. And in a difficult year he wouldn't give up his two executive jets. His words were suspect because they were not mirrored in his actions. When he began warning the company about a vulnerable market segment, everyone put down his statements as more hysterical manipulation. They were wrong; the company was in trouble, and it took two years to recover from the steep earnings dive triggered by the market "surprise" of which the CEO had warned. A history of less than absolutely truthful communication had left the organization with a case of terminal skepticism. In a climate like this, reengineering communications will be received as just more "lies and propaganda."

The second impediment to reengineering communications is "false familiarity"—the sense among employees that "we've been through this before." Over the years, successive waves of consultants have come pouring in over the battlements, waving the flags of Customer Satisfaction, Empowerment, Time-Based Competition, Theory Z, Economic Value Added, and Diversity, to name but a few. This nonstop parade of change programs has made skeptics of many employees, and justifiably so, because most of these programs were launched with great fanfare and then sank like stones without leaving even a ripple of real sustained change. Every organization has a history of such botched or insincere change programs. When employees first hear about reengineering, they have sound cause to view it as no more than the latest fad. Their rational response is to lay low until it passes.

The third problem facing reengineering communications is that, no matter what senior managers say, what employees will hear is, "I'm going to be fired." Day after day, articles in both the business press and the general media recount how one company or another is laying off 2,000 or 10,000 or 20,000 employees. Insecurity has become today's reality, and anything that sounds even vaguely threatening will be immediately interpreted in the worst possible light. No matter how carefully crafted the reengineering message, it will inevitably ratchet up an organization's level of anxiety.

Reengineering communications must therefore address the issue of layoffs head-on. Ignoring it will only cause people to assume the worst. If there are to be no layoffs, then say so loudly and clearly and often. If there is to be a reduction in staff, then get ahead of the anxiety curve with an early announcement; information is always better than uncertainty. Some executives fear that if they disclose layoffs, employees will respond badly. There is an almost touching degree of naïveté in this point of view. The reality of what reengineering will bring pales against what people's imaginations will invent. Moreover, taking the unprecedented step of telling the truth and treating employees like adults will earn management an unprecedented degree of respect and credibility. What should you do if you're not sure whether or not there will be a reduction in head count? Admit it. Craig Weatherup, president of Pepsi-Cola, N.A., stated at the onset of the company's reengineering effort that he didn't know if jobs would be lost, but guaranteed that if any were, the employees affected would be treated fairly and warned well in advance.

The fourth impediment to effective reengineering communications is the fact that the rumor mill, not official channels, is the real source of most information in any organization. What people say to each other in the cafeteria or on the elevator counts much more than any column in a newsletter. The grapevine usually carries a message quite different from the official line, and the grapevine is *always* operating.

The attempt to keep secrets always fails. If the White House can't prevent leaks, how can your organization? The minute an important decision is made, the news goes out on the jungle drums. Any attempt to keep it a secret will be self-defeating. Everyone will find out anyway, and the attempt to keep it secret will only increase the level of organizational mistrust. A noted communications specialist we know has said, "If you try to keep secrets, the only things people will know is what you don't want them to know."

The fifth obstacle to effective communications is poor execution, or falling into the following common traps:

Incomprehensibility: Too often, managers use a private, jargon-laden language rather than plain English. We recently heard a senior executive address a large group of shop floor manufacturing employees. His opening remarks included the following gem: "Our Q3 earnings are down and we have taken a big hit on our RONA target. Moreover, the recent FASB ruling has had a negative impact on our WIP inventory valuation, and the derivative loss we suffered has hammered our P/E ratio." This executive spent so much of his time talking with shareholders and investors that he forgot that their perspectives and concerns have little in common with those of employees. The big words, little acronyms, and mysterious references in this opening were bound to turn the group off— and they did. To succeed, you must speak your listeners' lingo. Otherwise, you might as well be speaking to them in Turkish.

Abstraction: All too often managers talk about ideas rather than things, concepts rather than experience. A conceptual statement like "We seek excellence" is flat and generic. "We've got to get our invoice accuracy to 99.99 percent" is far more tangible and specific. People understand the world through stories and examples. Alan Kay, the noted computer scientist, has said, "If a picture is worth a thousand words, then a metaphor is worth a thousand pictures." Effective communicators are teachers and storytellers; they use vivid images and specific anecdotes to illustrate their points. Most people are more comfortable moving from the specific to the general. So, first grab them with memorable events and powerful images. You must win people's interest before you can win their hearts and minds.

Complexity: Some managers, in their zeal for open communications, provide their audiences with too much detail. One leader we know loved to talk for hours about a new compensation system, reveling in every detail of the new, variable, nine-level, overlapping-band, multicomponent system. Needless to say, none of his listeners could grasp everything he was saying. More seriously, they weren't able to see the forest for the trees. The complexity and detail of the message obscured its meaning. Effective communications are simple.

Clichés: Trite and overused phrases like "best supplier to our customers" or "world-class performance" have no meaning. They are simply ritual incantations managers use either because they're not sure of what they really want to say or because they're unwilling to make the effort to find a unique and memorable way to say it. There's a simple rule of thumb. If you can envision another manager at another company giving your talk, then don't give it: You're not imparting any real information. You're just clogging the

DILBERT reprinted by permission of UFS, INC.

communication channel with sludge, making it harder for people to hear anything later on.

The sixth and final impediment to successful reengineering communications is that most companies suffer from too *much* communications. Official memos arrive by the pound and they go straight into the circular file. To be heard, reengineering communications must rise above the clutter, they must stand out, they must not be boring, they must grab and hold the audience's attention. This is not as daunting a challenge as it may sound; the opportunity for improvement is vast, given that the communications of most companies make the phone book seem fascinating by comparison.

THE TEN PRINCIPLES OF REENGINEERING COMMUNICATIONS

These obstacles to effective communications are serious. To overcome them, reengineers can learn from the practices of consumer goods companies, America's consummate marketers. As we have explored best practices in reengineering communications, we have encountered a recurring set of principles and techniques, which can all be expressed in terms of consumer goods marketing. So, forthwith, are the ten keys to successful communications.

1:   *Segment Your Audiences:* Marketers divide large diverse markets into smaller and more homogeneous segments; similarly, reengineers must segment an organization into specific constituency groups, each of which reacts to reengineering in a different and unique way. For example, a senior manager whose job is likely to disappear will approach reengineering differently from a sales rep who should make more money from happier customers. We have found that organizations may have as many as fifty of these segments, such as the executive team; the marketing department; the top 600 managers; the people in a factory that will change its manufacturing process; all first-line supervisors; and so on. All reengineering messages must be tailored to the specific characteristics and requirements of each constituency. This means different timing, different media, and different emphases. Telling managers that their departments are about to disappear, and possibly their jobs as well, requires a more personal and sensitive approach than is necessary when, say, informing salespeople that the number-one source of customer complaints is about to become history.

A reengineering communications plan must address the following questions for each of these segments:

Who is in this segment?
How will they be affected by reengineering?
What reaction will they have to it?
What behavior do we need of them?
What messages do they need to hear for that behavior to be stimulated?
When do they need to hear these messages?
What medium should we use for each message?
Who should communicate the messages to them?

This approach is analogous to the way leading consumer products companies segment their customers and target their communications. In reengineering communications, just as in selling soap, micromarketing is the name of the game.

2:    *Use Multiple Channels of Communication:* Effective advertisers use a mix of print, TV, radio, and other channels to reach consumers. Reengineers must do the same. It's not enough to place an article in the company magazine or to have an executive give a speech. Different media reach different people and affect them in different ways. Reengineers must use as many mechanisms as possible: presentations, articles, videos, design simulations, and so forth. There are many ways to tell the reengineering story, each most suitable for a different facet of it. Moreover, the reengineering journey can be a long one, and any particular medium can get boring after a while. In short, variety counts, and so does originality. Some organizations use an audiotape that people can listen to in their cars. Others have used comic strips, newsletters, team meetings, workshops, simulations—you name it.

Communication can take nonverbal forms as well. A bold, vivid, powerful logo can serve as a constant reminder of reengineering. Pepsi, for example, called its program 10X (tenfold improvement in performance). The logo has the same colors and typeface as the Pepsi-Cola logo. It's placed on everything at Pepsi that doesn't move. Hallmark created little globes to demonstrate the navigation of its reengineering program, called The Journey. Another company produced hundreds of hats emblazoned with its reengineering motto, "Innovation Masters." T-shirts, sweatshirts, coffee mugs, mouse pads, pens, and paper pads can all feature your reengineering logo or slogan to help reinforce the message. It may be cheap and vulgar, but that doesn't mean it won't work.

3: *Use Multiple Voices:* We have all seen how beer companies use a range of different sports personalities to promote their product. The idea is that not everyone will connect with a particular individual or identify with a given perspective. The same is true in reengineering. It's not a good idea for all communications to emanate from the CEO or from the reengineering czar. Other voices must also carry the message. It can be senior managers talking to their units, or members of reengineering teams visiting their peers and keeping them up-to-date on recent activities, or a plant manager telling his people what reengineering will mean to their site. This is more than just having a series of different mouthpieces for the same message. Each individual will describe reengineering from a different point of view, enriching *what* is said as well as broadening *how* it is said.

4: *Communicate Clearly:* Sizzle helps to sell, but it's not enough. The content of the message must be clear, specific, and comprehensible. Traditional marketing has "four *P*s" (product, price, promotion, position); so does reengineering: purpose, process, progress, and problems. These four elements should form the core of the reengineering message. By *purpose* we mean the *why* of reengineering, the reason for embarking on it. As we've said, this must be communicated in terms accessible and meaningful to the different constituency audiences. For some companies, the "why" is simple: If we don't do this, we'll be broke in a year. But many companies today reengineer to avoid problems rather than to react to them, and they face a special communications problem. Employees will look about, see a prosperous company with a record of success, and ask, "Why bother?" Leaders of reengineering must find compelling ways to convey the necessity of change despite apparent success. One company, number one in its industry, commissioned a video in the format of a news broadcast. Set in the near future, the video "documented" the decline and ultimate bankruptcy of the company because of changing technology, resurgent competitors, and its own process inadequacies.

Similarly, GTE has created a compelling video entitled *What Do They Want?* It consists of a series of vignettes, giving the perspectives of four key stakeholder groups—customers, employees, communities, and investors. Actors playing customers are seen commenting on what it is like to deal with inattentive salespeople, an older couple talks about their investment in GTE and their need for dividends, an employee inquires if GTE is the largest user of three-ring binders in the world—as the camera pans back to show him up to his neck in binders. This video has punch. Not just a collection of "talking heads," it shows real human beings in a way that makes viewers feel for them. Shown all across the company, it has effectively communicated GTE's complex set of reasons for needing to change. It also includes an explication of the nature of reengineering, what it is and how it addresses the company's predicament—and, as we have repeatedly stressed, couched not in abstract academic terms but in words that speak to everyone.

By *process* we mean an explication of how the organization will go about reengineering, so that the project plan becomes open to all. While the entire organization doesn't need to know every step in the reengineering methodology, it is important to share the outline of the approach so that everyone has a context for all the ensuing events.

The *progress* of the reengineering effort must also be communicated. Information should be flowing as the teams develop their designs and implementation schedules. Keeping the organization up-to-date on the work of the reengineering teams is vital for maintaining momentum.

Finally, and most unusually, it's also important to communicate reengineering *problems*. This is very countercultural for most organizations, whose communications are relentlessly optimistic and upbeat. Very rarely do companies acknowledge glitches, snafus, and errors. But when they do, they create a bond of trust between speaker and listener—the admission of fallibility purchases great credibility. Companies should admit failures, stress the lessons learned, and move on. If you admit your mistakes, your people will be far more inclined to believe you the next time you claim a success.

5: *Communicate, Communicate, Communicate:* We've all witnessed the power of market saturation. Who can forget Mr. Whipple or Ronald McDonald? Their images have been burned into our memories by the sheer force of relentless exposure. Repetition works in reengineering as well. It really, really works. (Get it?) Many managers seem to operate on the assumption that once they've said something, everybody has gotten the point. The key to effective communication is reinforcement in many ways, through many channels, and by many people. At Hallmark, for example, in the first year of reengineering alone, over a thousand talks were given across the organization so that people would know that this was no passing fancy. The sheer volume of repetition signaled the seriousness of the intent. Numbers like this are the rule rather than the exception in successful reengineering programs. Every leader we know has said that he or she seriously underestimated the magnitude of the communication effort required. One told us that in the first fourteen months of a reengineering effort, he held 120 small-group meetings with over 600 people, each lasting three to four hours. The time required for any given communication to penetrate and sink in can be formulated in various ways. One is the rule of seven times seven: The same thing must be communicated seven times in seven different ways before anybody will believe it. Another is the rule of the fifties: The first fifty times you say something, people don't hear it; the second fifty times, they don't understand it; and the third fifty times, they don't believe it. Repetition matters, repetition works.

6:   *Honesty Is the Only Policy:* Cynics might say that here is where the parallel between marketing and reengineering ends. However, smart marketers don't promise what they can't deliver because disillusioned customers won't come back. Similarly, lies about reengineering are not only unethical—they are foolish and counterproductive. As we have already said, reengineering can create a new paradigm for internal communications by being resolutely honest. If a mistake is made, admit it. If something is unknown, acknowledge it. If something is painful, face it. The truth is almost always less terrible than the fears that people build up; the truth buys credibility; and the mere fact of speaking the truth is another demonstration that something profoundly different is under way.

7:   *Use Emotions, Not Just Logic:* An analytical sales approach is only one way to convince buyers to acquire your product. Successful marketing plays on all the emotional strings—fear, greed, joy, hope, to name but the most obvious. Reengineering communications must also transcend a dry reporting of the facts to make an emotional connection with employees. A delivery style that works best in many organizations is what we call borderline evangelism. The reengineering leader must communicate passion. Like a preacher, he or she must be full of holy fire. People respond to burning and sincere enthusiasm—it's catching. But there should also be variety in the array of emotions driving the reengineering effort. Playfulness can be as productive as passion, especially if playfulness runs counter to the organization's traditional style.

8:    *Communicate to Heal:* Here we do diverge from traditional marketing. Reengineering affects real people with real lives and causes real pain. We have an obligation to use our communications not just to further the reengineering effort but also to help to minimize the stress and trauma that it causes. This may entail messages of hope, consolation, encouragement, or appreciation. When we tell people that we understand and share their fears and their pain, that their difficulties are in the service of a larger cause, that they are recognized and valued—then we do help to heal them (and incidentally, deflect their negative feelings away from resistance).

9:    *Communicate Tangibly:* Words are a start, but they are rarely enough. Just as consumer product companies provide free samples, reengineering teams must find experiential ways to convey important issues. At Texas Instruments, the reengineering team employs a communications device called the "Gameboard." Essentially a foldable strip of paper representing all the cross-functional activities associated with order fulfillment, Gameboard helps people feel the length and complexity of the process, makes them experience it through customers' eyes, and helps them realize how much change will be required. Each fold represents a significant change in the work required to meet the order fulfillment goals. Similarly, Hitachi Data Systems, a California-based division of the Japanese giant Hitachi, made the experience of reengineering a tangible one for its people. A month before the official launch of its reengineering program, Hitachi began issuing communications built around an old Elvis Presley song. On four successive Mondays it sent the following packages, consisting of a flyer and accompanying specialty items, to the 500 invitees to the reengineering kickoff meeting.

Week 1. "Tear it up." The flyer was printed on Tyvek, special paper that can't be torn. Message: Things are not what they seem. Go ahead and try to tear it up, but you'll fail if you don't find a new way of doing it.

Week 2. "Shake it up." This time, the flyer was accompanied by a hand warmer that remained inert until it was shaken up. Message: You can't be passive. You have to take some action to make reengineering happen.

Week 3. "Break it up." The flyer was accompanied by a plastic egg filled with Silly Putty. Silly Putty will not break until it is refrigerated. Message: Be resourceful.

Week 4. "We're going to have a ball." The flyer was accompanied by a tension-relieving soft rubber ball. Message: We *are* going to have a ball.

The "gimmicks" turned what would have been dry messages into memorable ones.

10:   *Listen, Listen, Listen:* Communication is not just talking; it must be two-way and involve keen, attentive listening. Marketers always listen to their customers, and reengineers need to as well. There are two reasons for this. The first is to have a feedback mechanism on the effectiveness of your communications program. How else will you know if your messages are getting through, if people understand reengineering, and if they are ready to accept it? The second is to offer people an opportunity to voice—even to vent—their feelings. People who feel they've been heard, who feel that they have a voice, who see themselves as participants rather than as victims, are much more likely to feel positive about reengineering and act accordingly.

There are numerous ways to make reengineering communications a dialogue rather than a monologue: focus groups, suggestion forms, questionnaires, surveys, interviews, "open mike" meetings, and so forth. The critical need is to use them widely and frequently, wisely and well.

These ten principles capture what we believe to be con-

> **The Ten Principles of Reengineering Communications**
> 1. Segment the audience
> 2. Use multiple channels
> 3. Use multiple voices
> 4. Be clear
> 5. Communicate, communicate, communicate
> 6. Honesty is the only policy
> 7. Use emotions, not just logic
> 8. Heal, console, encourage
> 9. Make the message tangible
> 10. Listen, listen, listen

temporary best practice in reengineering communications and must form the basis of any effective communication program. Each company is of course unique and will, through trial and error, create its own unique variation of these principles.

A SAMPLE REENGINEERING COMMUNICATIONS PROGRAM

Let's take a close look at how one company put these communication principles to work. The leaders of this large electronics firm, facing defense cutbacks and other broad industry changes, had determined that they needed to reengineer three of their major processes. They appointed a czar and a start-up team to assist in the launch of their program, and immediately set to work on communications.

Even before the design teams got to work, employees began to hear that reengineering was imminent. There were judicious hints at management meetings and mysterious advertisements in the company newspaper saying, "Reengineering is coming" and "Reengineering—watch this space for the definition."

In parallel with these teasers, preliminary one-on-one conversations were held by the CEO with key stakeholders and critical functional leaders. The CEO informed these important constituencies that a major change program was about to be launched.

> Even at this early date, it is evident that this organization is serious about communication. Catching people's attention is a good first step toward winning their hearts and minds. Conversing with key senior managers early also allows for personal concerns to be addressed and delicate questions to be posed.

Then the program was officially announced: 300 senior managers from across the company were invited to a local hotel for a half-day meeting. The invitations were personalized for each guest and signed by the CEO. At this kickoff, the CEO and several other senior executives spoke with passion and conviction of the importance of reengineering, communicating their personal enthusiasm for change.

> Many companies announce the launch of reengineering by issuing a dry memo that reads, "We're about to launch a very important new program. We really think this is critical stuff." But as Marshall McLuhan taught us, "The medium is the message." If you announce a program in a boring and traditional way, people will assume that it's a boring and traditional program. The initial advantage will be lost. Skepticism and inertia must be overcome right at the start if they are to be overcome at all. At this kickoff session, it was clear to all attending that the senior people were in alignment and had put themselves on the line. Their collective presence signaled a serious and unified intent from the top. The message was, "This is for real, and it's not going away." If passionate commitment and clarity of vision are communicated at the

kickoff, it is a sure bet that they'll be passed on to many others in the company the very next day. Word always gets around. In this case, leadership was managing that word.

Next, the executive team scheduled meetings with each department, to which everyone was invited. The executive team presented their reengineering plans: Here is what we're going to do; here are the processes we've selected; here is what is going to happen over the next three months; here is what we expect to happen over the next two years; and here is what we need from you. These meetings were conducted in an informal, interactive style, so that those attending felt comfortable asking questions. Precise information and timetables were communicated, but with the explicit qualification that, since this was a new experience for the company, there would inevitably be slipups. Each meeting closed with the executives' request that the department manager discuss the reengineering project with any employees who had been unable to attend the meeting.

> The executive team has segmented the organization and is talking with each of the segments. They are giving them real information, not fluff, thereby demonstrating they are both knowledgeable and irrevocably committed. Notice that even at this early stage the leadership is both talking and listening. These meetings have also been designed to trigger cascading communications downward through the organization. Cascading not only ensures the dissemination of the vision but also that it will be communicated to the right people by the right people.

Two months later, the reengineers began showing a twenty-minute video to everyone in the organization. By this point, the reengineering ranks had swelled to three process redesign teams, one coordination team, and a steering committee. All these groups collaborated with the company's communications group to produce this video in a very short time. In it, the CEO presented the reengineering Case for Action, spelling out how the competitive situation had changed, how the industry had changed, and why the company couldn't stay where it was. He concluded his remarks with this statement: "This is why we're reengineering. It's not a folly. It's not a whim. It is vital to our future success." Pictures of competitors' products then flashed across the screen followed by clips of dissatisfied customers. Each redesign team explained why their process needed to be reengineered and what its improvement would mean to the company. The CEO closed the video by saying, "We're starting this program now because we must and frankly we're not sure how it's going to end. I don't know if you will have jobs when we're done, so I can't promise that. But there are some things I can promise you. If your job is eliminated, we'll do everything we can to find you a similar position. If we can't do that, we'll do our best to train you for a new job. And if we can't do that, we'll treat you fairly and give you a generous outplacement package. You have my word on this."

This video had a powerful effect on the organization. The company had never made a video for such broad use before. Nor was the CEO accustomed to such high-profile activities; most employees had never seen his face before.

Of critical importance was how the video handled the issue of job loss. Rather than letting the rumor mill define the terms of the debate, management made a preemptive strike. By addressing this head-on, management deflected a speeding bullet.

The best treatment for uncertainty and fear is information and truth. Organizations reengineer for sound competitive and economic reasons—to survive, to cut costs, to improve customer satisfaction, to create the conditions for growth. In many companies, however, most employees have a very limited understanding of their company's overall business condition. If you doubt this, try going to a place in your company where the real work is done: a factory, a customer service center, a research lab, a warehouse. Ask the frontline employees, "Who are our most serious competitors? Our most critical suppliers? Our largest customers? What will determine our success in the future?" If your company is like most, your employees won't have the answers. They are focused on their individual tasks. They've never had the big picture explained to them. This company's video helped to explain the competitive context while linking reengineering to concrete current problems and to the requirements for a successful future. Management realized that all employees needed to understand the following chain of logic: (1) The problems that we face in the marketplace, such as high costs and long cycle times, are really process problems; (2) To succeed both individually and collectively, we will have to change how our processes operate; (3) Therefore, we are going to reengineer our processes. This kind of message can sink in deep and change people's perspectives at a fundamental level. By making people understand why reengineering is necessary, the company elevated it above the level of a passing fad.

Over the next six months, the reengineering team inundated the organization with a steady stream of diverse communications. Speeches were given, articles were published, results were shared. Following the launch of reengineering, senior management eliminated many of the other business change programs that had accumulated over the years. The empowerment program, the vacuous Vision 2000 initiative, and numerous others of the same ilk quickly disappeared. This had several salutary effects. From a practical perspective, shutting down these other efforts freed up some of the resources needed for reengineering. But it also sent two powerful messages: First, that the days of faddish, superficial programs are over;

and second, that reengineering is our only hope to prepare for the future.

> Many companies have dozens of unrelated change programs operating at any time, each with its own advocates, constituents, and ideologies. These all compete for time and attention, and usually have little real impact. It is necessary to pierce through this clutter, to make people see and believe that reengineering is not like all these other programs. The real goal is to position reengineering as the driver of all the changes that these disconnected programs were originally intended to make. Customer service, empowerment, innovation—all the contemporary catchwords—are in fact just facets of the reengineering enterprise. It is through effective reengineering that these goals can be realized.

The company's early and ongoing attention to communications paved the way to successful reengineering. By the time the reengineering teams had completed their designs, all the senior managers were aligned around a common vision of the future. When making the transition into implementation, the czar had a relatively easy time acquiring the additional 150 people needed for the various implementation teams. The intensity of executive commitment coupled with the broad dissemination and acceptance of the Case for Action had turned a potential crisis into a non-event. When the time came to test the design in pilot sites, the reengineers did not have to twist arms to find suitable locations. There were plenty of volunteers. And as the new processes were rolled out across the organization, there was little surprise and almost no opposition. The inevitability of reengineering had been communicated so long and so often that it had become a foregone conclusion. This company's communications program was not the only reason it succeeded; but it sure didn't hurt.

CHAPTER 10

You Are What You Believe: Reshaping an Organization's Values

As we have already explained, reengineering begins with process redesign but does not end there. A radical and fundamental change in process structure has ripple effects on all aspects of a business. As one CEO has put it, "If everything isn't changing, it's not reengineering."

One vital aspect of the reengineering revolution is a shift in the organization's value system. These values represent people's most basic beliefs about their work; inevitably, they shape people's behavior and how they perform that work. We do what we believe. As intangible as they may seem, as difficult as they may be to define, as slippery as they may be to grasp in conversation, values really lie at the heart of any successful attempt to reengineer.

Let's look at product development. Companies in many industries have discovered the power of the multidisciplinary product development team that is authorized to make decisions on its own. Everyone shares information about the new product with everyone else, from designers to financial planners to manufacturing experts, and everyone shares the responsibility for the outcome. When everyone communicates in this way, work becomes much more efficient because redundancy and rework can be avoided.

157

However, no process for rapid product development, no matter how carefully and cleverly designed, will work without one key ingredient: The people performing the process must believe that rapid product development is important. Without this underlying belief, people will not feel the required intensity and commitment and they will not be motivated to work hard as a team. Wonderful as your process design may be, its success will depend, in the end, on the value system embedded in the hearts and minds of the people performing the process on a day-to-day basis.

What kind of values, then, might be required to support rapid product development? One such value, certainly, is speed. If people don't believe speed is important, the process will not be fast, no matter what its design. Another one is recognizing that the needs of the customer come first, above those of any organizational unit or individual. Teamwork is also an essential value; people must truly believe in one for all and all for one.

The people working in product development can't simply be *told* to have these values; they must *internalize* these beliefs and embody them in their professional lives. Only a deep-seated belief in the right values can generate the passion and commitment that a reengineered process requires.

When reengineering a process, it is thus vital that values also be realigned. Trying to overlay a new process on people who have old-process values is a recipe for chaos. It leads to cognitive dissonance, confusion, and cynicism.

It is doubly important that people internalize the new values because they represent a key management tool for a reengineered environment. A hallmark of reengineering is that it creates processes with far greater flexibility than those they replace. Rule books and procedure manuals become largely irrelevant, as the members of process teams learn to focus on customers and results. In short, the days of "tell them and watch them" are over. When people have to check the rules every five minutes or ask their boss for permission and approval, the goals of flexibility, responsiveness, and speed will never be achieved. Moreover, in a world of relentless change, manuals are out of date before the ink is dry—in fact, even before they go to press. Today's reality is marked not only by constant change but by an extreme degree of complexity. A manual that could cover all the variables would probably stand taller than the high-rise in which the company was located.

Widely shared and deeply held values represent an alternative to traditional management control. If an organization's leadership can convince people to embrace a set of values and use them to guide their behavior, then that leadership can be relatively confident that people will do the right thing. The options for management control are three. I can watch you like a hawk and require that you check everything you do with me—a prescription for arteriosclerosis. Or I can write down every eventuality and expect you to consult my instructions before proceeding—which is impossible. Or I can take the time to instill my values in you so that when you are on your own, you will behave as I would have told you to.

Before examining the new values mandated by reengineered processes and the means of inculcating them, it is worth considering the value systems of traditional organizations as well as some contemporary attempts to dislodge or update them.

We often ask people who attend our seminars about the advice they would give to a newcomer to help them succeed in their (traditional) organizations; in other words, to identify the personal behaviors typical of their companies. Their answers usually include the following: Don't make waves; keep your boss happy; don't make mistakes; keep your nose to the grindstone; treat everyone like an enemy; if a problem lands on your desk, dump it on somebody else's.

What values must these people have, what must they

believe if these are the ways in which they operate? It is not hard to translate these typical behaviors into cultural norms: Avoiding mistakes at all costs is the consequence of believing that risk taking is unacceptable and that not failing takes precedence over succeeding. Concentrating on your boss's state of mind is the result of believing that your boss is the one who actually pays your salary and that your success results from this boss pulling you up the organizational ladder. Treating others as adversaries and passing problems along betrays a mentality that does not value personal responsibility or teamwork, and that prizes activity over result.

Needless to say, it is unwise to turn your back in this kind of an organization, to ask for help, or to extend it. Clearly, these values and the behaviors they generate are unsuited to reengineering and its aftermath. In fact, the values required for successful reengineering turn out to be exactly the opposite of the traditional ones we just described. It is not keeping the *boss* happy; it is keeping the *customer* happy. It is not keep low and keep moving; it is get things done and create value. If a problem lands on your desk, don't dump it on somebody else's—solve it. You must regard other people in your organization not as enemies or competitors but as allies and teammates. Your future depends not on their failure but on your own success, and by helping them today you can expect help from them tomorrow. In other words, reengineering requires a transformation of the basic values that have shaped people's behavior in large organizations for many, many years.

It is not especially difficult to articulate the kinds of values that modern organizations require. In fact, over the last several years, many executives seem to have suddenly recognized a pressing need for such a new set of values. Senior managers with time on their hands and no clear idea of what to do with it except latch onto any fad that will let them—

without working too hard—grab the spotlight often jump on this "values" bandwagon. One manifestation of this trend has been a very peculiar phenomenon called the mission-vision-values statement. It begins when a company's senior managers retreat into the woods to commune with nature and get in touch with the child within. After a week of self-indulgent psychobabble, they come back reborn, proclaiming a new set of values for the company to follow.

What ensues follows a certain inevitable progression. First, management distributes a memorandum communicating the new values. When this goes the way of all memos, the next phase centers on plastering large posters and wall banners everywhere. In the terminal phase, the values statement is printed on wallet-size plastic laminated cards that are distributed to everybody in the organization. (Some companies go even further in searching for ways to propagate the values statement—key rings, buttons, and notebook covers have all been pressed into service. One food company has even inscribed theirs on a trivet.) But cards are the most universal.

We have a collection of these little cards, which we have gathered in our travels over the years. They represent a touching affirmation of management's belief in the power of clichés to alter and modify behavior. These lists of homilies are always printed beneath the corporate logo and are given an ennobling title (Vision 2000 is a particularly popular name). The first thing that strikes you when reading through those cards is how much they are all alike, both in theme and language. For instance, in keeping with the precepts of the quality movement, the theme of customers figures prominently on these cards. A major oil company claims, "We are committed to anticipating and meeting our customers' needs, and will strive to exceed their expectations." A *Fortune* 500 manufacturer will not be outdone and counters that "Our first priority is to satisfy customers." A major maker of telecommunications systems insists that "We create superior value for our customers." A large retailer demands even more: "Customer satisfaction and delight are the focus of all our thoughts, plans, and actions." (Once upon a time, *satisfying* the customer was the goal; then this was set aside in favor of *pleasing* the customer; the stakes are now *delighting* the customer; we hesitate to speculate what might come next.)

"Excellence" may be hard to define, and even harder to achieve, yet everyone seems in favor of it. A semiconductor firm promises "excellence in everything we do." The telecommunications vendor proclaims, "We have only one standard—excellence." Integrity is also quite popular. "Above all, we will act at all times with integrity and honesty." "We will perform with unquestionable ethics and integrity." Another card calls for "an uncompromising integrity and adherence to the highest standards of personal and business ethics." Teamwork: "We share one vision/we are one team." "We build trust and worldwide teamwork with open, candid communications." "We believe that our success depends upon the participation and teamwork of all our employees." "We acknowledge all co-workers as valuable team members." And of course, people: "Our people are key to our success." "Our people are our strength." "We help our fellow employees improve their skills, encourage them to take risks, treat them fairly, and recognize their accomplishments."

Sometimes, at our seminars, we take out our laminated cards and read these bits of wisdom aloud. The response is always the same—gales of laughter from the audience. And when we ask the attendees *why* they are laughing, once again the response is uniform: "They are so empty." "It's all mush." "They don't mean anything." "They don't tell us what we're supposed to do." "They don't mean it."

DILBERT reprinted by permission of UFS, INC.

These are very serious indictments, but it is also notable what people are *not* saying. Nobody is saying that these values are *wrong*. Quite the contrary; the thematic consistency suggests that their authors are onto something. In fact, customer focus, teamwork, personal responsibility, speed, innovation, and the like are *exactly* the values required by a company that is seriously engaged in reengineering. No, the little laminated cards are not wrong; wrong is easy to understand and fix. The problem is actually much worse. Their weakness is, as our attendees recognize, that that's all they are—laminated cards. The noble principles printed on them are empty words, backed by nothing whatsoever. It is as if management believed in the talismanic power of laminated wallet cards, that somehow the messages printed on them would be absorbed through magical osmosis by all who touch them.

Clearly, cards don't work. However, it is possible to inculcate new values and to do so in a systematic way. But it takes work, using the five measures outlined below.

The first step is to ensure that the desired values are designed into your processes. If you tell people that you care about customers, yet nobody ever has the chance to interact with them, your words will be at best hot air and at worst a symptom of hypocrisy. If you declare speed a competitive advantage, then make damn sure that you design your processes to be fast. If your goal is flexibility and innovation, then the ways in which people work must be structured to accommodate variation. If you proclaim change, be sure you can handle it. An order fulfillment process locked into a fixed mode of operation speaks louder than any talk about flexibility and change.

The second requirement is a personal, demonstrated commitment to these values by senior executives. It's that good old "walk the walk." All executives will *say* that their first priority is to satisfy the customer, but when they spend all their time in meetings or dealing with investors and never actually get close to a customer, their words ring hollow. Albert Schweitzer summed it up when he said: "In trying to communicate values, example isn't the best way, it is the only way."

In one insurance company, every member of the executive team adopted a small set of customers as his or her own personal concern. In a large manufacturing company, senior managers carry beepers. A customer with a problem can reach a senior executive directly, without any hassle. In another manufacturing company, senior executives, very busy people, each spend an hour or two a week in the customer service center answering phones. Are they much better at answering phone calls than anybody else? Not at all, but their behavior sends a strong and unmistakable signal throughout the organization that customer contact is crucial. Clearly, these are all merely symbolic gestures, but that is precisely what is needed.

The third requirement is seriousness. It is very easy for a company to proclaim a belief in integrity (or people or teamwork) when everything is running smoothly. The real question is: What are you prepared to do when the chips are down? Johnson & Johnson's Tylenol experience is an excellent example of how one company's deep commitment to its values saw it through a turbulent period. In the early 1980s—with Tylenol the number one analgesic in the marketplace—a homicidal maniac started tampering with bottles on pharmacy shelves. People were poisoned, and several died. J&J's management faced a difficult choice. If the company admitted that Tylenol was questionable, consumers might switch to another product. If it recalled Tylenol, it would fall prey to Aristotle's dictum "Nature abhors a vacuum," a corollary of which is "So do retailers' shelves." A recall would open up shelf space to competitors; Tylenol's management had no way of knowing if they could ever regain any of that shelf space. And to top it all off, the recall would cost a fortune.

The alternative was to issue a press release proclaiming that the scientific data wasn't conclusive and that the overall situation was under control. All that was needed was a little PR, some smoke and mirrors, and an attitude like that of the pet shop owner in a Monty Python sketch who assures the customer his parrot isn't actually dead—"It's just sleeping."

And so what did Johnson & Johnson do? The decision wasn't hard, because it actually adhered to a genuine set of values, called the Johnson & Johnson Credo. It opens as follows: "We believe our first responsibility is to the doctors, nurses, and patients, to mothers and fathers, and all others who use our products and services." (Incidentally, elsewhere the Credo states explicitly that this responsibility takes precedence over J&J's responsibility to shareholders.) The J&J Credo reads much like other companies' mission and values statements. The difference is that the Credo is taken seriously.

If, as a company, J&J truly believed its number one concern was the well-being of its patients, then it had no choice and there was nothing to discuss. Its product had been poisoned; it had to be recalled. J&J did so, and it cost a pretty penny too. Did the company lose shelf space? Absolutely. But where is Tylenol now? Number one again. If you hold the right values, you will do the right thing and, in the end, achieve the right results. Seriousness—the willingness to make a stand and accept the consequences, particularly when times are tough—is essential to creating an environment in which values are shared and practiced, not just preached.

No one, however, should wait for a crisis to establish his or her commitment. Values must be practiced all the time, whether business is prospering or troubled. Yes, the right values are vital to surviving a crisis, but those values must already be in place, solidly established in daily practice, the battles of war won on the playing fields of Eton. No one should ever forget what counts just because there are no great problems in the "peacetime" between crunches.

The fourth requirement, whose importance cannot be overstated, concerns measurements and rewards. Imagine management insisting to employees that the focus of the business is customer satisfaction. People say, "Sir, yes sir," and proceed to concentrate on satisfying customers. At the end of the quarter, management inspects customer satisfaction measures, which are way up. Then they ask to see cost figures, which turn out to be up by one-eighth of 1 percent. Typically, management's response is to regretfully announce that they will be forced to shoot off everyone's knees. In other words, the message is that cost counts, regardless of all the rhetoric about customer satisfaction.

The lesson here is that the way to people's hearts and minds is not through their ears but through their wallets. A company's management systems shape its values. If you want people to share your values, you have to specifically measure and reward them for exhibiting those values. Otherwise, they will be confused about the importance of the values you espouse and will experience no positive reinforcement for adopting them.

Financial incentives can also be accompanied by disincentives, negative measurement for not participating or achieving. At Levi Strauss, a major fraction of everybody's evaluation is based on the extent to which they have behaved in accordance with Levi's values (called the Aspirations). Failure to have followed the Aspirations is reflected in lowered evaluation and bonus.

The fifth and final requirement is the effective articulation and communication of the new values. This may even include handing out plastic cards to everyone, but it is much more than that. It means stating your values clearly and in a way that makes them unique; you don't ever want to sound like everybody else. Values and goals must be presented with clarity, freshness, and a certain edge so that people will have a sense of what they really mean and not hear them as mere slogans. If you are doing everything else—designing your processes consistent with your values, exemplifying those values, remaining true to them in tough times, and measuring and rewarding people accordingly—then a brief and clearly articulated summary of your values can serve as an effective reminder of everything you stand for and intend to accomplish. And it can even be printed on a plastic card.

Making New Values a Reality

Ensure they are reflected in process designs
Have executives demonstrate them through
    personal behavior
Use them in difficult situations
Incorporate them into measurement and reward
    systems
State them clearly and uniquely

Ultimately, the measure of success in reengineering values could not be clearer. If the new values are no more than just another plastic card in someone's purse or wallet, then this essential ingredient of reengineering is missing. But if these new values live in people's minds and hearts, shaping their behavior and their work, then the magic of transformation has occurred.

CHAPTER 11

Combating the Counterrevolutionaries

In the world of physics, Newton's Third Law asserts that every action has an equal and opposite reaction. Adapted to the world of human organizations, this law would say that every revolution spawns a counterrevolution. Reengineering is a revolution, and like all other revolutions—political, economic, social—it inevitably gives rise to its own counterrevolutionaries. Their mission is to prevent reengineering or to roll it back.

Counterrevolutionaries are nearly always motivated by one overriding belief—things were better as they were before, in the days of the *ancien régime*. While counterrevolutionaries loudly proclaim this to be true for everyone, it is in fact usually quite true for them as individuals. In reengineering, not everybody will be a winner. In particular, many people who are well situated in an existing organization and have a great deal invested in the status quo are likely to come out behind, and they will be hard-pressed to see any good reason for risking everything on a game of pitch and toss. From their point of view, a rational weighing of the odds clearly shows the reengineering game is not worth the risk. The company may come out ahead, but they themselves are not likely to. Because their opposition is based on the sincerity of self-interest, such counterrevolutionaries are always a formidable foe. They'll do what it takes to win or go down in flames.

Opposition to reengineering can be based on a variety of motives and expressed in a variety of ways. Some foes generalize their own self-interest and take what masquerades as a principled and pragmatic stand against change. Others will pretend to accept the need for change, yet contend that the specific proposal under discussion just happens to be ill considered and inappropriate. Others, the "true believers" of the counterrevolution, are moved more to save a way of life than a way of making a living. Then there are those who crave the limelight, who try to call attention to themselves by railing against whatever happens to be the prevailing wisdom. If everyone is saying that reengineering is a very good thing, then they will declare it very bad. Whatever their motives, these people are opposed to the revolution and will try to stop it.

You are likely to find such counterrevolutionaries in your own organization. For that reason, we want to prepare you for the criticisms that they are most likely to offer—and to give you the best responses we know to nullify their arguments. Here are the most common arguments and our responses.

Argument 1: Reengineering does not work. The most audacious of all the counterclaims, this is nothing but a contemporary version of the Big Lie. Some people feel that if they say something that is completely false but say it repeatedly, with a straight face, and in a sufficiently loud voice, that something will in time become true (or at least be believed). Mark Twain once observed that if you tell a lie three times you begin to believe it yourself.

Believing that you can fly is fine, but you should nonetheless stay away from the window.

The claim that reengineering doesn't work must strike terror in the hearts of the great many companies that have used reengineering to achieve striking improvements in their performance—such oddball companies as AT&T, American Express, Federal Mogul, GTE, Progressive Insurance, Pepsi, Hallmark, and Taco Bell. No doubt these companies will be startled to learn that their operational improvements and increases in customer satisfaction are illusory. Perhaps they will be moved to refund their increased profits.

Many of the critics who take this line of attack actually have the gall to cite us in support of their argument, using the common trick of quoting out of context. Claiming that we have said that reengineering has a 70 percent failure rate, they offer this statistic as "proof" that reengineering doesn't work. However, as we've stressed time and again, the reference they cite was a historical observation, not a normative one. While many companies *have* failed at reengineering, no companies *need* fail. The failures failed because they did it wrong. Success is virtually guaranteed for companies that go about reengineering with will, intelligence, and passion, and failure is similarly guaranteed for those that don't.

The successes make for a monumental presence. In fact, many more companies have achieved much greater results than we ever dared hope. The eighteenth-century man of letters Dr. Samuel Johnson was once asked how he would refute Bishop Berkeley's doctrine of immaterialism, the philosophy that maintained there was no substance to physical reality. In reply, Johnson kicked a curbstone and proclaimed, "I refute it thus." The stone's obvious physicality was enough for Dr. Johnson. Arguments that reengineering does not and cannot work should not put you on the defensive. You need only point to the dozens of companies that have reengineered successfully and invite your opponents to kick that curb.

Argument 2: Reengineering is nothing new. Some naysayers claim reengineering is at bottom nothing more than old-fashioned notions of automation or industrial engineering or quality improvement wrapped up in new packaging. Our response is based on the old joke in which Eddie, a well-known burglar, is arrested for robbing a jewelry store on a certain Tuesday. Eddie is indignant. First of all, it wasn't a jewelry store, he says; it was a bank. Second of all, it wasn't Tuesday, it was Wednesday. And thirdly, it wasn't him, it was his brother Charlie. (Lawyers call this "arguing in the alternative.") Similarly, we have multiple responses to the claim that reengineering isn't new. The first is: It is new. The second is: Who cares?

The argument that reengineering is nothing but a rehash betrays a deep ignorance of the subject. Reengineering does in fact represent a radical departure from previous approaches to business improvement. It differs from conventional automation techniques in that it does not merely apply technology to processes that already exist but rather uses technology to create new processes. Traditional automation begins with a detailed description of existing processes in order to fit technology to them. Reengineering takes the exact opposite position—technology should not be adapted to processes, but processes must be totally reconfigured to exploit the full potential of technology.

Reengineering is also different from total quality management, although the two do have certain points in common. Both start with customers. Both seek improvements in performance, and both are centered on cross-functional processes. There, however, the similarities end. The quality movement is essentially incremental in its worldview; it employs a set of structured problem-solving techniques whose purpose is to isolate narrowly confined difficulties within existing processes in order to apply focused solutions to them. By contrast, reengineering takes a macro perspective; it doesn't seek to solve problems in an existing process but rather to discard the process entirely and to replace it with something new.

Reengineering also has little in common with traditional industrial engineering techniques. By and large, those have focused on optimizing the individual tasks and activities performed within a process. In contrast, reengineering examines the process as a whole, the aggregate of these activities. Instead of attempting to improve the ways in which individual tasks are performed, reengineering reorganizes and restructures how tasks are combined.

In any event, even if the "we've-seen-this-before" criticism were valid, it would make little difference. The purpose of reengineering is not to win prizes for intellectual novelty but to achieve "dramatic improvement." It doesn't matter if reengineering is new—it only matters that it works. Even if the ideas are old, the fact that a new label is energizing organizations to apply these ideas makes the label a success in our view. Someone who helps reengineering succeed while scoffing at its newness is nonetheless on the side of the angels. The goal of reengineering is to enable organizations to achieve breakthroughs in their operations. Whoever serves that end is welcome in the church of reengineering.

Argument 3: Reengineering is not radical enough. Admittedly, this is a criticism we don't hear very often, but it is sometimes voiced by those with a particularly Machiavellian turn of mind. After all, if reengineering claims that radical change is necessary, then one way to thwart it is to contend that it doesn't go far enough. The counterrevolutionary co-opts the message and attempts to block its call for radical change by finding reengineering insufficiently extreme. This assertion always leaves us somewhat dumbfounded. We have not been the least shy in stating again and again that reengineering involves the complete reinvention of virtually every aspect of an organization. It entails a fundamental reconsideration of a company's ways of creating value, with ripple effects on all aspects of the organization. In some cases, reengineering even leads to a fundamental reconception of the identity of the company, of the nature of its products and services, and of its basic strategies. If that is not radical, then what is?

That question should be enough to destroy this argument, one that was never serious in the first place, only a bluff with no backing and one easily called.

Argument 4: Radical change is dangerous and inhumane. A certain school of criticism concedes the business validity of the reengineering vision but contends that organizations are unable to survive the kind of dramatic change that reengineering entails. This argument has two variations—the pragmatic and the moral. The pragmatic argument is that such drastic change is too disruptive to an organization, causing people to panic and retreat into their shells. Corporate culture is shattered, and any sense of common purpose disappears. Thus, the argument goes, reengineering ultimately does more harm than good. The moral argument admits that while it might be feasible to implement such change, it is cruel to inflict it upon one's employees. Uncertain gain should not be purchased with certain human suffering. Reengineering is therefore to be avoided by any manager with a shred of morality and decency.

These are serious objections, but they can be overcome. Our response to the practical argument is the plain fact that while reengineering does create some turmoil and real pain, neither is fatal. The experience may be dislocating, even wrenching, but as the expression goes: No pain, no gain. The laws of thermodynamics remind us that you can't get more out of a system than you put into it. Dramatic improvement has to be paid for in some way, and the coinage is usually denominated in units of suffering. When a situation calls for drastic change, drastic actions must be taken—and endured. The long list of companies that have successfully navigated this passage gives the lie to those who maintain it cannot be done without life-threatening damage and trauma.

As to the so-called moral argument, our reply is: What is the alternative? Given the choice, we too would rather not induce the kinds of travail and confusion that reengineering often engenders. However, organizations do not undertake reengineering lightly. As Bruce Marlow, chief operating officer of Progressive Insurance, puts it: You only do reengineering because you have to. "Have to" is an elastic term. You may "have to" do reengineering because you are on the verge of extinction. You may "have to" do reengineering because you are facing radical shifts in your environment. You may "have to" do it because it is the only way to stay ahead of an eager and ever-hungry competition. In each case, the alternative is a serious decline in a company's fortunes. This has consequences even more disruptive and unpleasant than reengineering's for the people in the organization—foreshortened careers, huge stress, lost jobs. The pain of reengineering inoculates a company against the much greater pain of decline. The counterrevolutionaries may use compassion as their camouflage, but in fact the moral high ground belongs to reengineering.

Argument 5: Reengineering isn't for us because we are different. This argument is one of the favorites of people wishing to avoid the imperatives of reengineering. They claim that in some way their industry, their company, or their process is different from those to which reengineering can usefully be applied. This is a clever argument because it avoids the broader and more easily deflected criticism that reengineering in general doesn't work; its adherents hide behind the claim that while reengineering may work *else-*

where, it has no relevance to *their* situation.

People in the public sector will say that reengineering is only for profit-making companies. Small companies will claim that reengineering is only for the *Fortune* 500. Product development groups maintain it only has value for routine processes. Sales organizations assure us that reengineering is only for the back office.

These are all excuses. Reengineering is not about profit, size, routine, or the back office. Reengineering is about changing the way work is done.

Reengineering is based on the principle and premise that you need a total reexamination of the way your work is done—its purposes and its processes. This includes everything from developing a new sense of the customer to finding new ways of performing the activities that create value. The public sector is as focused on doing work—and producing results—as any profit-making enterprise. Small companies, R&D, sales—they all perform work. The only people to whom reengineering has no applicability are those who do not work. And those are beyond our help.

Reengineering applies equally to processes that are creative and to those that are routine. Formulating a strategic plan, developing a new product, and conducting scientific research are processes that are as structured as any other. It is the individual tasks within these processes that make them "creative." Reengineering does not intrude on the performance of these tasks but rather addresses how they can be better coordinated to make the processes as a whole more effective. Work is achieved by processes composed of tasks, and reengineering applies to processes whether the tasks be mundane or highly creative.

And so, the best and obvious answer to the objection that "Reengineering doesn't apply to us because we are different" is: You're not. Work is work.

Argument 6: We can't afford it. Some may find our response to this—"Good for you!"—somewhat surprising. If the executives of a company tell us that they cannot afford to dedicate the human and financial resources that reengineering demands—or that they can't devote the requisite amount of their own energy to it—we offer them our sincere congratulations. To us, that means that reengineering is not vitally important to them. If reengineering is of vital concern to you, then you *will* find the resources to do it. You *will* allocate your best people. You *will* make it your own top personal priority. If you can't, it means you have other, higher priorities. And that in turn means that you are doing well now and have every reason to believe you will continue to do well far into the foreseeable future. And that indeed is cause for congratulation. But, to be honest, we think that there are few organizations that fall into this category today. Contentment and complacency are dangerous feelings. We live in a world in which the future comes faster than expected and arrives with a jolt.

Argument 7: We've already been doing reengineering for years. This argument is a variant on the previously mentioned "reengineering is nothing new." Some companies have claimed that they were doing reengineering long before *Reengineering the Corporation* was published and the term became a household word. Maybe they're right. We never claimed to have *invented* reengineering. In fact, if we *had* invented reengineering, we wouldn't believe in it. At the most, we *discovered* reengineering. When we encountered it, reengineering was being practiced by a number of companies that had stumbled onto it after they had exhausted virtually all other avenues for improving their businesses. It was our good fortune to come across a number of these companies and to recognize the common elements in what had previously been seen as a series of unrelated and somewhat haphazard efforts.

Reengineering today is no longer haphazard. There now exists an organized body of knowledge on how to succeed at reengineering. Companies that originally stumbled onto reengineering can now apply and implement it more consistently and effectively than in the past.

So when someone tells us they're old hands at reengineering, we don't argue (even though we don't always believe it). Our reply is simple—keep up the good work. And it must be kept up because reengineering is an ongoing response to a constantly changing world. Previous experience and success at reengineering do not excuse you from continuing it; they merely qualify you for the next round.

Argument 8: Reengineering is just another name for downsizing, and downsizing doesn't work. This statement is half true—the second half. Downsizing is indeed an ineffective response to a business crisis. It is usually an act of desperation—throwing people overboard to lighten the financial load. However, downsizing rarely pays off in the long term. Why? Because downsizing almost always means eliminating people, not work. Desperate to improve short-term financial performance, some companies take extreme measures to reduce costs without taking the time and trouble to rethink what is actually driving those costs. Eventually, however, the piper must be paid. In many cases, the reduced workforce must struggle to cover the workload formerly performed by the terminated employees. While this may be feasible in the short term, over time it will result in high levels of stress, resentment, and burnout. A widely practiced—and somewhat disingenuous—alternative is to covertly rehire many of the people just laid off. This is done often by bringing them back as "consultants" (so they don't appear on official company rosters) or by "outsourcing" the work to newly created firms operated by those same former employees. In either event, the strategy of eliminating people without eliminating work may lead to short-term payoff but definitely leads to long-term disaster. Among sophisticated managers, it has become widely recognized that downsizing only works if a company has gross amounts of excess fat or is confronting a long-term decline in demand for products and services. In such cases, shrinkage may be the appropriate strategy, but for the great majority of companies, downsizing is a detour on the road to success.

In contrast, reengineering is not about downsizing, no matter how many people persist in confusing the two. We suspect that many naysayers and counterrevolutionaries in fact understand the difference between the two but deliberately interchange them in order to attack reengineering. Reengineering is *not* about getting rid of people or jobs; it is about getting rid of *work,* specifically work that does not create value for the customer. Such work cannot be merely tossed overboard along with the people who perform it. It needs to be *designed* out. It requires the rethinking of the overall structure of processes, the identification of the meaningful value-adding work, and the discovery of novel ways to maximize that value-adding work while minimizing any less productive work. This is not easy. It cannot be done overnight. Although reengineering must not be allowed to drag out over a long period of time, it cannot be done with the ease and immediacy of downsizing. Reengineering offers a more thoughtful and textured way of improving operations. It has little in common with the crudities—and limited applications—of downsizing. So our reply is, "Downsizing indeed doesn't work—but reengineering does."

Argument 9: Reengineering is just a cost-cutting tool, but we need growth. This is one of the newest slurs being leveled against reengineering. Those who make it grudgingly admit that reengineering may be of help to companies in trouble or economies in downturn, but they claim that it has little to offer companies seeking growth in a robust economy. This position reflects both ignorance and misunderstanding on the part of those who take it. Nowhere in the definition of reengineering do the words "cost reduction" appear. Rather, reengineering is about dramatic improvement in process performance, in whatever ways matter to the customer and the company: cycle time, accuracy, quality, and, yes, cost. There are many ways to realize the benefits of reengineering. While many companies have reengineered to reduce their costs substantially, at least as many have had cycle-time reduction as their primary objective.

As we have stated repeatedly, reengineering is fundamentally focused on customers and their needs; by scoring major increases in customer satisfaction through reengineered processes, companies can gain market share, attack new markets, and achieve major growth. For instance, Liberty Mutual Insurance, Vortex, and Matthew Thornton Health Care (discussed in chapters 13 and 15) all had growth as their primary objective; even companies that begin with a cost-cutting goal often later redirect their efforts toward growth (as Engelhard Chemicals did—see chapter 13).

Those who make this argument are frequently people who see themselves as "strategic thinkers" and who view operating details as beneath them. Do not be taken in. Reengineering, by creating operating-performance breakthroughs, can contribute to growth as much as any elegant strategy. So when people say that reengineering is just cost-cutting, we reply, "No, it isn't"; and when they say that reengineering doesn't contribute to growth, we reply, "Yes, it does."

Argument 10: Reengineering is just common sense. Some people who have become familiar with the reengineering concept say to us, in tones that range from indignation to confusion, "But isn't this just common sense? Isn't this the most natural way for work to be done?" Our initial response is to thank them for their words of praise, for this is how we take them. An idea that is simple, readily understandable, and consistent with people's intuition is likely to be accepted and to work. Complex and esoteric concepts may make their developers feel clever, but they are rarely of great practical value. Moreover, as the old saw goes, there is nothing so uncommon as common sense.

On the other hand, we suggest that it is only now, after the fact, that the ideas of reengineering are called common-sensical. At the time they were formulated, they were seen as anything but that. With its emphasis on processes, its embrace of the radical, and its disdain for organizational structure, reengineering flew in the face of the "common sense" of the time. It is only in retrospect that good ideas seem obvious; rarely do they seem so in prospect.

In any event, this "criticism" is one to which we scarcely object.

These are the most common critiques of reengineering that we encounter, and our responses to them. However, we must close with one caveat: It is important for both the leaders of reengineering and members of reengineering teams to distinguish between deliberate (and ignorant) verbal sabotage on the one hand and intelligent criticism on the other. There are legitimate and important concerns that can be raised about reengineering: its difficulty, its cost, the disruption it causes, the challenge of managing in its aftermath. While reengineering does claim to deliver dramatic improvement, it does not claim perfection. Certainly reengineering is—and should be—subject to sober, constructive analysis, but that is not the agenda of the counter-revolutionaries. It is in how objections are raised that the friendly critic is distinguished from the fifth columnist. If the question is, "How do we deal with these issues so that reengineering will succeed?" then you are among allies. But

Counterrevolutionary Arguments and Responses

Argument	Response
Reengineering doesn't work	Tell it to the winners
Reengineering's nothing new	Who cares?
Reengineering's not sufficiently radical	Huh?
Reengineering's dangerous and inhumane	Compared to what?
We're different	And so is everyone else
We can't afford it	Congratulations
We've been doing it for years	Keep up the good work
Reengineering's just another name for downsizing, and downsizing doesn't work	The premise is wrong
Reengineering is not for growth	Yes it is
Reengineering is just common sense	Thank you

if the tenor is, "How can we possibly proceed in the face of such insurmountable problems?" then you have fallen into the hands of the opposition.

Actually, even some of those who express the kinds of criticisms we have outlined here do so not out of malice or ill will but simply from lack of knowledge. It is necessary to deal with them gently but insistently by pointing out the gaps in their understanding and the errors of their ways. By means of repeated communication and clarification they can be brought onto the straight and narrow.

However, those who are deliberately trying to obstruct the reengineering effort through bogus arguments, who are trying to sow doubt and despair, must be dealt with differently: They need the back of a hand. It is a waste of time to argue the merits or demerits of criticisms made by people who do not even believe them but are merely using them as sticks with which to attack reengineering. You will never convince them.

Of course, you must always be alert to the possibility that your reengineering efforts contain flaws in either conception or implementation. Before automatically dismissing critics as carpers or saboteurs, you should listen carefully to determine whether they are merely throwing stones or are, in fact, raising real issues. Reengineering not only can withstand intelligent criticism, it will be strengthened by it.

PART III

Tales from the Road

CHAPTER 12

The Case of the Overdue Orders

This is an interactive chapter. You, the reader, will be asked to put yourself in the role of a reengineering team leader confronting a series of crises. At each crisis, the narrative will pause and you will be asked how you would handle it. Think through your options and decide on the best course of action. (You may wish to work through this chapter with a group of co-workers, probing and discussing each other's ideas.) The narrative will inform you of what transpired in this case—a real one albeit heavily disguised. The quality of your responses will depend as much on alertness as intelligence. And so, whether reading alone or with a group, it is now time to shift from beta waves to alpha.

BACKGROUND

The company under consideration manufactures and sells electronic equipment for commercial use. Most customer orders require some customization; therefore, the company builds system components for stock and does final assembly and configuration to order. In the good old days, the order-processing, distribution, and finished-goods inventory departments were all part of the manufacturing operation. The marketing organization, then known as the "new kid on the block," was primarily responsible for customer service.

Some time ago, customers began complaining about the performance of order fulfillment. Management recognized that the majority of "service" calls were about order fulfillment rather than postsales support. In an effort to improve customer satisfaction, order processing was transferred to marketing; yet little really changed. The four departments— order processing, customer service, distribution, and inventory control—continued to function independently. Each had its own information system; cross-departmental communication was accomplished mostly by phone.

THE PROBLEM

Despite the reorganization, customers still complained that delivery took far too long. A customer could not place an order or get an answer with a single phone call; it was often necessary to call all four departments. Customers claimed that many orders were delayed or filled incorrectly. Company management recognized the validity of these complaints. When things worked smoothly, they knew, it took three weeks to fill an order. However, in 30 percent of the cases, delays added an average of twelve more days per order. Moreover, 20 percent of all orders had errors that led to billing disputes. To compound the problem, the company was unable to give preferential service to its best customers. Their orders were handled just like everyone else's.

The vice president of marketing commissioned a study to diagnose the situation and recommend solutions. This study confirmed the weaknesses of the order-fulfillment and customer-service processes. However, it also concluded that the competition performed no better. Thus, reengineering these processes would give the company a huge edge in the marketplace.

THE VISION

The marketing VP took the study results and articulated a vision of future performance. His vision centered on streamlined and coordinated processes with two key themes:

One-stop shopping: A newly designated "order representative" would complete a customer's order—including reserving inventory and locking into a delivery date—during a single phone call.

One-stop service: A "service representative," again a new designation, would handle all postsales needs—including order changes—with one call from the customer.

The vision also included ambitious performance goals to be achieved within two years, to wit:

Same-week delivery (which would be an improvement of more than 70 percent).

Error and delay rate of less than 5 percent (reduced from 50 percent).

95 percent of orders and inquiries handled during the customer's first call.

The VP recognized that a process that would realize this vision would require changes in organizational boundaries and would also create two key new job titles, those of order representative and service representative.

INPUT FROM I/S

Information systems management was part of this reengineering effort as well. I/S assured marketing that the new plan was workable. However, it would mean creating two new integrated databases: inventory availability (currently spread across three departmental databases) and customer information (still pegged to an obsolete geographical structure). I/S also pointed out the need for new systems to support the order and service representatives, recommending a new software package to handle the revised order fulfillment process.

THE PROCESS OWNER

The VP of marketing made this vision his personal crusade. Young, a real "comer" in the company, he also had lots of contacts, including many in manufacturing whom he knew from his days in the old order-processing department. The VP presented the results of the study to his CEO and board of directors. Enlisting their support, he got a commitment of real funds for one year and a provisional budget covering two more. He also won the support of the VP of manufacturing. This was a delicate task, because reorganization meant marketing would add the distribution and finished-goods inventory control departments, while manufacturing would give them up. To make things worse, the manufacturing VP was an old crony of the CEO. The two VPs agreed that any formal reorganization would happen only after they had tested and "proven the concept" of the vision.

THE KICKOFF

The company formed a reengineering team, mostly "functional leaders" (insiders) drawn from the departments, and the rest information systems personnel (playing the outsider role). The team leader came from order processing. She was

dynamic and uncompromising, generally respected as someone who "produces results." The team formulated a game
plan centered on supporting the new roles of order representative and service representative. They divided the overall
implementation plan into four phases:

1. Knitting together existing computer systems in order
   to provide customer-inquiry support as quickly as possible.
2. Implementing the core of order fulfillment with the
   new software package.
3. Integrating order processing with distribution and
   inventory management; this is where the heavy database integration would take place.
4. Finally, integrating order fulfillment with the production planning and control system.

According to the plan, these four phases were expected to
overlap somewhat as design changes adapted to evolving
needs.

There was much hoopla at project launch. The kickoff
meeting was attended by almost everyone in the four departments. It featured introductory remarks by the CEO, presentation of the vision by the marketing VP, and remarks by the
manufacturing VP.

The reengineering team went to work on phase 1 with
enormous energy. They succeeded in designing, constructing,
piloting, and installing the new capability even faster than
anticipated. Customers loved it. Previously they had been
calling all over the company to get answers to their questions; suddenly the information was available almost
instantly. In fact, everyone loved the new system, especially
those who had once been on the receiving end of all those
bothersome phone calls. They could get back to their real

jobs now, without unnecessary interruption. Life was easier and more productive all around.

The team leader and her teammates felt things could hardly be going any better. And then . . .

EPISODE I:
The Process Owner Vanishes

Phase 2 was launched and seemed to be going smoothly. The new order fulfillment system initially affected only one department directly, and that department reported directly to the VP of marketing, who was, after all, the process owner. Unfortunately, a slight glitch arose.

The VP of marketing's star was on the rise. It rose so far and so fast, in fact, that he was abruptly promoted to head up the company's European operations. With many loose ends to tie up in a hurry, he had no time to devote to a project that was apparently chugging along quite smoothly. In three short weeks, he was gone.

His replacement, the new marketing VP, came from the sales side of the company. While she was a strong leader, she also, understandably, wanted to dig in and get a hands-on, operational feel for her new role before focusing on the reengineering effort. Nevertheless, she supported the project in principle and instructed the team leader to proceed as planned.

The VP of manufacturing agreed to become the titular process owner, even though he made no bones about wanting to tone down the changes and delay any organizational restructuring. The CEO, the team leader, and the team all agreed that this was a practical approach, given the departure of the initial process owner. They also felt the project had the funding and momentum needed to move forward even with a less active process owner.

The new marketing VP was seldom available for consultation. She kept a low profile as project reviewer, preferring to concentrate on her other responsibilities. Soon the pace of change began to slow. Two of the functional leaders—one from distribution and one from inventory control—were pulled from the team because of what were called "more important" duties; they were replaced by less experienced individuals. A third team member, also from inventory control, was cut back to half time. The phase 2 schedule quickly slipped by three months. Concerned, the project leader tried to regain momentum by adding more I/S people to the team. New problems began to crop up, though. In particular, the new team was having trouble agreeing on key aspects of phase 3 design. People started referring to the reengineering effort as a "computer project" and talking disparagingly about why it would "never work." The schedule slipped some more.

You are the team leader. What do you do?

EPISODE II:
The Data Disagreement

The team leader made the case—first (diplomatically) to the manufacturing VP and then (more forcefully) to the CEO—that the project could only be rescued by an infusion of leadership from top management. The root cause of the problem, she argued, was a poor transition from the original process owner to his replacement. The VP of manufacturing was admittedly less interested in the effort, she noted, and there was no contingency plan to cover the departure of someone as valuable and dynamic as the ex-VP of marketing, who, most realized, had been ticketed for promotion soon anyway.

The CEO agreed to assume responsibility as interim process owner. The CEO, the team leader, and the two VPs further agreed to meet weekly as an ad hoc steering committee in order to monitor progress and get the project back on track. Their first, and highly visible, move was to revitalize the team by restaffing it with a full complement of first-rate insiders. The steering committee meetings continued for twelve more weeks, effectively functioning as a reengineering seminar for the two VPs. At the end of three months, the new marketing VP assumed the role of process owner.

With this leadership issue resolved, happy days were here again. Phase 3 began, even though a few important matters regarding the new databases appeared unresolved. All parties agreed on the need for a single inventory database; however, they disagreed on who should have the authority to update it.

The finished-goods inventory control people insisted they remain in control of both physical and reserved-for-orders inventories. They proposed that order-processing and distribution personnel (who actually picked, packed, and shipped product) should post on-line "notices" of their desired inventory adjustments to the database. Inventory control would then review these notices and make the actual changes; they alone, in other words, would commit inventory to orders and adjust the necessary inventory balances. After all, they reasoned, they were the ones responsible for inventory accuracy and minimizing inventory levels, and their performance was measured accordingly. If things got out of control, inventory levels would rise and/or production planning would be in chaos.

Others, including the team leader, felt the whole idea—the basic vision, the entire process model—hinged on order representatives being able to make immediate and firm commitments to customers. Their design called for the initiator of the transaction to perform the associated database updates. They felt that order representatives should update reserved-for-order inventory and distribution people should handle actual inventory.

DILBERT reprinted by permission of UFS, INC.

Discussion continued over a period of several weeks. It grew increasingly rancorous, and the team sought executive advice. First to reply was the VP of manufacturing, who sided with the inventory control people and refused to budge. The two VPs met with the team leader to try to settle the issue, but the three simply could not reach a consensus. The team leader suggested going to the CEO to break the impasse. The manufacturing VP replied, "If either of you go over my head on this, you lose my support. I'll kill the project, slowly if necessary, by pulling my resources."

You are the team leader. What do you do?

EPISODE III:
The Shadow Function Knows

The team leader and the process owner discussed the situation at length and concluded that the CEO would not overrule his old ally, the VP of manufacturing. The disagreement had become public knowledge, and the CEO would not allow his pal to lose face. Moreover, appealing to the CEO at this time would surely incur the wrath of the manufacturing VP, exactly as he had threatened. The two leaders agreed that the politics of the situation required a delicate diplomacy.

So the team devised a compromise, a build-around. First they designed a "pure" process whereby order representatives would do the updates directly. On top of this they overlaid a "notice" feature: a feedback loop from inventory control to order processing, informing them which notices were not followed and why. In this fashion, representatives could get back to their customers quickly if they had to change a commitment. According to this plan, this notice approach would remain in effect until inventory control agreed the system was working perfectly (i.e., they were following all notice advisories and were becoming tired of doing the updates themselves). No fixed time frame was placed on the transition from one version to the other. The team leader and process owner figured that at most they would have to wait three years until the manufacturing VP retired. The manufacturing VP agreed to this compromise plan.

The next step was implementing phase 3—integrating order processing, distribution, and inventory control. It began with a three-month pilot project, using orders for a single, moderate-volume product line as a test case. For five weeks, things went splendidly. Same-week shipment was being realized on a regular basis. Order and service representatives were performing admirably; well trained in their new duties, they had reengineering team members on call and often sitting at their sides. Inventory control personnel followed instructions to the letter and updated data as "notices" required.

In week six, all hell broke loose. Three items had stockouts. Manufacturing quickly shifted production schedules to compensate. This move had a cascading effect, causing stockouts on other items. By week eight, 50 percent of all orders were late, and customers were furious. The project manager and two VPs met with all concerned parties, but nobody could pinpoint what had gone wrong. Because the situation was deteriorating so rapidly, however, they agreed to put the pilot on hold and appoint a special team to push existing orders through—plus another team to investigate the system breakdown. As the emergency meeting broke up, the manufacturing VP said, rather smugly, "I told you it would never work."

It took the two teams four weeks to reprocess the orders and establish what had gone wrong. The problem occurred where the new process interfaced with production planning and final assembly. As the investigative team discovered, inventory control had been performing a subtle, essential, but undocumented function: adjusting the trade-off among order fulfillment, manufacturing efficiency, and inventory levels. For example, they might delay or invent orders, or inflate or deflate the length of a manufacturing run, to keep manufacturing in tune not just with received orders but with anticipated orders as well. Blindly following the "notices" instructions, inventory control stopped making these unofficial adjustments, throwing the whole system out of balance.

The special team brings this report to you, the team leader. What do you do?

EPISODE IV:
In Which It Hits the Fan

The reengineering team, team leader, and the process owner discussed their options. They believed that, despite problems with the pilot, the new process was fundamentally sound and close to being workable. To implement a fully functioning system, however, they would have to delay six months in order to merge phase 4 (the production planning interface) with phase 3. They saw no way to divide the project into smaller deliverables. They also concluded that the subtle balancing act performed by inventory control was probably too complex and risky to model directly. The revised design would include a semi-automated interface between the two functions. Inventory control would have responsibility for "batching" inventory commitments and advising production planners, thus continuing their role as buffer.

The process owner and team leader first presented their analysis and proposed redesign to the CEO, who backed the project's continuation. They then made a conciliatory approach to the manufacturing VP and his staff, who, after the requisite amount of grumbling, agreed to go along with the new plan.

The second tryout of phase 3-plus-4 was a success; the project progressed smoothly until the full rollout occurred. Then, despite hours of training in their new roles, order and service representatives began making mistakes and proving not nearly as productive as they had been in the pilot. The quality and accuracy of order fulfillment and customer service were far below performance expectations. New procedures were seemingly being followed, new computer systems were being used, but the process as a whole was misfiring on several cylinders.

The reengineering team discovered three basic (and related) problems:

1: Many representatives were unaccustomed to their new levels of responsibility. They were therefore tentative in their actions and afraid of fouling up.

2: Many continued to rely on old work habits in case the new procedures failed completely. For example, even though inventory-availability information was right in their own computers, order reps would still put customers on hold (or even call them back later) while they phoned inventory control or distribution to check on physical stock. They also kept manual lists of inventory levels, comparing notes with one another as if they were shopping at their local supermarkets.

3: Many representatives objected to their extra duties. As one said, "You raised my pay $1.00 an hour and are asking me to do the work of three people. Why should I break my neck?"

You are still the team leader (somehow). Now what do you do?

EPISODE V:
Virtue Triumphant

This story ended happily, though it took much longer than planned to reach (and eventually exceed) anticipated productivity levels. The team leader, process owner, and reengineering team took four steps to wean people from manual "shadow systems" and thus fully implement the new process:

1: The team provided an additional round of training, focusing not on specific tasks and procedures (in which the reps were well-versed) but rather on the business vision and goals—overall process design, their roles and responsibilities in making it work, and the support structures and management systems that would help them succeed. In other words, they (belatedly) provided the kind of education that changes people's thinking and understanding.

2: The reengineering team established and staffed a temporary support organization that offered the reps telephone help and field service. Whenever representatives had problems or questions, they could call for help and, if necessary, have someone assist them in person. A basic ground rule stated that these assistance calls would not be reported to management; the goal was to help representatives succeed, not to measure their productivity or to establish their short-comings.

3:   Information systems were enhanced to provide the individual representative with feedback about the quality, accuracy, and timeliness of his or her work. Also added was an expanded "tickler" list of orders and actions pending. Again, this information was provided for the representative's self-improvement. It was not reported to management except, of course, in summary form that described the effectiveness of the entire process.

4:   The team leader and the process owner worked with department managers and human resources staffers to upgrade the job levels and compensation of the representatives.

And all was well that ended well.

The Case of the Overdue Orders illustrates some of the challenges, pitfalls, and critical factors in implementing reengineering. The four crises detailed here are among the most common that afflict reengineering projects:

1. Loss of the process owner/project sponsor.
2. Interorganizational strife and stonewalling, usually over issues of turf and control.
3. A pilot phase that proves disastrous, often traceable to a process design flaw.
4. The persistence of "shadow systems," as employees find it difficult to discard old work habits and become comfortable with new processes.

Aside from the question with which each of the five episodes end—What should the team leader do?—we must also address two other key points: What is the root cause of each problem? What should have been done earlier to address this root cause and prevent the problem from ever occurring? We offer the following suggestions, points for discussion, and food for thought:

EPISODE I:
The Process Owner Vanishes

You will get nowhere without a strong process owner/project sponsor. You cannot settle, even temporarily, for an absentee owner like the VP of manufacturing. It is entirely predictable that a strong process owner is unlikely to remain in position for the duration of a multiyear business change. (Why? Because strong managers are typically on fast-track promotion ladders.) Thus, the team leader and CEO should have had a backup or owner-in-waiting plan. The original owner should also have given a firm commitment (part of his original pact with the CEO) to ensure an orderly and effective handoff.

Another dilemma crops up here. A project derives much of its energy and momentum from the owner/sponsor's personal commitment; at the same time, however, it is essential to spread some degree of sponsorship among all senior managers, especially the owner-in-waiting.

EPISODE II:
The Data Disagreement

The root cause here was the failure to appreciate—and explicitly address—political resistance. Failing to do so early, a team may find it necessary to make awkward compromises later on, as happened here. The manufacturing VP would have been more inclined to compromise had he shared direct responsibility for the project's success. True, he was not the original project sponsor. But as a key functional executive, he should have had responsibility for helping this initiative succeed. The reality, though, is that compromise on process design is sometimes necessary to work around political barriers.

EPISODE III:
The Shadow Function Knows

Sabotage by the VP of manufacturing? Conspiracy in the inventory control department? Such things are not unheard of. But the real issue here is the "invisible process." The reengineering team did not have a deep enough understanding of the business processes. Inventory control's balancing act should not have been invisible. Note that the requisite understanding would not have come from meticulous interviewing or documenting existing manual and paper processes. The reality of the process could only be appreciated by sitting in the inventory control and production planning departments for a few weeks apiece. A generic mistake being manifested here is failing to pay sufficient attention to factors at the "perimeter" of a process.

EPISODE IV:
In Which It Hits the Fan

One problem exhibited here was an inappropriate mix of education and training. The representatives were taught new tasks but not the purpose and context of their new work. Another problem was insufficient support by the reengineering team during the rollout of the new process. A third was that inadequate attention was paid to job design and compensation systems. Shadow systems are inevitable to some extent; the key is to anticipate and eliminate them. Clichéd as it sounds, it is essential to help people unlearn old ways as well as to master new ones.

It is also useful to think about overall responsibility for these problems. There is no lack of candidates for the role of scapegoat: the team leader, who failed to recognize the potential pitfalls; the original process owner, who abandoned the project for a better job; the new VP of marketing, who exhibited timidity rather than leadership; the CEO, who tolerated (and perhaps encouraged) such a politicized organization; and, of course, the parochial folks over at inventory control and the nefarious VP of manufacturing. More to the point, what were the underlying errors that made these problems inevitable? We nominate the following three culprits:

- Not anticipating the challenge and effort that would be required, especially at implementation time.
- Not addressing organizational resistance early and directly enough.
- Avoiding the issue of organizational restructuring in the name of political expediency.

To be fair, none of these pitfalls can be entirely avoided. They arise out of human nature and the nature of reengineering.

And of course reengineering itself, like any other exceedingly complex endeavor, offers ample opportunities for error.

As always, the game is to the quick.

CHAPTER 13

The Realities of Reengineering I: Three Roads to Success

Legend has it that Euclid once told a monarch impatient for knowledge that there was no royal road to geometry. We tell managers today there is no single road to reengineering. Though the laws of vehicular physics apply everywhere—take a corner too fast and you career off the road—the routes that vehicles take vary greatly. Starting in different places, different organizations will have different priorities, proceed at different speeds, and employ different techniques. Here are tales of three roads to the promised land of reengineering: one broad, one fast, one indirect. The differences among them are apparent; so too, we believe, are the commonalities.

ENGELHARD: THE BROAD ROAD

Some reengineering efforts are narrowly focused, concentrating on a single process in a single part of the company. Others attack across a broad front, touching many parts of the corporation. The latter strategy can yield extraordinary results, but it requires extraordinary ambition and commitment. These elements were present at Engelhard, a specialty chemical and engineered materials company headquartered in New Jersey, whose special expertise is surface chemistry and whose biggest business is catalysis. Engelhard has six business units and aggregate revenues of approximately $2.2 billion.

Reengineering has had a major impact at Engelhard. "Business reengineering," Donald LaTorre, president and COO, said recently, "has been a significant part of our major cultural change at Engelhard. Our company is going through a dramatic transformation. We are aiming to dramatically increase our revenues by the year 2000, and reengineering is a major component of our effort. Without reengineering, we wouldn't be as far along as we are. It has helped us deliver record earnings in each of the past three years by dramatically reducing costs in our manufacturing facilities."

Engelhard's reengineering story has its roots in the late 1980s, when the company undertook several rounds of restructuring, culminating in a 1990 effort that eliminated more than 500 jobs from the salaried workforce. This restructuring aimed to reduce costs and increase speed and flexibility by eliminating bureaucracy in corporate staff and operations management. However, "We learned that we really didn't change the work, we just eliminated people," LaTorre admits. "This made us realize that we really had to change the work as well."

In November 1991, the company brought all its senior managers to an off-site meeting to explore what would be needed to make Engelhard the world's leading catalyst company. At that meeting, management realized they could not get there from where they were. The improvements of the past would not be enough to fuel the future growth of the company. It was time to reengineer.

Since manufacturing was the dominant driver of the company's costs, Donald LaTorre announced that reengineering would begin with an immediate goal of "reducing manufacturing costs 20 to 33 percent—or 10 percent below best in class, whichever is the most favorable—in at least one site in each of our business units, within twelve months." This goal was quite a stretch, since the company's restructuring and quality programs had long been hacking away at costs. No one, moreover, had the slightest idea how to achieve the goal. LaTorre also mandated that the effort be self-funding. The clock began ticking on January 1, 1992: twelve months to go and counting . . .

Stephen Pook, then director of information systems, was assigned to manage the effort. Pook was selected because he had introduced the concept of reengineering to Engelhard, force-feeding his colleagues with article after article, dragging them to seminars, and generally championing the idea. His frustration with traditional information systems, which merely automated existing ways of doing things, was what had originally attracted Pook to reengineering. His championship had been so intense that when the decision was made to proceed, his colleagues took their revenge by making him reengineering czar.

During the next year, Pook would spend 80 percent of his time on reengineering. Despite his information systems background, he did not turn reengineering into a "technology trip." This was reflected in the composition of the two teams he quickly organized: a Sponsor Team, consisting of the COO, the CFO, and the vice presidents of human resources and corporate development; and an operating group called the Reengineering Task Force (RTF), which included Pook himself, a finance director, the vice president of R&D, a manufacturing vice president, and a director of corporate development.

The RTF started by convening six teams, each to focus on one manufacturing site in a different business unit. Each team was composed of from three to six people from that site. Staffing these teams took very little time or energy, thanks largely to the intervention of the Sponsor Team, especially LaTorre. "We put a lot of pressure on those sites, and they came through wonderfully," he says.

The RTF's job was to enable and facilitate the six teams. Its support was built around a series of critical meetings held over the course of the year, at which major problems were explored and decisions reached. The first session, held right at the start in January 1992, focused on organizing and targeting the effort. The Sponsor Team, the business units' senior management, and the six teams gathered for what Pook called "a balloon ride over the organization—an elevated look at our business and processes." The goal was to provide everyone with a holistic view of the business, a perspective unlimited by organizational myopia and inherited biases. Many organizations find this a powerful experience, the business equivalent of seeing Earth from space.

The January meeting attendees discovered that hardly anyone, even—perhaps especially—senior executives, truly understood how the business worked as a whole. This realization spurred the teams to create process models of the six units, consisting of six to twelve key processes each. They also identified *leverage points* for each process. A leverage point is some aspect of a process where small improvement will produce a disproportionate impact on overall process performance, making it an important target for reengineering. For example, production scheduling is a leverage point in many manufacturing processes, since even a small improvement in its accuracy can reduce inventory levels dramatically.

Following the January meeting, the teams began to study their processes and to pinpoint specific areas ripe for improvement. Their results were presented, shared, and validated at the next RTF session, in March—which launched the teams into an intensive planning effort. The June meeting focused on action plans, project schedules, and resource requirements. It's really remarkable what executive commitment and a process perspective can accomplish. In the first six months, Engelhard had gone from a vague and seemingly unachievable goal to an organized program.

During the next six months, the six teams worked on project implementation. Each member of the RTF was responsible for one of the teams, functioning both as an internal consultant and as an enabler who could provide resources as needed. The final meeting was held in December, and results were presented. Pressure and urgency had borne fruit. All six teams had achieved *at least* a 20 percent cost reduction. Several managed to reach the 33 percent target.

The seriousness of Engelhard management's approach to reengineering is illustrated by their actions in the petroleum catalyst business unit. Its reengineering team was able to reduce costs as mandated—and at the same time they increased the plant's manufacturing capacity by 45 percent, obviating the need for a previously authorized multimillion-dollar plant expansion. Understandably, the reengineering team wanted to claim those millions as project benefits. However, the Sponsor Team ruled that additional capacity in itself is not a bankable benefit; only its output, when sold, could be considered part of the reengineering outcome. The sponsors were not being greedy or arbitrary: Their decision gave the team a powerful incentive to find customers for the enhanced capacity.

To meet the challenge of selling the additional capacity, the team proceeded to reengineer the unit's customer acquisition process. In the past, Engelhard's greatest success had come from selling to a particular segment of the petroleum catalyst business—specifically, smaller independent customers. It had been less successful at selling to major multi-site companies, which required long-term relationships, team selling, and the involvement of many departments, from purchasing to R&D. The company simply wasn't set up for that kind of cross-functional sales approach.

To sell to a new kind of customer, the team created a new selling process, in which cross-functional teams were paired with major target accounts. The process also focused on cross-company linkages so that Engelhard's distribution specialists, for example, could understand exactly how customers wanted to receive their products, in terms of packaging, delivery schedule, and so on. This new approach worked so well that the new capacity was sold out in six months. Thanks to reengineering, the petroleum catalyst unit increased its worldwide market share in this segment by 35 percent and achieved an important improvement in profits.

While the first year of reengineering met its stretch objective, it was in the second year that "reengineering really got interesting," according to LaTorre. "We started to do exciting things. Our initial activity had been so successful that people began coming to Stephen Pook for help in changing the business everywhere." Reengineering was extended to larger-scale efforts, such as the sales process just discussed. It was also extended to enabling processes, such as information systems and finance, and to international operations.

All first-year reengineering efforts had taken place in Engelhard's American plants. When those efforts proved successful, the company decided to export reengineering know-how to its facilities abroad. While cultural obstacles quickly became apparent, success was eventually achieved. In the Netherlands, for example, "Once they got it, they became true converts," according to Donald LaTorre. "They were able to take 35 percent of their costs out in the first year. Now we're rolling out in France and the UK. We're also beginning to see some very promising results with our Japanese affiliates."

Needless to say, not everyone was happy or remained with the program. "We've had to move some of our resisters out," LaTorre says. "But we got such good early results that there's been a lot of peer pressure to go along with the change." Not surprisingly, the greatest problems were encountered in middle management, where people felt very threatened by the changes. Management hierarchy in the plants is being flattened, with the worker-to-foreman ratio increasing from eight-to-one to fifteen- or even eighteen-to-one.

But there's no turning back. Reengineering has become a way of life at Engelhard. Stephen Pook, now vice president of I/S, quality, and business reengineering, best sums up the outlook: "Change is a central part of our lives now. We'll never be done and we'll never be 'normal' again."

What Engelhard Did Right

Began with, and held to, explicit stretch goals and
   timetables
Developed a process perspective on the business
Achieved, and built on, early successes
Propagated the effort through all parts of the
   company

LIBERTY MUTUAL: THE FAST ROAD

Liberty Mutual is an insurance and financial services company with over 20,000 employees and owned assets in excess of $25 billion. Despite its overall success, the Boston-headquartered company had persistent problems in its middle market unit, which concentrated on selling business insurance—workers' compensation, general liability, property, commercial auto—to small and medium-sized companies. Its profitability was far from satisfactory, and key performance measures were below industry norms.

Initially, the company thought the difficulty stemmed from the underwriting department, where decisions were made about which risks to accept and what premiums to charge. But closer examination revealed that the entire process of risk selection, underwriting, and policy production—everything involved in customer acquisition and order fulfillment—needed reengineering if inefficiencies were to be eliminated and profitability improved.

The symptoms of distress were many and varied. Most tellingly, value-added work time was a tiny fraction of elapsed time. For small accounts, the elapsed time from initial contact with a potential customer to issuance of a contract averaged sixty-two days, of which the value-added work time was three days. To put it another way, customers waited twelve weeks for a contract on which Liberty Mutual employees worked for only twenty-four hours. The primary cause of this long cycle was the fifteen to twenty interdepartmental handoffs that each application had to endure. Moreover, the sales, underwriting, and production departments used independent computer systems, with each group rekeying data into its own system. This led to errors, of course—and to more delays.

On top of this, the traditional conflict between sales, which wants to close the deal, and underwriting, which is concerned about holding the line on price, had reached epic proportions. Almost all differences between these perpetually warring units had to be resolved by a formal appeals process, often involving four levels of management. These process dysfunctions raised costs, slowed cycle times, and reduced customer satisfaction. This was the challenge facing Liberty Mutual when it began reengineering in September 1992.

Only twenty-one months later, in mid-1994, Liberty Mutual had implemented a solution that eliminated almost all the handoffs, avoided appeals, and reduced the cycle time by more than half. The performance consequences have been dramatic. Liberty Mutual is now offering quotes to a much higher percentage of prospects than before, and to a lower fraction of unsuitable accounts. (That is to say, it is not simply chasing bad business.) It has also doubled the percentage of quotes that turn into closed business, from 15 percent to 30 percent. At the same time, the quality of the risks Liberty Mutual accepts, as measured by claims paid as a percentage of premiums, has improved significantly. In other words, the company has not increased its business by lowering its standards. Overall, the annual benefits of the new process exceed $50 million a year.

The new process that delivers these benefits is based on cross-functional teams responsible for all customers in a given part of a district. (The company divides the United States into eight divisions and forty-three districts.) Each team includes sales, underwriting, and loss prevention experts, who are collectively responsible for everything from sales planning through application processing, underwriting, and policy issuance. The teams are supported by a new integrated information system. Team members work under a shared incentive system that reflects both sales effectiveness and account profitability. In effect, everyone must think like both a sales rep and an underwriter, since the teams must satisfy two sets of criteria. In short, a fragmented process was transformed into a coherent, integrated way of doing business. And it's worth repeating that the new process was in operation, nationwide, only twenty-one months after reengineering had begun from a standing start.

How did Liberty Mutual achieve this seeming miracle? Not by good luck. Five company qualities enabled it to do so much so quickly: strong sponsorship; the right people organized in the right way; disciplined project management; intensive field involvement; and a commitment to rapid implementation.

Strong Sponsorship. The driving force behind the reengineering was Therese Maloney, executive vice president of underwriting. The project's executive team was composed of the COO (Edmund Kelly), Maloney, and the EVP (Gary Lia) responsible for all field operations—a leadership cadre representing all the company's key power centers. Simply put, the executive team's role was to ensure that the project succeeded. They served as a liaison between reengineering, and the executive committee and the board. They ensured that the project secured the right staff. They reviewed and approved redesigns and implementation plans. They provided funding, monitored progress, and assisted in the development of contingency planning. Meeting with the project leadership every two weeks, they stayed close to the actual effort at both macro (policy) and micro (tactical execution) levels.

The project also had a sponsor group composed of the vice presidents of underwriting, sales, loss prevention, operations, and I/S. They served as devil's advocates, challenging findings and ideas in order to make certain that they were well thought out. In addition, to ensure that the reengineering was integrated with other Liberty Mutual initiatives, they acted as functional ambassadors to key constituencies throughout the company.

Over the project's lifetime, these two advocacy groups not only spread the word of reengineering while overcoming psychological resistance in the company's ranks, but also resolved innumerable dilemmas, removed obstacles, and provided the clout that powered the entire expedition. Without their intensive, ongoing involvement, the project would have died a thousand different deaths.

The Right People in the Right Structure. As reengineering shifted from design to implementation, project organization became more complex. Initially, the project was conducted by a small redesign team composed of six full-time people and headed by a strong project manager who reported directly to Therese Maloney. The redesign team members were selected on the basis of their knowledge of the old process, their ability to think out of the box, their credibility in the organization, and their willingness to work exceptionally hard. As the project progressed, this stamina proved to be an invaluable asset.

The implementation phase sent the number of teams soaring. There were teams dedicated to pilot site preparation; information systems development; training and human resources development; communications; pilot implementation; and rollout. Each was staffed with three to ten full-time members, with much overlapping membership for the sake of alignment and cooperation. This allowed the teams to work concurrently, addressing pilot and rollout in parallel. Since many team members didn't know each other—having come from different organizational units—extensive team-building exercises were employed throughout the program's duration. This investment of time paid off in the integrated operation of all the teams.

Disciplined Project Management. The large number of implementation teams required strong coordination efforts to ensure that the pieces of the effort all fit together. To this end, each team was responsible for developing detailed project plans that were folded into a master project plan. The teams also made use of a formal set of conflict resolution mechanisms. Conflicts and differences of opinion are unavoidable and even desirable aspects of teamwork; the key is to resolve them quickly rather than let them fester.

Liberty Mutual accomplished this resolution by maintaining explicit databases of open issues, so nothing could be swept under the rug, and by insisting on rapid closure, with the project manager intervening quickly when necessary.

The company's stance on scope management was particularly important. As soon as the middle market redesign looked real and promising, the large-account group petitioned to be included in the reengineering effort. All the reengineers, from Ms. Maloney to individual team members, united in opposition: no, no, a thousand times, no. Why so adamant? Why not take advantage of the enthusiasm to reengineer the whole company? Because the larger the scope, the longer the time frame; the longer the time frame, the higher the risk. And the higher the risk, the greater the chance that no benefit would be achieved. Although sympathetic to everyone's needs, the reengineers never allowed themselves to be distracted from their original focus and never succumbed to seductive scope-creep, the slow growth of scale and functionality that inevitably leads to missed schedules and overrun budgets. They expressed their discipline in a slogan: "Refuse all comers!"

Field Involvement. The project was born in Boston. Most of its leadership came from corporate headquarters, and that is where the design team operated. Nonetheless, the focus of the reengineering activity was the field. Success would be attained only if all the divisions and districts accepted the redesign. At every step, therefore, the reengineers ensured that field perspective and field personnel were represented and involved. When conducting a diagnosis of the old process, for example, the redesign team interviewed over 150 managers from all eight divisions, soliciting information and ideas for improvement. Every person to whom they spoke became a partner in the project, an evangelist who helped ensure the field's buy-in to the new design. The reengineering team also interviewed every division leader and most district managers. Field personnel were asked to "dream your dreams." How would they do things if they were starting afresh? What would they like to see in the new design to help improve their performance? On this journey, they were drivers, not freight.

Another mechanism for ensuring field involvement was the Field Advisory Board (FAB), an ad hoc field committee composed of senior field managers from districts not involved in the early pilot implementations. In an unusual wrinkle, it was decided to vary the FAB's composition over time instead of keeping it a fixed group. Nor did it have a fixed meeting schedule. Meetings were convened when the implementation teams had new deliverables to share, when field communications were being developed, and when important questions arose about field perspective and its acceptance of the redesign. Many field leaders served on the FAB during the course of the project. Each left a thumbprint, adding value and deepening the FAB's commitment to the effort.

Commitment to Rapid Implementation. Of all the factors that contributed to Liberty Mutual's success, this was the most important. By demanding rapid progress and rapid results, the company forced itself to find effective shortcuts at every step along the way.

With relentless devotion to the 80/20 law—Pareto's principle, which states that 20 percent of the effort delivers 80 percent of the benefits—the reengineers compressed the design phase to ten weeks by triaging their design in the interest of speed. Similarly, they accelerated the testing and validation of their design through simulation exercises that re-created actual sales situations. Each simulation was followed by a formal debriefing to document the findings and improve the design. The simulations were open and publicized, allowing field personnel to attend and observe the new process at work. Some of the better simulations were captured on video and used for publicity and training purposes.

The emphasis on speed was extended to information systems development. Rather than construct traditional monolithic systems, with their long lead times and inflexible specifications, the information systems development team used an iterative prototyping approach to software construction. They quickly created small, imperfect applications, assessed their performance, and rapidly improved them. Each of their five new systems went through countless versions, multiple revisions, and constant upgrading. They also used outside system development organizations to augment their own resources, which enabled them to develop their systems in less than a third of the usual time.

The new sales process had to be installed in forty-three districts around the United States. To ensure that this rollout would proceed quickly, the reengineers decided to test the new design at two pilot sites. The goal was to "make as many mistakes as possible in the pilot," where the stakes and investment were smaller. The criteria for pilot selection were several: The divisional and district management had to have a genuine desire to play the role of pilot; it had to have a good representative mix of business; the business climate and recent history of the area had to be at least average, since it would be unwise to select a poorly performing district. For logistic reasons, the two districts also had to be in reasonable proximity. Given executive management's explicit devotion to reengineering, it's no surprise that many districts volunteered to host the pilot program, and that suitable sites were quickly selected.

The reengineering team deployed a variety of mechanisms

to monitor the pilots' progress. "Pilot rovers"—members of various reengineering teams—visited the sites to gather information, conduct on-the-job training, and solve problems on the spot. Electronic mail and focus groups were used so that the people involved in the two pilots could communicate their feedback to the reengineers. These mechanisms allowed problems to be identified and resolved quickly, before they became entrenched.

Liberty Mutual also accelerated its rollout by using a "lead district" approach. After the successful pilots, the forty-one remaining districts had to be trained in the new process, have their computer systems switched over, and adopt new daily routines. It would have taken years to execute those transitions had they been done sequentially, using only the reengineering teams. In order to save time—a great deal of it—the reengineering teams set off a chain reaction by training and converting one district in each of the divisions, after which this lead district would help train and convert the others in its division. To prevent degradation of the redesign's integrity and to avoid defective training as districts prepped other districts, the reengineers conducted strict quality reviews all along the way.

Liberty Mutual's obsession with speed paid off. After taking only ten weeks to develop the new process design, it took only four months to get to the pilot tests, four more months to complete them, three months to roll out the first sixteen districts, and three more months to convert the remaining twenty-five. (Alert readers will notice that this doesn't add up to twenty-one months; this is because some up-front time was required for crafting the vision and mobilizing the effort.)

"But at my back, I always hear Time's winged chariot hurrying near," wrote the seventeenth-century poet Andrew Marvell. Liberty Mutual heard the same thing, and it stood their reengineering effort in very good stead.

> **What Liberty Mutual Did Right**
>
> Created a strong sponsorship cadre
> Staffed the effort with the right people
> Adhered to a rigorous project management discipline
> Involved the field from start to finish
> Made rapid implementation the number one priority

AMOCO: THE INDIRECT ROAD

Most companies begin reengineering by addressing a key value-adding process, one of the mechanisms through which customer value is created. This can be order fulfillment, product development, postsales service, and so on. This approach is logical, since reengineering, at its heart, is customer driven and these are the processes that most matter to the customer.

In some cases, however, a company begins with an enabling process, an internally focused process that creates no direct value for customers but supports or enables the processes that do. One major insurance company, for instance, addressed corporate purchasing early in its reengineering program, not because the acquisition of paper and pencils was critical but because it could be easily and quickly accomplished, giving reengineering a boost in momentum and credibility. At other companies, enablers like information systems development or human resource acquisition were high priorities because their condition was so poor that they inhibited the reengineering—even the effective operation—of other processes. That was the case when Amoco began Project Spring, the reengineering of its budgeting and planning processes.

Amoco is a $30 billion petrochemical company headquartered in Chicago. Having heard about reengineering in the early 1990s, management invited one of us to address their top 150 executives. At this event, the conversation turned to which of Amoco's processes might be suitable for reengineering. Since Amoco is an integrated oil company, including upstream (exploration and production), downstream (refining and marketing), and chemicals, it has many disparate parts and so it was hard to find a common concern. The discussion remained somewhat desultory—until someone mentioned the budgeting process. Then the room exploded with the excitement normally experienced when the home team hits a grand slam in the bottom of the ninth.

This enthusiasm reflected management's frustration with the bureaucracy and resources involved in budgeting and planning, enabling processes that in effect determined who got the money and who didn't. This was known as control budgeting, with the accent on control.

The workings of the old control budgeting process began in February or March and lasted through November or December. This nine-month gestation period virtually guaranteed that the results, when finally certified, would be obsolescent or nearly irrelevant. Control budgeting also consumed the equivalent of 750 full-time employees, spread over a much larger number of people who were actually involved part-time. But no numbers can capture the contempt in which the process was held at Amoco. It had been designed in a bygone era, when all wisdom was presumed to reside at the top of the organization. Operating managers found themselves devoting inordinate amounts of time and energy to preparing budget numbers, only to see them rejected. The antiquated process condemned droves of workers to endless varieties of essentially vacuous work.

The budgeting process began at the operating unit level: an oil field in Egypt or a refinery in Texas, for example. Each unit prepared and submitted a budget for the coming year to a regional headquarters, where the proposed numbers were massaged to fit into the region's budget. Another massage was administered at the national level, to which the regional headquarters sent their budgets. The reworked national numbers were then sent up to the sector, whose management often said, "We don't have that much money. Redo your budget." This dictate would leach down the hierarchy to the hapless local unit, and the roll-up cycle would be repeated.

When the cycle was "complete" at the sector level, a similar one ensued involving the sectors and corporate headquarters. These countless iterations explain why the 750 person-years were required and what those poor souls were doing: constantly revising spreadsheets to fit new requirements, ignoring and discarding all previous calculations. The process that started with grass-roots activity—with each local level identifying its precise spending levels, capital needs, and head-count requirements for the coming year—eventually degenerated into a set of seemingly arbitrary top-down decisions.

This endless number crunching was a major priority and preoccupation at Amoco. John Carl, executive vice president and the reengineering project manager, remembers the mindset as one of "great precision beyond accuracy." One wag's description was more vivid: "Our budgeters had more numbers to the right of the decimal point than to the left of it." The budgeting process had become a ritual in which bureaucrats rather than the business units were the winners. At the end of the day, a business unit was held more accountable for hewing to its final numbers than for its profit or growth figures. "What's the worst thing you can do at Amoco?" went a company quip. Answer: "Overspend your budget." "And what's the second worst thing you can do?" Answer: "Underspend your budget." Hitting your numbers was the definition of success.

Actually, we've heard this jibe at many companies like Amoco (these companies also often have departments named "Profit Planning," a sign of arrogance if ever there was one). Such companies share a notion that performance can be managed by controlling input. Convinced that if x dollars are spent or invested on a business activity, y dollars of output can be expected, they believe that controlling x controls y. This may have worked in a stable business environment; however, today's pace of change has rendered it a dysfunctional and nonsensical ritual.

Much has changed since the completion of Project Spring. Now the equivalent of only 250 full-time employees are involved in budgeting: a two-thirds reduction. The entire budgeting process is completed in a three-month cycle, from September to November, and entails two or three iterations at most. The reams of paper that were submitted under the old system are gone.

The reengineering of control budgeting actually extended beyond the boundaries of that process. Amoco came to realize that many of its problems resulted from budgeting being disconnected from the larger strategic planning process.

Now every Amoco business unit develops a strategic plan describing how it will attain a set of key long-term objectives. These multiyear plans, which provide the context for yearly budgeting, specify required resources and a set of performance measures for tracking progress. Each business unit also develops a one-year tactical performance plan that specifies the near-term results to which it will commit, the steps it will take to achieve them, and the funds required to support each step. The units develop their plans in consultation with senior management, and they are approved by the company's executive committee.

All plans are developed using a set of corporate assumptions—about such things as oil prices and taxation levels—that ensure consistency and relieve each unit of the burden of making and justifying such assumptions. Since the funds requested in the unit's annual budget are related to the achievement of previously agreed-upon strategic objectives, the budgeting process has become relatively deterministic instead of random. Business units can essentially determine for themselves whether the budgets they're about to submit will be approved, since the criteria for the allocation of funds are explicit. The process has lost its mysticism and arbitrariness. Since higher-level management can easily evaluate a budget's validity, there are only two levels of roll-up and almost no iterations. Thanks to this, not only are far fewer people tied up, but better decisions are reached and managers have time to manage instead of functioning as clerks.

This extension to a larger purpose was a critical aspect of Amoco's reengineering effort. The company followed a winding—although not overly long—road to reach its goal. Project Spring began in early 1992, with a charter to concentrate solely on the control budgeting process. A cross-functional project team of twenty people was formed, comprising both line and staff managers with a good geographic distribution. At the outset, nervous team members suspected they were being exiled to corporate Siberia, since two previous attempts to fix the budgeting process had failed ignominiously.

This time, however, they tried a different approach. Rather than first developing a long-term (six-month) project plan, which would have been the usual Amoco method, they decided to collect some data—a remarkable notion!—before taking any other action. Their first step was to conduct a diagnostic of their control-oriented management processes.

The team decided to use focus groups as their main data collection mechanism. Over the next several months, hundreds of employees across the organization participated in facilitated small-group discussions similar to the focus groups consumer product companies use to assess consumer preferences. This was a highly unusual step for Amoco. By listening carefully to employees in the field rather than telling them the answers, the team signaled to all focus group participants that their input was being taken seriously and that Project Spring was committed to real change.

The focus groups enabled the team to generate a multifunctional, multibusiness-unit, multisector, multigeographic database of perspectives on the process. Even more important, it allowed them to develop a constituency of people who, having expressed their points of view, had a stake in the outcome.

After forty workshops in which more than 800 employees in seven countries aired hundreds of complaints about wasted time and bad decisions, the team concluded that control budgeting was broken beyond repair and that it was not an isolated process, but one of several interdependent enabling processes that would become known as the Strategic Management System. Control budgeting could not be reengineered on its own. Strategic planning, performance planning, performance reporting, accountability management, and a number of other processes would have to be addressed in unison and in their entirety.

This meant a change of mission and scope. The team had to invent an entirely new management system that would align all resource expenditures with business strategy, eliminating the costly internal number crunching endemic to the old approach.

Fortunately, Amoco was in the midst of a set of changes that were consistent with the direction in which the team wanted to take the company. CEO Larry Fuller, who was relatively new to his job, was trying to shift the company's culture and systems from a traditional command-and-control orientation toward a more decentralized approach, with dispersed responsibilities and increased decision making at the business unit level. He was looking for ways to turn "empowerment" from a concept into a reality.

But Amoco, steeped in the old culture for decades, had much inertia to overcome. While senior executives proclaimed decentralization and empowerment, the company continued to operate with the old, constraining top-down management systems. Project Spring's sponsors came to view reengineering not only as the solution to the specific problems of budgeting and planning but also as a critical step toward reorienting the company's culture and a concrete demonstration of its commitment to undertake major change.

Strong sponsors are always important for successful reengineering. At Amoco, they were to be found on the Strategic Planning Committee (SPC), the equivalent of the company's executive committee. The SPC supplied whatever Project Spring needed, from more staff for the team to access to senior managers to assistance during implementation. But the contribution of an ad hoc group that became known as "the breakfast club" may have been even more vital to the project's success.

The breakfast club started as an informal advisory group convened by the reengineering team. It grew to include the heads of information systems and human resources, several business group managers, a pair of operating company presidents, and a variety of other line and staff managers. Initially, the club met for an hour over breakfast every other Tuesday to get feedback on the reengineering project. However, it soon evolved from a passive group into an active nucleus of influential reengineering proponents.

The club was in effect an unofficial leadership group, working without an explicit charter but united in its support of change. Over time, it played a variety of roles, especially acting as a sounding board for the Project Spring team's ideas, challenging their depth and real-world application. Club members served as informed listeners at "dress rehearsals" before the quarterly SPC meetings. Holes in the team's logic could be mended and their presentations refined before a friendly audience.

One instance of the breakfast club's valuable support occurred early in the project, when the team was preparing to recommend that the company's entire management system be redesigned. After reviewing the proposal, breakfast club members volunteered to lobby the SPC for approval. Between the review and the subsequent SPC meeting, many breakfast club members met with, called, and wrote to the SPC, reinforcing the team's findings, signaling their personal support, and urging approval of Project Spring's scope expansion. Without this aggressive promotion, the SPC might have balked at this controversial proposal that was so different from what they had been expecting.

Shortly thereafter, the team recommended nine quick hits that would, they promised, dramatically reshape and redefine that year's budgeting. Many were surprised when the SPC approved all nine, saying it wanted to allow real-life testing of the design. The focus groups had made a clear case for change, and Project Spring had provided Fuller and the executive committee with an opportunity to demonstrate their commitment to making it happen.

The Project Spring team then split into two groups. A quick-hit team was charged with implementing the nine projects. The other team would work on implementing the complete design for the following year.

Meanwhile, a variety of communications about the new processes flowed throughout the organization. Workshops were held in every business unit to train people in the new approach to strategic planning and budgeting. For six months, every major company meeting on any topic was attended by someone from the Project Spring team, the breakfast club, or the executive committee, to explain the new system and its rationale. They also leveraged their internal training programs. Each year, 3,500 managers attend Amoco's Management Learning Center. Both implementation teams conducted workshops there, informing the attendees about the reengineering effort and training them in the new processes.

The new enabling processes are now in place, under the banner of the Amoco Strategic Management System. Project Spring's results have been striking. The cost and complexity of the company's enabling processes have been slashed, while their effectiveness has soared. Instead of spending money counting and recounting money, Amoco spends it where it counts. Project Spring has also been a catalyst for more extensive reengineering of Amoco's value-adding processes: Buoyed by its success, budding reengineers are transforming many of the company's business units. In short, the energy freed from make-work budgeting has been channeled into reengineering and the creation of productive processes that harness energy rather than waste it.

What Amoco Did Right

Found and addressed organization's hot button
Extended scope to address the real issues
Reconfigured project to support expanded mission and
    scope
Developed an effective advocacy group

Three companies, three different roads. The bottom line is that reengineering is always uncharted territory and every company must map its own route to the promised land.

CHAPTER 14

The Realities of Reengineering II: Three Who Failed

While reengineering successes are celebrated and legion, there have been many failures as well. As we've suggested, this should come as no surprise, since reengineering is among the most difficult and complex endeavors an organization can undertake. Few firms are eager to publicize the details of their mishaps. This is understandable but it is also unfortunate, because failure probably teaches more lessons than success. Success stories may illuminate the road but rarely show where—or, more important, how and why—some "vehicles" broke through the guardrail and plunged over the cliff. For that, we must examine the accident sites, hoping that knowledge about others' wrong turns will help us avoid similar fates.

This chapter traces the recent history of three companies that began with high hopes and admirable determination but failed nonetheless. Just as there is no single formula for winning at reengineering, there's no one way to lose. Each of these companies fashioned its own style of failure—but the common denominator was that each style reflected the company's corporate identity. Their reengineering difficulties, real enough in themselves, were also symptoms of deeper problems, chiefly a dysfunctional culture, weak leadership, and a surplus of arrogance.

George Bernard Shaw's dictum, "The road to hell is paved with good intentions," was never more true than when applied to reengineering. No one *wants* to fail; no one starts a day by deciding to make stupid choices. In fact, failed reengineering efforts are full of reasonable decisions at every juncture—but reasonable only in a traditional context. These decisions are, however, fatally inappropriate for reengineering, whose core and mission is the transformation of precisely such contexts.

Woody Allen once said that 90 percent of success is just showing up. We might say that 90 percent of reengineering failure is showing up, but with the wrong attitudes, leadership, and approach. That makes reengineering failure more a matter of error than of accident, as our three cautionary tales illustrate. We hope they help you discover your own potential for failure and learn how to prevent actualizing it.

THE RELUCTANT UTILITY

Utilities have long been considered the American economy's most stable—some would say most boring—industry. No longer. The electric power industry is in the throes of enormous, unsettling changes, caused largely by deregulation. Many of these changes have come with the birth of "wheeling," a practice that puts an end to the monopolistic sale of commercial power. No longer must a business in Chicago, for example, receive all its kilowatts from local Commonwealth Edison. If the price is right, it may decide to buy some or all from, say, Pacific Gas & Electric, and rent transmission lines to bring them from California to Illinois.

This is the context in which a midsized, middle-of-the-road Midwestern electric power utility decided to reengineer, chiefly because the population base in its service territory was declining. Traditionally, utilities have relied on population growth as a major source of revenue growth. That was until deregulation derailed all the old assumptions about where growth could come from.

The company knew that it had always been difficult to get the state's Public Utility Commission to approve rate increases. And even if approval could be won now, higher rates would make them more vulnerable to competitors with lower costs. Consequently, new sources of revenue had to be found in order to increase profits. Having heard about reengineering at a consultant's seminar, the chairman decided that this was the way to turbocharge the company's lackluster product development effort. The chairman and his executive team had watched competitors develop innovative products, such as off-peak commercial-pricing schemes, and new services, such as consumer consulting on energy conservation. Although this bureaucratic, monopolistic utility was unaccustomed to the marketplace, its leadership had now concluded they must take the competitive path.

The recently hired senior vice president (SVP) of marketing was appointed sponsor for the reengineering project. He quickly assembled a study team, composed of representatives from corporate staff functions such as finance, R&D, and continuous improvement (its name for the quality group) to consider various reengineering approaches. Unfortunately, the group suffered from an excess of self-direction due to insufficient precision in their mandate. For instance, several of their meetings were spent debating whether the company was contemplating actual reengineering or just another form of total quality management. The disputes had a theological intensity, with the proponents of radical and incremental change trading management biases and corporate body blows. The study team did everything but debate whether to spell reengineering with or without a hyphen. A full six months passed before the group concluded that the company should truly reengineer. However, they avoided setting specific revenue improvement targets, perhaps out of fear of being held personally responsible for achieving them.

After these six months had passed, an impatient marketing SVP interceded. He formed a new team whose mission was to implement a new product-development process as quickly as possible and to begin stocking it with new-product ideas. However, many operating managers were unwilling to release their high performers from their daily jobs to join this NPD (New Product Development) team. Needing high-quality people for the team but unable to get them without the compelling business case that the team itself would create, the SVP was caught in a Catch-22. He had to settle for part-time commitment of a number of middle managers.

Over the course of a year, the NPD team developed a detailed process design and identified several potential new products and services to apply it to. The old product-development process had essentially been a marketing activity, which tried to sell existing services under new names. The new process centered on cross-functional teams developing entirely new products and services, which were seen as flowing through a pipeline, with rigorous evaluations and investment decisions being made at key junctures. The NPD team developed a substantial amount of design detail for this new process and walked through its every conceivable implication. Working in splendid isolation, freed from distraction, the team was confident that they had solved the problem.

However, the sponsor was not sanguine about reengineering's prospects. Since joining the company, he had not been very successful at finding kindred souls for his market-oriented views. He did have the chairman's blessing for reengineering, but the chairman, who was scheduled to retire soon, was somewhat removed from the business—and most of the other executives viewed the sponsor as the proverbial bull in a china shop. They spent much of their time jockeying for position in the coming succession, maneuvering for power and promotion, and considered reengineering a sideshow at best. Nor did the senior management team agree about the organization's long-term business strategy. Many of the younger executives advocated growth and supported both reengineering and a campaign to acquire other utilities. They saw deregulation as a blessing that would liberate the utility from the stifling attitudes and habits of a monopoly. But the majority of the executives, especially those with many years of service, were far more conservative in their vision. Convinced that the industry would evolve much more slowly than the "young Turks" predicted, they argued for a slow and cautious approach to change. Why change things that had worked well? Why shake up a company with a history of success? The sponsor's concerns about senior management were justified.

The NPD team was also seriously distracted by an ongoing war with the CI function. The utility's quality function, which had been in place for five years, had achieved commendable results in eliminating waste and had won the support of most senior executives. But the experience of both the first study team and the NPD team made it clear that the CI facilitators, as they were called, resented the reengineering activity. They had paid their dues, having overcome significant resistance in the early days of their own effort. But now accustomed to being the utility's only change-oriented group, they felt that process-oriented change was their exclusive province. They also resented the fact that no one from CI had been invited to participate in reengineering. CI facilitators muttered that the marketing SVP and his upstart band of reengineers were poaching on their territory. They waged passive-aggressive warfare, professing support while undermining the NPD team's efforts. Privately, they maligned the team's work, suggesting that the whole effort was nothing but a passing fad. To friends in the field, they suggested avoiding participation in order to escape guilt by association. And they challenged all requests for resources or management time as distractions from CI, the company's number one priority. The attacks could not be met head-on, since it was "politically incorrect" to criticize CI. The sponsor found himself constantly fighting brush fires, politely and sometimes less politely untangling issues and resolving disputes.

Another source of friction was the tepid attitude toward the marketing SVP on the part of the three senior executives who formed the project's steering committee. The three had been selected on the basis of their pledged support for change, but then the personal chemistry turned sour. To put it plainly, they didn't like the SVP because he wasn't like them. Brash and confident, he was seen as an outsider who hadn't earned his stripes at this utility. When the project began to flounder, they didn't throw him a life jacket, preferring to see him go under.

One year into the reengineering program, the team, the sponsor, and the steering committee held a watershed meeting. Everyone listened quietly while the NPD team presented their vision of the new process. For many of the attendees, this was their first exposure to the group's work—and although it impressed them, everyone wanted to see which way the wind would blow around the team's controversial recommendations. Specifically, they waited for the chairman's reaction, and since he remained silent, they did too.

The room grew increasingly quiet as the presentation continued: page after page detailing the redesign, without comment or feedback. The lack of reaction made the SVP increasingly angry. Finally, after the redesign concept had been presented in full, he asked for questions. Everyone looked at the chairman. The chairman looked at his lap.

There were no questions. The SVP saw a full year of work—along with his future—begin to unravel. Something in him snapped. He launched into an angry, impassioned defense of the reengineering effort. He castigated the steering committee for their failure to support him. He upbraided the senior executives for not recognizing that the new product-development process was vital to the corporation's future. He called them cowards.

When his tirade subsided, the chairman spoke up. "Thank you very much for your opinion," he said. "We all agree that reengineering is important, one of the most important things we're doing. But as I'm sure you've noted, we have many other important activities as well. I'm sure you can appreciate that this company has many places where we can invest our capital and only a finite pool of investment funds. Before we can move ahead in considering this new process, we must follow our formal procedure for capital allocation. While your redesign is interesting, we must insist—*I* insist—that you provide us with a well-documented business case that supports your recommendations. We must understand the economic implications of reengineering, both the costs of implementation and the expected benefits. Do you have this information?"

The SVP looked at the team. The team looked at the SVP. All shook their heads. Pressed for time and working intensively, the team had decided to create fewer but better deliverables, specifically the redesign and the implementation plan. The business case had been put aside. All they had to show for it was a one-page high-level pro forma of expected revenues from new products. They hadn't quantified the costs of implementation.

"Without this documentation," the chairman continued, "we cannot and will not proceed. When can you get it to us?" Sensing the approach of a humiliating failure, the SVP swiftly promised a two-week turnaround on the business case.

The team spent two arduous weeks struggling to assemble the business case. With little baseline data and few benchmarks from other utilities to guide them, they had to rely on unverifiable estimates. They had experience in assessing cost reduction, which was much more concrete—and much simpler—than what faced them now. Projecting new revenues is notoriously difficult. The CEO had asked for the virtually impossible (which may have been his intention).

The sponsor tried to finesse failure by proposing a different approach to implementation. The team, he explained to the steering committee, wasn't ready to quantify the benefits. In order to develop the data needed to justify full implementation, they first needed to pilot a few new products in a test market. The SVP proposed taking money from his own budget to fund a new group for testing some of the team's ideas. Accepting this recommendation, the steering committee bought time for its own temporizing while giving the SVP enough rope to hang himself.

The story's unhappy ending is hardly surprising. Having spent all his financial and political capital, the sponsor grew bored managing the introduction of some product pilots in a remote district of the utility's service territory—and suddenly took a new job. He left believing he had tried hard for over a year to move the company into the twenty-first century, while the company itself seemed content to stay in the nineteenth. After his departure, no one wanted to assume leadership of the reengineering program.

For several months, the new product pilot project was leaderless. Finally, a midlevel manager—from CI, of all places—was assigned to the job. His first act was to dismantle the remnant of the NPD team and integrate their work into his organization. The new product pilots were soon forgotten. Reengineering had died.

This failure was inevitable. In a company more comfortable looking backward than forward, the reengineering team never had a chance; the project was doomed from the start. The team lacked allies. Its sponsor was temperamentally unsuited to building a coalition of advocates and supporters. Nominally supported by a distant, lame-duck chairman, it was essentially opposed by a group of managers preoccupied with power politics.

Moreover, the majority of executives were uneasy with the action-oriented, risk-tolerant style demanded by reengineering. "When EDS saw a snake, we'd kill the snake," Ross Perot once said. "When General Motors saw a snake, they'd form a task force." This utility went GM one better by forming a study group to determine whether it needed the task force. Its hesitation in getting started was an omen that should not have been ignored. But ignore it is precisely what the sponsor did when he filled his first team with staff people who preferred theorizing to moving quickly.

The NPD was also burdened with fatal problems from its inception. Its charter was both unclear and unreasonable. The dual mission of designing a new process and populating it with new products and services was overwhelming. Either mission alone would have been difficult; together they were impossible, since each required different people with different skills.

Settling for less than the best and the brightest in staffing the team was also a fatal error. In an undertaking as critical as reengineering, talent counts even more than it does ordinarily. Strong leadership—the chairman mandating that first-rate people be made available, for example—could have won the day. Seeing no such leadership, the sponsor should have folded his cards immediately. "If the rules say you can't win, don't play," goes one of our mottoes.

Mediocre people usually do mediocre work. A better NPD team would have done a better job. Instead of staying isolated and aloof for months, they would have conducted an effective outreach campaign. Traveling across the organization to solicit ideas, share their designs, validate their results, and preview their recommendations, they would have recruited many more allies and supporters. The fateful review meeting would have been a rubber-stamp approval, a foregone conclusion, since its participants would have already bought into the design. Instead, the team found themselves facing skeptics rather than friends.

Clearly, the sponsor's outburst did not help. Rather than rail at his colleagues, he should have educated them. He should have taken them to other utilities that had successfully reengineered so they could see for themselves what could be achieved.

Conflict between the reengineers and the "quality police" was probably inevitable—but no one anticipated it or tried to mitigate its consequences. No attempt was made to put the two activities in a coherent framework, no effort was spent helping the two groups understand their different but complementary missions. So they fought, consuming rather than generating energy.

One of the underlying causes of the fiasco was the utility's failure to make a genuine transition from a monopoly mindset to a customer focus. Utilities have traditionally been internally focused, concerned with generating and transmitting power; demand had always been a given. Although the company realized in principle that its dwindling consumer base required it to find new sources of revenue, it hadn't truly embraced the need to rethink attitudes and redesign processes for the customer's benefit. Reengineering was seen as just another project rather than a strategic imperative, and the delay in quantifying benefits tended to reinforce suspicion of it.

Consolidation is about to transform the entire industry. The CEO of one major electric power company has told us he believes that within a decade only ten utility companies will be operating in the United States. All will need bold leadership and a compelling vision of their future in order to survive. If the industry does consolidate into ten—or even twenty or thirty—the company in this story is not likely to be among them.

What the Utility Did Wrong

Failed to secure strong and committed leadership and the consensus of the executive team

Fashioned a complex and unrealistic charter

Accepted second-best people for the effort

Did not develop an intensity for results and fast action

Paid insufficient attention to political agendas and conflicts

---

THE ARROGANT ELECTRONICS COMPANY

Our second tale of failed reengineering takes place at a global electronics company we'll call ABC. ABC sells high-technology hardware and services in an intensely competitive industry where success requires a steady stream of new products. ABC had excelled at this, producing winner after winner—and lacing the company with a belief in its own invincibility.

ABC's many successful years had also masked several serious and worsening problems. While profits were high, the mushrooming size and cost of corporate staff groups caused little concern. Few objected that new R&D investments were increasingly focused on product extensions rather than breakthrough products or technologies. And there was scant worry about low customer service ratings. After all, the products were selling extremely well.

One of those products, a major new device for the communications industry, had been a huge winner: the dominant source of the company's revenue and profit. It was so unique that ABC enjoyed a virtual monopoly for many years. But it had been launched over a decade earlier, and like everything else, was beginning to show its age. Although sales were still increasing in new and emerging markets, growth had stalled in the United States and Europe.

Although ABC continued to be profitable, its product leadership position, the source of its pride and identity, was rapidly fading. Competitors were introducing a new generation of products, and ABC found itself unable to respond; its development process was lagging years behind.

To catch up, the company had to cut costs rapidly in order to free funds to invest in new technology. At the same time, many of ABC's not-very-happy customers—customer service had never been a strong suit—were eager to move to a more "user-friendly" vendor. Having been left behind in the frantic rush of mergers, acquisitions, and strategic alliances during the information highway's early days, ABC was also starting to feel unpleasantly irrelevant.

Over the years, a succession of executives had undertaken a variety of fashionable initiatives to revitalize the company. Restructurings, early retirement options, and moral exhortation had been tried, but with little effect. The grandest scheme, a program called VisionQuest 2000, was intended as a major effort to achieve empowerment and excellence. Many speeches were given, the annual report lavishly praised the program, and heroes were celebrated—but little changed in substance: Management still focused on products and prices, not on people. Most employees considered "empowerment" an empty slogan and "excellence" a joke. They were aware of their competitors' superior products, had listened to customer complaints about product quality and service, and witnessed old-style managers killing innovative ideas. They saw arrogance, not excellence. In the end, VisionQuest 2000's slogans and speeches left them even more cynical and disillusioned.

The CEO heard about reengineering from peers, consultants, and trade journals—and decided to take the plunge. He began by creating a reengineering task force. Thirty midlevel managers from across the company were assigned, part-time, to develop a reengineering strategy and to recommend action. Their own first action was to develop a company process model. Over the next two months, the team identified 25 primary and 150 secondary processes, most of which were given names very similar to those of existing functions and departments. (No doubt this was done to minimize potential confusion.)

The task force presented the processes and subprocesses, displayed on an attractive set of four-color charts, to several management groups. Its second and final activity was to commission twenty-five process teams to identify reengineering opportunities. Since each team was staffed by people from the affected organizations, the reengineering effort would thus be owned by the business units and the line. Each process team formed its own steering committee and began to analyze the current process. In fact, many assumed that the real purpose of their work was to produce an exhaustive assessment of the current process. The teams believed that if they immersed themselves in the details, they'd be able to identify and resolve any problems. A sense of action and progress was enhanced by publication of a glossy reengineering brochure that announced the program's launch and displayed the process map in full color.

A year later the process teams were still analyzing and identifying opportunities for improvement. Meanwhile, ABC's condition had worsened considerably. Competitors were introducing new technologies much more quickly than ABC had anticipated. Industry standards were changing, and the company's customers were getting ever more frustrated and hostile. Large accounts were defecting, key employees were leaving, the board was angry. Recognizing that dramatic action was needed, the executive committee decided to reinvigorate and elevate reengineering.

The vice president of administration was named reengineering czar. He seemed ideal for the job. As the head of corporate services—such as legal, corporate purchasing, and office support—he'd been very effective at cutting costs. And he was the only member of the executive committee, other than the VP of human resources, not preoccupied with finding breakthrough new products. The czar was also bright and well-meaning; but since he lacked reengineering experience, he decided to hire a consultant. Which one to choose? ABC had never used consultants before; they'd never felt they needed them. The czar used an approach that had served him well when selecting office-equipment vendors. He asked eight consultants to spend two weeks with the company and then identify how much money they could save ABC. The firm promising the greatest cost reductions was selected. They were less expensive than the others, though admittedly they hadn't done much reengineering before.

A reengineering design team was named, and the twenty-five process teams were disbanded. The design team sifted through their predecessors' work, focusing on a few major reengineering opportunities. However, company leadership was preoccupied with a swarm of short-term problems, and making time for reengineering was not given high priority. So the CEO delegated responsibility to the czar and began pressing him to deliver payoffs within ever shorter time periods. The czar grew obsessed with developing a business case that would validate his—and the consultants'—pronouncements that reengineering could save the company a lot of money.

ABC's organization structure presented a further complication. The company had five primary business units, defined in terms of products, each with a complete set of support functions. There was very little cross-unit sharing or cooperation. In fact, talk of integrating service, sales, or even purchasing was virtual heresy, since each unit was convinced it was "special." Besides, each unit now had a multitude of projects under way to improve their operations: a total of more than 200 active but uncoordinated improvement programs. ABC suffered from powerful tribal rivalry and from tremendous clutter. "If you reengineer order fulfillment," unit X would say, "don't forget we're different from unit Y. We buy, sell, and service differently." Although the data showed that common processes would result in significant cost reduction and that customers were asking for cross-unit consistency and integration, the czar's team could not convince the units to agree on standardizing processes. This was a perfect case of Pareto suboptimization; no one would sacrifice anything for the common good.

ABC also suffered from an acute case of "structuritis." Reorganization was a regular company ritual. Its motto might have been, "Reorganization's the answer; now what's the question?" Management apparently believed that redrawing the lines and boxes on an organizational chart would somehow transform reality. In fact, reality remained unchanged; despite some reshuffling, the same work was done by the same people, although they reported to new bosses. There had been five reorganizations during the past six years, each costing six months of reduced productivity as employees relocated, budgets were redrawn, and managers were introduced to their new employees.

But superstitions die hard. Now the ritual was to be performed again. Three months after reengineering began, the CEO decided to reorganize, in this case largely to divide financial accountability among a larger number of business groups. For better focus on customers, the company decided to reorganize around customer segments. Twenty-three new business group managers were named, each with full profit and loss responsibility.

That rang the death knell for reengineering. Early rumors about this latest major restructuring diverted everyone's attention—even the reengineering team's—from reengineering. Discussions of process redesign were replaced by whispers about who'd be the new boss, who'd be the winners and losers. Release of the official announcement virtually halted all forward progress for three months as employees tried to determine who was in and who was out and where the power would lie.

The czar was among the reorganization's first victims. His department was dismembered and dispersed among the new business groups; he himself was asked to leave the company. A centralized reengineering approach did not fit with the new structure. Although the reorganization brought ABC closer to the market, it also further reduced the likelihood of cooperation among the business units. Each planned to do things its own way, further weakening the faint movement toward common processes.

Some of the new business groups went so far as to hire their own reengineering consultants. They had come full circle, from twenty-five process teams back to twenty-three business group teams. But this "reengineering" was no more than a label for ad hoc cost reductions. There had been no real reengineering at ABC. Now it seemed there never would be.

ABC used almost every bad reengineering technique in the book, and may have invented a few new ones. It took far too long to diagnose its current processes; it merely renamed its functions as processes; thirty people on a team is twenty-four too many; twenty-five is far too many top-level processes; and on and on. . . .

But it's not certain that even impeccably executed technique would have made a difference. ABC spent more time admiring itself than it did in any real reengineering effort. Like generals who are still fighting the last war in supposed preparation for the next, the senior managers believed that the sources of their past triumphs would sustain them through their current problems. However, success can be a double-edged sword. While winning is gratifying, it can generate complacency and arrogance. "Nothing fails like success" should be emblazoned on the walls of every high-flying company.

ABC was inhospitable ground for the tender seed of reengineering to sprout and bloom. Widespread cynicism and congenital "structuritis" do not encourage people to stick their necks out and try new things. Reengineering requires humility, a deep acceptance of the need for fundamental change. But why change when once you were perfect and you're convinced the same methods will make you perfect again? Far from a program of radical change, ABC's "reengineering" was merely an overlay of a process veneer on a conventional cost reduction exercise.

ABC may not have been an appropriate candidate for reengineering in the first place because it was too close to the edge. Reengineering can do astounding things, but it's not a miracle drug and it doesn't work overnight. ABC's crisis situation—its excessive costs and weak competitive posture—may have necessitated some emergency surgery before beginning reengineering's long-term restoration. A dramatic first step, such as selling off some business units or removing the management team that had gotten the company into the hole, might have been the way to start. When the company did neither, the unrelenting pressure for immediate cost relief colored and distorted everything it did do.

When your house is on fire, it's hard to concentrate on reinforcing the foundation. It's easy to see why ABC never made reengineering its first or even its tenth priority; why it never invested the needed management time; why it didn't use its best talent; or why it never bothered to design a real reengineering campaign.

As the song says, "You've got to know when to hold 'em and know when to fold 'em." ABC should probably have folded its reengineering hand very early on.

What the Electronics Company Did Wrong

Started too late

Spent too much time planning instead of doing

Selected an inadequate czar and an inexperienced consultant

Did not overcome skepticism and cynicism

Allowed organizational structure to get in the way

THE OVERLY AMBITIOUS MANUFACTURER

Even superior companies don't always produce superior reengineering results. This was clearly the case at a major food manufacturer, considered by many to be a paragon of excellence. Over the years, company X had grown mightily through acquisitions, amassing an impressive array of products, brands, and businesses under one umbrella. But like many companies in the consumer products business, this one was forced into reengineering by a dramatic power shift in the industry.

Fifteen years ago, consumer products manufacturers—especially those in the food business—held all the cards and had almost all the power. Their brands were kings, after all.

Ad-prepped consumers entered stores looking for a brand name and went elsewhere if they couldn't find it. Therefore, the manufacturers could tell retailers what to do—which new products to stock, when to order, when to pay—or face being cut off. This would hardly damage the manufacturers, who had thousands of retailer customers. But it could cripple the retailer.

This has all changed dramatically. Now the once lowly grocers call the shots. The rise of generics, private labels, and house brands, together with the consumer shift to "value," has eroded the manufacturers' position. Moreover, consolidation among retailers has created far fewer and far more powerful customers, with greatly increased purchasing leverage. New technologies, especially bar coding and point-of-sale (POS) systems, that give retailers the inside track on consumer buying patterns have played a critical role in this shift.

Retailers have used their newfound information, and the power it confers, to demand major price concessions from their suppliers. As a result, the profit margins of consumer products manufacturers, including X, have steadily declined. This has led to enormous pressure to reduce costs and an explosion of interest in reengineering.

Exploring possible cost reduction opportunities, X's management committee quickly identified logistics as an area of very high potential for reengineering. If the company could integrate the purchasing, manufacturing, and distribution activities spread across its myriad manufacturing sites and warehouses, it would achieve true economies of scale.

This possibility electrified senior management. The scope of the venture fit with their aggressive self-image and their equally aggressive profit plans. A high-level team was named to plan and launch the reengineering program, which was named ISC: Integrated Supply Chain, an industry buzz phrase.

True to their marketing legacy, the ISC steering committee

planned an exciting program launch. Buttons and brochures were designed and manufactured. Detailed project plans, however, were left to an ISC design team to be named later.

The project was kicked off to considerable fanfare and media attention. It made the cover of the company magazine and was trumpeted in the annual report. For many years, senior executives had dreamed of weaving their many units, products, and activities into a seamless entity. Now they believed that reengineering would be the means to achieve that awe-inspiring goal. Senior management promised they would soon have the world's most formidable integrated logistics process.

At the heart of their ambitious plan was a massive new computer system—which, as they envisioned it, would link all existing purchasing, inventory management, manufacturing, forecasting, and order fulfillment processes and systems, providing any data on demand, anytime, anywhere. Beyond realizing enormous economies of scale, it would enable them to manage the business with pinpoint accuracy, assessing the profitability of individual products and customers.

The ISC design team was named at the launch. Most members were information systems personnel. Recognizing the central role of the new computer system, the steering committee believed that I/T professionals should lead the charge. The design team spent several weeks exploring options, then reached their first major decision: They would develop the new logistics information system themselves rather than turn to outside sources. None of the software packages they had assessed contained sufficient functionality to satisfy their requirements. Reluctant to compromise, they resolved to rely on themselves.

Thus began a descent into technology hell. The design team had bitten off far more than anyone could chew. Only a handful of internal MIS organizations—typically in such industries as telecommunications and aerospace—are ever called on to build systems approaching that scale. It required technology sophistication and project management skills that only systems integrators and software vendors find it useful to develop. (This was not a unique situation. Systems to support reengineered processes are typically five times the size and complexity of traditional information systems.) X was in way over its head. Although the signs were not immediately apparent, the effort was destined to fail.

The first year saw a prodigious amount of activity as hundreds of people began working on ISC 2000, as the new computer system became known. New technologies were acquired; vast, all-encompassing databases were designed; much software was written. But when the first release was due to be delivered, it became clear that things were seriously amiss. Many subsystems had been designed and built as components of the grand infrastructure that ISC 2000 would require, but none of them were yet able to actually do anything useful. Moreover, these subsystems did not integrate into a functioning whole, since the groups developing them had been out of touch with each other. As the functionality of ISC 2000 had grown, its complexity had increased exponentially, making the system essentially impossible to consummate. It wasn't even clear anymore precisely what the system as a whole was intended to do. Its specifications had become a moving target, subject to much debate and interpretation.

Many of the new technologies the system required—such as handheld data-entry devices and a new generation of bar-code readers—operated less quickly and reliably than their vendors had promised. X had wandered into the "bleeding edge" of advanced technology, where empty promises—"vaporware"—is an important product category and skepticism and pessimism are essential survival skills. In desperation, more people were assigned to the effort. X had forgotten the old adage that the best way to make a late computer system even later is to put more people on it. At this point, a visitor (actually, it was one of us) suggested that ISC 2000 be renamed ISC 3000, since it just might be completed by then.

How did X's management allow this situation to develop? The short answer is that they were intimidated. As the ISC design team focused on technology, the project came to be seen as an MIS effort. Business managers felt excluded from a program whose lexicon was replete with terms like "client-server architecture" and "object-oriented databases." They were hesitant to intrude on this domain and were beaten back when they tried. Eyes glazed, management decided that technology was best left to the experts. This, too, was another key error; technology is far too important in modern business—especially in reengineering—to be left solely to technologists. The longer answer lies in the long, troubled relationship between MIS and non-MIS people, who represent two different cultures, with different languages and different norms.

Two years after launching their reengineering project, X's senior management realized that they had spent $25 million on ISC 2000, which existed in the company's mythology and jokes but had delivered no concrete results. Management faced a Hobson's choice. Scrap the project? But that would mean writing off the huge investment. Continue on course? But there was no guarantee that it wouldn't end as a $100 million disaster.

The executive committee, who hadn't seen much of the project recently, opted to relaunch it, but with far less fanfare and sizzle. A new and consolidated governance committee was created. The ISC Sponsor Group was comprised of senior functional managers, headed by the senior vice president of logistics. ISC II was born.

A new design group, the Restart Team, was assembled, with high-quality staffing from all key functions. Their charter was to "finish the job," as the CEO bluntly put it. The first team had considered ISC primarily a systems effort. The new team would implement ISC from a business perspective.

Searching hard for redesign ideas, members of the Restart Team conferred with experts inside and outside the company. They researched the industry and studied reports on trends and directions. They talked to every consultant and academic they could find. With such extensive input, it is not surprising that after six months they came up with a long list of ways to reengineer the logistics process for breakthrough performance. The team had hundreds of good ideas, far more than they could handle. While many of the ideas were truly attractive, their cumulative effect was to expand the project's scope farther and farther. Soon virtually every aspect of the company's operations, from production scheduling to labor planning to supplier negotiations, was involved in ISC.

X had escaped from technology hell only to descend into idea hell. Lacking the ability to focus, to pick a few high-payoff ideas from the mass they had gathered, the Restart Team could not concentrate on the practical issues of turning ideas into reality.

The team had accumulated so many ideas partly because they couldn't agree on a prioritization scheme for narrowing them down. This, in turn, was a result of the Restart Team being a team in name only. Actually, they were more like a mob of egos: They had trouble compromising and cooperating; they spent more time bickering than producing. Team members also assumed that it was their responsibility to represent the interests of their home departments. To America's Founding Fathers, suspicious of activist government, representative democracy was an inspired solution. At X, it was a killer because it retarded decision making.

The Restart Team rejected team building. Its members were too intent on reinventing logistics to allow themselves to be sidetracked by touchy-feely stuff. "Real men don't bond" was a popular, if unofficial, saying at X.

Pressed for recommendations, the Restart Team presented no less than six binders crammed with ideas to executive management. The total price tag was in the hundreds of millions. Deciding that discretion was the better part of valor, the corporate management committee effectively removed themselves from the scene by declaring that implementation would be paid for by business unit heads, hitherto essentially uninvolved. The Restart Team sent them their six binders and waited for responses. They're still waiting.

In retrospect, ISC was fated to fail, thanks to the program's grandeur, the enormity of its scope, and the magnitude of change required. Company X would have done much better to focus on a few high-value areas rather than attempting to create an integrated logistics system all at once. A narrower focus would have allowed the reengineering teams to identify more manageable projects. Success in a few starter projects would have generated the goodwill and momentum needed for tackling more ambitious ones.

Company X's approach to technology contributed heavily to the failure. Its technology decisions—thinking it could build a system of ICS 2000's magnitude in the time frame of reengineering—were an extreme manifestation of hubris, which is what the ancient Greeks called the pride that goes before a fall. It should have sought the outside help that it deemed unnecessary.

What the Food Manufacturer Did Wrong

Began with a grandiose and ill-defined scope
Focused too narrowly on technology
Formulated unrealistic plans
Pursued too many ideas
Did not concentrate on delivering near-term results

DILBERT reprinted by permission of UFS, INC.

Reengineering often ends not with a bang—be it of celebration or catastrophe—but with a whimper, to paraphrase
T. S. Eliot. Some fear that reengineering failure means the
business is destroyed by ineffective new processes that drive
costs up and drive customers away. We have never seen that
happen. In reality, what happens in reengineering failure is—
nothing. The reengineering army that marched to war with
unfurled banners and gleaming swords is not slaughtered by
the enemy. But it often gets lost in the swamp on the way to
the battlefield, never to be heard from again.

CHAPTER 15

Small Companies Can Do It Too

In the early days of reengineering, we, like many others, thought that it was meant exclusively for large organizations. Our assumption was that reengineering solved the problems of bureaucracy and complexity that existed only in companies with more than $100 million in revenues. We were wrong. In fact, a great many small companies have successfully reengineered, all displaying the same verve and creativity as their larger brethren. Small companies reengineer for the same reasons as big ones: to significantly improve the performance of their key processes, and thereby compete more effectively in an ever more difficult world economy.

Having revised our earlier view, we now believe that reengineering is potentially relevant for every organization with more employees than can fit around a kitchen table. Once an organization grows to this size, it begins to encounter fragmented tasks, ballooning overhead, and internally focused activities. All companies, great and small, are candidates for reengineering.

When smaller companies reengineer, they follow the same approach and principles as larger organizations, but with a few interesting twists and variations. And so, without further ado, here are three tales of small companies that succeeded at reengineering.

VORTEX INDUSTRIES

Here's a company that reengineered not once but twice without ever using the term. None of the participants had read the book, but they nonetheless did it *by* the book, happening on the principles themselves. No matter what they called it, the result can only be called success.

Vortex is a small, Southern California–based organization founded in 1937 by the current president's grandfather. Its business is repairing and replacing commercial warehouse doors.

Its first attempt at reengineering began in 1987 when Frank Everett, the company president, sensed something was wrong. His organization was still small but had somehow grown bureaucratic, sleepy, and overstructured. It was going nowhere. In 1984, sales had been $2.5 million; in 1985, they were the same; in 1986, they were up to $3 million; in 1987, $3 million again. As Frank Everett said in 1987, "I asked myself, if I were an employee, would I want to work here? No. If I were a customer, would I want to buy here? No. We were so boring. I knew we had to change."

Vortex's key business process was structured like those at organizations many times its size; it was characterized by handoffs between specialists with very narrowly defined duties. Vortex salespeople spent their time knocking on doors, giving out business cards, and getting to know warehouse managers. The idea was that if someone needed help with a warehouse door, he or she would call Vortex. When that did occur, the customer's call would go to Vortex headquarters, where it would be handled by the receptionist. The receptionist would take the customer's number and try to find an estimator, either at headquarters or on the road, who would visit the customer and assess the situation. The estimator would inspect the door, determine if it needed replacement or repair, estimate the cost and submit a quote to the warehouse manager. If the manager, who might or might not shop for other quotes, decided to use Vortex, he or she would have to call Vortex HQ, talk to the receptionist again, and request the services specified in the estimator's bid. The receptionist would then try to find the dispatcher, who maintained the installers' schedules, and get him to schedule the actual work. After many calls back and forth, the dispatcher and the customer would agree on a time for the work to be done. If a new door was needed, the dispatcher would deal with Vortex's materials manager to acquire the appropriate door and associated hardware. The dispatcher would send an installer (usually from the closer of Vortex's two satellite service locations) to pick up the replacement door and go to the customer's warehouse to perform the work. Finally, the installer would write up a work order, submit it to the A/R clerk for billing, and a bill would be sent. All of this for a small company! A simple piece of work in a small, low-tech company could involve as many as five people and a half-dozen handoffs!

Looking at this process, Everett realized that no one was really responsible for putting everything together for the customer; in other words, no one was responsible for customer satisfaction. The company was also overwhelmed with difficulties caused by the many handoffs. Dispatchers would double-schedule the installers. An installer would get to the customer site and discover that he could repair a door for less money than the replacement ordered by the estimator; he would do so, but the bill would still go out with the estimator's initial quote. Although centralized, the operation was virtually out of control.

To break this impasse, Everett decided to try an experiment at the company's Orange County satellite office. He selected one of his better salesmen and told him, "From now on, you are a branch manager and this location is your branch. You're not a salesman anymore. Your job is to do everything needed for the customers served by the Orange County branch. You are going to quote a price, get the materials, get the trucks to the site, and manage the people who repair the warehouse door." And to a woman who worked in the same office, he said: "You are not going to be a secretary anymore; you are now an office manager. You are going to answer the phones, take care of paperwork, do the billing, talk to the customers, be our receptionist, provide clerical support, manage accounts receivable, and act as a customer service representative. You are going to manage the resources in the Orange County branch to ensure that we make our customers happy."

The new, experimental process was far more integrated than the previous way of doing business. Now, the branch manager, not HQ, sold the job, ordered the materials, and dispatched the installers. Results were immediate. The company actually started keeping its promises to customers. When the company said something would happen, it happened. The reason was that one person was now doing and coordinating the work. Customers were thrilled. Everett extended the experiment, turning more and more people from narrowly focused specialists to customer-focused generalists.

To support this initiative, Everett created a profit-sharing plan in which each branch kept 25 percent of its monthly profits. When a branch made money, the people who worked there made money. Business volume increased, and Vortex became a better place to work. The secretary whose functions and responsibilities had been greatly increased said, "This is much more fun than just typing." Everett soon rolled out the new process to the entire company.

These process changes allowed Vortex to evolve from a highly centralized company into one with four semi-autonomous branches. In the transition, however, it had to overcome some serious problems. One unexpected issue was turnover. "I thought people would want expanded responsibilities, but as it turned out, not everybody did," says Everett. "That was especially true in the sales department. They just wanted to sell." In fact, he experienced a 75 percent turnover in the sales department in the first year of the new design.

Everett was forced to fire a number of people, primarily specialists who did not wish to be cross-trained. In hiring new people who would fit the new process design, Everett changed his hiring criteria. "I used to hire people based on their specific skills. Now, I hire based on attitude, aptitude, and experience, in that order. In terms of attitude, I want happy, enthusiastic, and honest people. In terms of aptitude, I am looking for particular abilities, whether they are mechanical, sales, or detail—whatever is appropriate for the job. In terms of experience, we can do the training. We have done much better with green people with the right attitude than experienced people with rotten attitudes."

Vortex undertook unprecedented levels of training, both for new hires and for veterans who had to be cross-trained; creating generalists out of specialists is no easy task. For two years, there were weekly training sessions at each of the company's locations, for each employee.

However, Everett did not own the company by himself. He had a partner who did not support the trend toward integration and decentralization, who didn't want to see his employees empowered. Eventually, in late 1988, Everett bought him out. The former partner immediately started a competing firm and tried to attract salespeople, customers, and suppliers away from Vortex.

Nonetheless, increased sales indicated that the company was on the right track. In 1988, revenues were $3.5 million, and by 1990, they had jumped 33 percent to $5 million.

However, in 1990 the business environment suddenly

changed. California was hit hard by recession—especially the defense industry, a major Vortex customer. To make up for declining demand, warehouse door manufacturers themselves began entering the repair and replacement business. Everett realized that it was going to be impossible for Vortex to compete on price with large manufacturers. His only option was to become the company the customer liked the best—this became his goal. "We switched our focus from doors to customers," he said.

As Everett moved to an emphasis on quality and customer service, he began Vortex's second wave of reengineering. He held meetings with the branch managers to explain what they needed to do in order to survive. In April 1990, he articulated a formal Vortex Vision, which communicated the urgent need for change. In the vision, he told his people that they couldn't simply invent a new door. (In fact, through all of history, there have been only five innovations in doors: the rock rolled in front of the cave, circa one million years B.C.; the swing door, invented by the Romans in about 100 B.C.; the sliding barn door, invented in the American West in 1860; the sectional overhead door, invented in 1913; and the roll-up door, invented in the 1930s.) "Since we can't invent a new door," he said, "we have to innovate in customer service, our sales approach, and all of our business practices."

Fast response became a priority. The response time for door repair or replacement was twenty-four to forty-eight hours at best. The new goal was completion the same day as the call—Vortex was to be the fastest in the industry. Customers judged Vortex quality as good; now the company sought perfect quality ratings. Another key goal was "no second visits"—get everything right the first time.

While the first reengineering effort had integrated the process, the second wave was focused on changing attitudes and behaviors. "We had to change from making the door happy to making the customer happy," Everett explained.

Making the *door* happy meant taking a technical point of view: Did the door fit properly? Did it work as needed? Did it lock? Making the *customer* happy meant having the product arriving on time, with a clean truck and a smile, and submitting accurate bills.

To achieve "instantaneous response" Vortex added more people. It opened earlier and closed later. The branches became customer service centers. "Our terminology was wrong. Headquarters sounded like the trunk, and branches felt like the leaves, distant and unimportant," noted Everett. "We changed the name to service centers because what they do is the most important part of our business. 'Branches' was actually an inside word, it focused on our internal relationships; customer service is outward focused. That is where we wanted our employees' attention." At the same time, branch managers became known as team leaders. With growth, the branch manager's job had evolved from performing the process themselves to supporting others as they performed it. Everett went on: "We, those few of us who remained at headquarters, became coaches, showing people how to do things like repairing unusual doors, and providing training and expertise. One important new role we played was capturing good ideas from one customer service center and spreading them to others. As branch managers became team leaders, our installers became customer service reps rather than foremen and helpers. We wanted the guys in the field with tools in their hands to become service oriented. They did. It worked."

The company became very innovative in its compensation policies, making use of bonuses and incentives to solve specific problems—like that of uneconomical travel time. Typical arrival time at the customer site was between 8:45 and 9:00 A.M. Investigation revealed that this was because the customer service reps had to stop at Vortex first to pick up their work orders, materials, and tools. But, since they were being paid to start at 8:00, the company was losing money. Vortex started offering performance bonuses to those who got to their first jobs by 8:30. Soon, employees were arriving early, loading their trucks, and making it to the job site with time to spare.

The results have been impressive. Today, Vortex is a $12 million company with 190 employees. Strikingly, much of its growth occurred during the recession, at a time when many of its competitors were going out of business. "We are opening in Las Vegas and in Denver," Everett says proudly. "Nine out of ten of our service center team leaders have been promoted from inside. We are continually reinventing what we do."

In mid-1994, Vortex was fielding sixty-five trucks across its many service centers. And Frank Everett's former partner, the enemy of reengineering who left to start his own company, had a grand total of three.

Vortex didn't use the word "reengineering," but that's what it did and did right. It focused on its basic process and compressed a complex assembly line of tasks into a single job, employing the caseworker concept we have seen in many other organizations. It used a process-oriented organizational form at the service centers and turned its headquarters into a resource center, where skills are honed and best practices are shared.

In the true reengineering spirit, Vortex focused all its work around the customer. It had an ambitious vision of success and supported that vision with training and incentives. And everything that it did was driven from the top of the organization. Without Frank Everett's relentless leadership, no change would have occurred.

However, there are also some unusual aspects to this story, facets atypical of larger firms. For example, Frank Everett single-handedly led and executed this revolution. He had no management committee, no cadre of designers, no reengineering czar to support or hinder him. Vortex's small scale allowed him to know everyone personally, to hold all the power, and to do what he thought was right. He could literally reach out and touch every member of the staff and discuss with them the company's direction. Selling reengineering is easy with that kind of personal touch.

Finally, small scale meant speed. The time between decision and rollout was close to the "instantaneous response" Vortex was seeking in the market. Executives at large companies may well envy this ability to execute so swiftly.

IVI PUBLISHING, INC.

IVI, a small Minneapolis-based start-up firm, is an electronic publisher of medical and health information in interactive and multimedia formats. Its initial product, *The Mayo Clinic Family Health Book* on CD-ROM, was released in December 1992 and has sold three-quarters of a million copies. In 1993 the company released a second product, and by mid-1994 it had produced eight more titles. These products have been very successful, and IVI has developed extensive marketing and distribution arrangements with companies such as Time-Life, McGraw-Hill, and The Mayo Clinic.

This enthusiastic market acceptance, however, led IVI to recognize a problem: the length of its product development cycle. *The Mayo Clinic Family Health Book* took twelve months to produce, and its second title took nine months. Given its strategic objective of producing forty to fifty new titles a year by 1995, it was clear that a new approach was needed. The old approach was slow, cumbersome, resource-intensive, and complex. There also was strong staff pressure to change. As one manager noted, "We did the first product with guts and long hours, and no one wanted to do it that way again." The long development cycle was also noted by

IVI's investors, who began putting pressure on management to shorten it.

The old process was like a job shop; that is, each title was produced differently from the one before. There were no economies of scale or experience. The title creators operated like artists, molding a series of unique products. The early titles were produced by hordes of specialists operating in a disorganized crazy-quilt version of an assembly line. This process was never really documented, but on the whole, it operated in the following manner.

First, the marketing department determined the need for the title. Then the title design organization, a group of marketers and technicians, determined the basic flow and format, and an outline of the contents. They then produced an extended storyboard, which served as a concept demo for internal review, after which a detailed design was created. The next major phase was title production and assembly, where most of the work occurred and most of the time was consumed. Here, packaging was designed and developed, photos and text were created, and software was written to guide the viewer through the contents; testing and debugging concluded this phase. The final phase of the process was the creation of what IVI called the "golden master," the master copy of the title from which all other copies would be made.

Everyone agreed that this long, sequential, and time-consuming process needed to be reengineered. Unlike Vortex, IVI was very conscious of reengineering: Management read the book, talked to other companies that had reengineered, and actively sought reengineering assistance. As they began, they had two explicit objectives: to halve the time it took to produce a title, down to four months or less; and to improve the replicability of the process so that each title's producers could learn from others' experiences. However, this latter goal produced a certain tension. For the most part, IVI's employees were refugees from large bureaucratic organizations. They didn't want the new process to turn out to be another boring, mindless, assembly-line activity. On the other hand, management wanted to add enough structure so that the process was orderly and duplicable. This tension had to be managed through the reengineering program.

The company put together three teams of six to ten part-time people each, with every team member expected to spend 10 to 20 percent of his or her time on the reengineering effort. The first team documented the old process. The second, appropriately called the Clean Plate Team (CPT), designed the new title-development process. The third focused on education—keeping all employees current on the progress of the effort.

The CPT patterned their redesign on a popular reengineering "move"—the integrated team. They compressed their lengthy and convoluted process into a set of parallel and linked activities conducted by a single cross-functional team. After this concept was approved by management, the CPT split into several subteams, each focused on a different aspect of the business system. They met every two weeks as a complete team to ensure that their pieces would fit together.

As they moved into detailed redesign, the process subteam identified three primary subprocesses: develop the business plan; design the title; produce the title. In the past, all three had been performed by separate groups, with little communication between them. This resulted in fragmented accountability and a diminished sense of ownership. With reengineering, all three subprocesses were to be overlapping, interdependent, and conducted by a single title team.

The first subprocess, business plan development, was designed to take only three weeks. This pace was enabled by a newly standardized template for a title business plan, to make it easier to organize the information needed for an early go/no-go decision. Assuming that the title got a green light, it moved on to title design, which was to take four weeks. Title design now had two components: concept prototyping and title refinement. Concept prototyping was a new activity, in which the title was "mocked up" so that the business case could be validated before a lot of time and money had been expended, and so that implementation requirements (such as animation) could be identified early. Title refinement is as its name implies, an iterative development of the concept based on implementability. Rather than trying to create a possibly unrealistic implementation plan, this subprocess culminated with a production prototype that provided a strong basis for final title development. The last subprocess, title production, was designed to take only nine weeks; this compression was possible because of the work done earlier in producing the prototype and by the anticipation of long-cycle activities.

The structure, skills, and staff subteam envisioned the title development process being performed by a cross-functional title development team (TDT). Each TDT was to have a certain amount of latitude to adapt this process template to their unique requirements. The constant objective, however, was speed and quality. Each team was composed of three concentric circles. At the center was a core team, six people who would stay with the title from beginning to end. These would include: an executive producer, who would codevelop the budget as well as manage and hire the rest of the team; a producer, who would be responsible for the title's content; an engineer, who would translate the product design into programming and other technical requirements; a designer responsible for the graphics and packaging; a marketing representative, who would manage the launch, packaging, and product promotion, as well as codevelop the budget; and a team administrator who would support the clerical and administrative needs of the team.

The next ring would be composed of a number of special-ists involved with key aspects of development but who would not be with the team throughout its entire life cycle. These would include quality control experts, text prepara-tion staff, various technical virtuosos, and product testers. In the outer ring would be people who supported the team indirectly or for very short periods of time, such as a finan-cial analyst who might help in preparing the financial fore-cast, an HR person brought in for team building, or a salesperson who could speak with the voice of the customer.

Because the title development process is the *only* value-adding process at IVI, the CPT also had to redesign much of the company's basic structure. They declared that people's natural homes would be these title development teams and that when they weren't on a team they would reside in a tal-ent pool, a "home room" focused on skills enhancement in areas such as software development, animation, and market-ing. They envisioned having six to ten such home rooms, where people would return after a three- to four-month team assignment.

The reengineers also identified several technologies, such as groupware and videoconferencing, that would be needed for title development team communications and group sup-port. These were becoming increasingly important because during the reengineering IVI had set up several new offices in other states and had also begun to use more outside subcon-tractors. These technologies would serve as a critical "glue" to link dispersed team members.

Finally, the CPT also devised team-based financial incen-tives. If a team stayed within its budget, there would be a small initial bonus. But the real money came from the royal-ties the teams would earn if they completed development within their time window and succeeded in the marketplace. A successful title would be good both for the company and for the team; their interests were now identical.

The design team completed their process redesign in three months. Given the company's urgent need for a new approach, and the simplicity of the new design, they decided to go immediately to pilot.

The first of the titles developed under the new process was published in January 1995. Even before then, reengineering had left its mark. The number of employees had more than doubled during this time, and, as a result, IVI needed to move in late 1994. The company reflected the new process design in its new office and production facilities. Its new headquarters is predicated on the notion that people work in integrated teams. The facility includes movable cubicles organized around shared space to support employees moving into and out of teams on a frequent basis. Reengineering has reshaped both the title development process and the work environment.

One interesting aspect of this story was the fact that IVI wasn't *re*engineering at all; rather, it was engineering the process from the outset. In a sense the phrase reengineering has always been a misnomer. Most organizations' processes were never engineered in the first place. They had evolved over time, generally without intent or explicit architecture. Because IVI was literally a "green field," it had a real opportunity most reengineers only have in theory: It got to start with the proverbial blank piece of paper.

MATTHEW THORNTON HEALTH CARE

Larger than Vortex or IVI, this New Hampshire health maintenance organization (HMO) has been so successful with reengineering that its work was profiled on CNN. Every high-level process and critical subprocess in the company has been redesigned, and the results in terms of market share have been significant.

Founded in 1971 and named after a New Hampshire signer of the Declaration of Independence, Matthew Thornton Health Care is one of New England's oldest HMOs. For those who slept through the debates on health care, an HMO works as follows: "Members" sign up either on their own or as part of an employer-sponsored group, and, for a fixed fee, the HMO supplies them with all needed medical care. This care is delivered by providers (nurses and physicians) who are either employees of the HMO or are affiliated with it. In the latter case, the HMO strikes a deal with physicians and hospitals (sometimes called its network); in return for providing them with a steady stream of patients, the physicians offer the HMO a discount and agree to follow its approach to medical practice. This "network" strategy is the one followed by Matthew Thornton.

When their reengineering story began in 1990, Matthew Thornton's 150 plus employees were divided into twenty-seven units, each with its own budget. More than forty of these people had managerial titles, ranging from supervisor to president. Throughout the 1980s, as medical organizations were passing rising costs onto the customer, Matthew Thornton did what most companies did: Every time it had a problem, it hired another smart person to solve it. As COO Everett Page put it, "We were a little pond with a lot of whales." Not only that, the firm was stagnating. Matthew Thornton had not introduced a single new product in the twenty years since it was founded. Enormous time was spent on internal issues, such as budget allocations and job titles. Its sole external focus was on its affiliated doctors; very little attention was expended on its participating members. During the mid-1980s, membership had peaked at 80,000; by 1990–91, membership was below 63,000 and the company was losing 300 members a month. Executives knew they would have to sell the company if membership fell to 50,000. Nonetheless, because Matthew Thornton was not yet in a cash crunch, no immediate action was taken.

Starting in 1990, however, the health care market began to change radically. Rising medical costs were causing consumers to demand more alternatives. The latest buzzword was "point-of-service product," which essentially meant allowing customers more choice in how they acquired and paid for health care. One such alternative was the member's ability to purchase medical services outside of an HMO network rather than exclusively from affiliated physicians. (Typically, these new offerings were structured to include a copayment and a deductible.) Matthew Thornton spent a year designing a point-of-service offering, only to see a mere 200 of its 63,000 members sign up for it. According to COO Page, "The new product had been created by the underwriters, actuaries, and operations types. It was designed to be easy to administer and easy to underwrite and to minimize our risks. It was also designed to force the customer back into our HMO network. It presented the illusion of choice without any real options at all. Consumers wanted something innovative and attractive, but Matthew Thornton failed to provide it."

By February 1992, it was clear to everyone that the new product wasn't working. The experience of failure was devastating. Matthew Thornton Health Care's executive team realized that they had to create a new product that actually delivered. The one they finally came up with—offering members the true ability to go outside the network by assuming more personal risk—sold like hotcakes.

This product was created in only six months. Page formed a small, cross-functional "skunk works" team. For six months, they labored outside the HMO's mainstream, protected by Page. Just as the product was taking off in the market, however, problems arose within the company. Many middle managers, whose input hadn't been sought by the skunk works team, decided not to support the product. As one of the managers who was resisting put it, "If they don't want my opinion, okay, fine. I will just sit around and watch it fail."

Given the initial product's failure, the declining membership, and the open resistance to the new product, Page, who had attended one of our reengineering seminars, concluded that major change was a must. He convinced the other executives of their need to reengineer. He stated his goal as "ensuring we are organized around what we are paid to do, rather than around what is easy to administer." At this point, three vice presidents, all opponents of the new product, left the company. The rest of the company's leadership accepted his proposal, realizing that their old ways of medical management were over.

In August 1992 Matthew Thornton started reengineering in earnest. Page formed a small, part-time design team, consisting of a set of managers from across the organization, and brought them to an off-site kickoff meeting. Given his own recent training, he was able to guide the team through the initial steps. Over the course of only a few days, they received background training and began to model the organization's processes. Over the next few weeks, they refined the model, eventually identifying five major processes: service and education; medical care management; developing quality provider networks; claims processing and payment; and customer acquisition. Next, they developed preliminary work plans for attacking each process.

In addressing the "quality provider network" process, the team quickly put together focus groups in which unaffiliated doctors from around the state were asked what they wanted from an HMO. Based on these findings, the team decided to change Thornton's entire relationship with its affiliated physicians. The old relationship was based on capitation, a payment mechanism by which an affiliated doctor is paid a fixed monthly amount per member for all potential medical services, whether those services are used or not. The most common flaw of capitation is undertreatment; doctors have an incentive to provide less care. The focus groups indicated that capitation made them view affiliation with Matthew Thornton as undesirable.

In their first action, the team quickly recommended (and the company swiftly adopted) a new pay scheme that gave doctors what they really wanted: a fixed monthly amount for managing each patient, plus discounted payments for the services they rendered. The amount of payment per patient varied according to the cost and quality of the treatment. But the basic idea was a very old one: Doctors were paid for the services they rendered. The system was conceptually simple, and doctors saw it as fair.

The result was a complete turnabout for Matthew Thornton. Within seven months of adopting the new payment scheme, Matthew Thornton Health Care had overtaken its competitors in number of affiliated physicians.

However, the most breathtaking changes came in the medical care management process. The team managed to unite two seemingly incompatible perspectives: the business and the medical. The HMO overhauled its medical management practices so that doctors and nurses would focus on good medical *outcomes* and not on the patient's *symptoms*. Page put it this way: "We realized that good medicine was good business and that focusing on outcomes, not just symptoms, was the key to success." In Page's view, medicine had something in common with manufacturing. If you buy the cheapest parts, you end up doing a lot of extra work dealing with rejects and returns, which costs you more in the long run. The real objective is the lowest overall cost, not the lowest cost per unit.

He explains this line of reasoning with a real-world example, one that shows how everyone in the reengineered process—the patient, the doctor, and Matthew Thornton Health Care—emerged a winner.

The story goes like this: A mother is brought into the hospital in premature labor. In the past, the mother would have been sent home after her immediate symptoms had subsided. Under the new process, however, the Matthew Thornton team may decide to keep her in the hospital for two more days should they feel that she was at risk for premature delivery. The HMO may also provide child care for the mother's children at home. All of this cost Matthew Thornton Health Care about $5,000. If the purpose of the health plan were merely to minimize its costs, the woman would have been sent home as soon as her symptoms were treated, that is, when her labor had stopped.

But that's not the way Matthew Thornton now sees it. Its new measure is the best medical *outcome,* which would be the delivery of a full-term baby. In the HMO's view, good patient treatment leads to the best outcome, which in the long run leads to lower costs. The average cost of treating a premature baby is $500,000, as opposed to the $5,000 just cited. For every twenty cases of unmanaged premature labor, at least one can be expected to end with premature delivery. In other words, Matthew Thornton is spending $100,000 to avoid spending $500,000, and in the process it gets healthier mothers and babies. Everybody—mother, baby, physician, HMO—is a winner.

Matthew Thornton's affiliated doctors are extremely pleased with this focus on final medical outcomes. In fact, it has become even more of a draw than the payment scheme that attracted many of them in the first place. Members, feeling they are receiving higher quality care, are delighted as well.

Over the next year and a half the company moved from a fragmented, internal focus to a customer-driven process orientation. Page notes the HMO instills a simple and consistent philosophy across all of its processes: to articulate a good medical outcome and work as a team to achieve it. That's all. For instance, the baby-sitting service in the previous story was not part of the coverage specification. Yet, in effect, the new process allowed nurses and physicians to override the specification if they felt it necessary for achieving the best outcome. This has had a powerful effect of liberation and empowerment.

Since its reengineering program began in mid-1991, the HMO's enrollment has increased from 63,000 to 107,000. Staff has grown from 150 to 200, but administrative overhead has been reduced: There are now twelve budgeting entities and twenty-one managers (both reductions of 50 percent). As a result of reengineering, Matthew Thornton has one of the highest profitability and liquidity ratios of all the HMOs in the United States. Perhaps more important, it came in first in a recent nationwide customer satisfaction survey. Reengineering has made this company better, larger, leaner, and more profitable.

As these three cases indicate, reengineering a small company is much the same as reengineering a large one. The ideas and principles are identical and so are the key ingredients for success: obtaining executive commitment; taking a process perspective; focusing on customers and their needs; and starting with a clean sheet of paper. Moreover, techniques for process redesign (like assumption breaking) work just as well for small company processes. However, there are also some real differences between the two environments. On the one hand, reengineering can be accomplished more

DILBERT reprinted by permission of UFS, INC.

quickly and with fewer resources in a small company than in a large one. A smaller organization suffers from less bureaucratic overhead, and its processes lie closer to the surface; therefore, its reengineering teams can be smaller, and they can usually operate more quickly. Moreover, employees of a small business typically have a better appreciation of the overall condition and activities of their company, and so it is usually easier to enroll them in the reengineering effort.

On the other hand, the leader of a small company reengineering effort has an even larger role to play than his or her large company counterpart. In a small company, the reengineering leader will often have to fill the roles of czar, process owner, and team member, and may even bear the brunt of the change management effort. The president of a small company can expect reengineering to take the lion's share of his or her time. However, these differences, while real, are nonetheless minor compared to the similarities.

Large Company vs. Small Company Reengineering

Similarities

Concepts and principles
Focus on processes and customers
Techniques for design and implementation

Differences

Time frames
Resource requirements
Leader's time commitment

Who says reengineering isn't for small businesses?
Not us—at least not anymore!

CHAPTER 16

Beyond the Bottom Line: Reengineering in Mission-Driven Organizations

One of the great misconceptions about reengineering is that it applies only to businesses, and large businesses at that. As we hope you've gathered by now, reengineering is not primarily about profit and loss, the stock price, or any of the other appurtenances of modern capitalism. It is about *work*. Reengineering is concerned with the redesign of work so that it can be performed in a far superior way. Therefore, reengineering is relevant for any organization in which work takes place: large or small, manufacturing or service, profit or nonprofit, private or public sector.

It's true that when corporations reengineer, they do so for financial benefits. They're interested in reengineering for the same reason that Willie Sutton was interested in banks: because that's where the money is. But while Protagoras may have been right in saying that man is the measure of all things, money is *not* the measure of all organizations.

Think of the United States Army, Planned Parenthood, the Metropolitan Museum of Art, the American Civil Liberties Union, the John Birch Society. They certainly need money, often plenty of it, to pay their staffs, buy equipment, cover their rent. But to them, money is a means to a noneconomic end. Their purposes transcend economics. We call these *mission-driven* organizations.

There are tens of thousands of them: government agencies, charities, hospitals, universities, schools, think tanks, benevolent societies, veterans' associations, communities of bird-watchers. While improving their financial situation may be important, what really motivates them is performing their mission more effectively. Such institutions often consider finance a necessary evil, and not to be confused with their fundamental mission, which usually seeks to improve or even transform lives.

Still, reengineering has much to offer these organizations, and some—the United States Army, the Church of Latter-Day Saints, and the Social Security Administration, to name just a few—have embarked on the adventure and are reaping its benefits. Reengineering is not just a capitalist tool. It enables *any* organization—those in the service of ideals as well as of stockholders—to rethink its processes and find breakthrough ways of improving them. And although there are fewer reengineering tales to tell about the mission-driven world, where it has arrived more recently than in the private sector, those tales are still worth examining. They demonstrate many similarities with profit-driven reengineering—and certain meaningful differences.

Perhaps no organization seems more remote from the world of business than the university. Since its inception, the academy has been a retreat from the hurly-burly of commerce, a refuge where scholars and researchers expand the frontiers of knowledge for its own sake and share their wisdom with succeeding generations. Still, reengineering has won admission to the hallowed halls of academe.

American universities are currently facing many of the pressures that have squeezed their business counterparts over the last decade: escalating costs, intense competition for a more sophisticated—and shrinking—pool of customers, a world of constant change. Unable to run deficits forever, universities have concluded that they must do more with less. After trying the usual palliatives, many now believe that reengineering may be their only salvation.

Universities have discovered that under the surface they're often not so very different from the businesses they frequently disdain. A recent Stanford University School of Medicine study concluded that:

> Even though its model is flat and decentralized, we found that the school has the unmistakable feel of the hierarchical setup described by Hammer and others. These hierarchies, the webs of responsibilities and accountabilities, are duplicated in dozens of departments. Each department's organizational chart is a mini-hierarchy, overseen by central hierarchies in a multitude of functional areas: personnel, finance, sponsored projects, and the like. Furthermore, the smaller hierarchies are often mirror-images of the larger ones. The problems arise from the labyrinthine route a project or a piece of paper takes to reach its final destination. Routine items lumber from one approval or review to another, oftentimes doubling back for small clarifications. When an item needing special attention comes across someone's desk, it becomes petrified as it sinks under a morass of piecemeal work.

Sound familiar? To paraphrase Gertrude Stein, an organization is an organization is an organization.

Universities are responding to the challenge in various ways. Many, including MIT, are concentrating on their administrative processes, the so-called business side of educational institutions. The expense budgets of colleges and universities routinely run to the hundreds of millions of dollars. (MIT's is $1.2 billion.) Therefore, it's useful to think of them as medium-size or even large businesses, especially since their operating infrastructures are only indirectly connected to education and research. Their finance organizations, procurement offices, and publications departments are almost identical to those of their private-sector counterparts and can be reengineered in much the same way. Other activities—admissions, student aid, registration, resident housing—may bear special names and seem unique to universities, but they are actually the functional equivalents of business processes. MIT's reengineering effort is focusing on such processes as management reporting and appointments (i.e., hiring). By reengineering such processes, MIT and other schools are cutting administrative costs and freeing faculty from paperwork burdens so they can concentrate on their real work.

De Paul University in Chicago—America's second-largest Catholic university, with more than 16,000 students—is rethinking its administrative processes to focus on its key customer, the student. In the span of his or her lifetime, a college student interacts with many nonacademic departments: admissions, student aid, registration, career placement, alumni relations, development (the academic euphemism for fund-raising), and so on. In most schools, those interactions take place in independent, nonintegrated processes. Lacking the means for maintaining consistent, ongoing relationships, a school rarely develops the kind of rapport with its students/alumni that leads to a lifelong connection and sustained giving. Moreover, fund-raisers are hard-pressed to understand their graduates/prospects when possessing only a narrow view of their histories. But now De Paul is implementing a computerized contact/response system that will provide a longitudinal view of a student's history. The system will support a new integrated set of administrative and fund-raising processes—and will also support the university's mission of lifelong learning, which is particularly important because a majority of De Paul students are older than traditional college age.

De Paul's work illustrates an emerging pattern in both

mission-driven and commercial organizations: namely, to develop a set of customer-focused processes based on an integrated database. The Boston Lyric Opera Company is developing new processes for ticketing, communications, and fund-raising, all centered on an integrated database containing a variety of information about its donors. In health care, this is known as "patient-centered care." Similarly, some corporations, particularly banks, are using integrated customer profiles to support a relationship-based approach to sales and service.

Yet reengineering efforts like MIT's and De Paul's, however worthwhile and successful, do not touch the heart of the university and its mission: teaching and research. That barrier is being breached only in rare places, one of which is Brandeis University. There, in the Boston suburb of Waltham, Professor Marc Brettler has applied reengineering in what would have seemed a most unlikely venue: study of the Bible. Specifically, Professor Brettler has reengineered the instructional process for his graduate course, "The Book of Exodus: A Study in Method."

Brettler was attracted by what he calls the "ongoing spirit of reinvention" in *Reengineering the Corporation*. As an academic, however, he had mixed feelings about what appeared to be a business-oriented process. He writes:

Many if not most academics are deeply suspicious of the business world. There are often legitimate reasons for this suspicion. We have seen our universities run more like businesses with attentiveness to class size, departmental budget, and other issues that affect the financial standing of the university, but that often get in the way of the pursuit of scholarship and the teaching of students. In some universities and colleges, a state of war exists between the administration with its business considerations and the faculty with its academic ones. Being a professor far removed from any administrative role, I am generally wary of importing models from the world of business to the university. Yet in reengineering I found a concept from the business world that could be beneficial to the university. I speak here not to administrators, some of whom have begun to consider the principles of reengineering, but to professors, who can constructively use reengineering in teaching courses.

What's striking about Brettler's appreciation of reengineering is that he actually applied it, paying strict adherence to its principles. First, he was committed to breakthrough improvement. While his course had previously been well received, he did not subscribe to the axiom that "if it ain't broke, don't fix it." He was determined to make his course even better.

Second, Brettler was willing to start with a clean sheet of paper. Rather than incrementally improving the course, he decided to set it aside and start afresh. He began by asking the same fundamental question asked by companies from Procter & Gamble to GTE: What is my true objective and what is my real end product? In doing this, he was applying the reengineering principle of focusing on outcomes rather than tasks. Brettler identified student understanding of the basics of biblical scholarship as his primary goal.

Most importantly, Brettler now conceived of his course as a process rather than as a disconnected set of individual elements like class preparation, class sessions, readings, and writing assignments. Rethinking all those components together, working backwards from his objectives, he decided that the best way for students to learn the nature of biblical commentary at the deepest level was for them to try their hand at writing one. So, he then refashioned three formerly independent writing assignments into modules of a larger paper—the commentary—to be submitted at the end of the semester.

In addition, formal classes were periodically dispensed

with in favor of informal learning sessions, held in the library, where Brettler demonstrated research techniques and tools while giving students the chance to ask for help. (Brettler was partly motivated by a desire to avoid the conflict most students experience when they must both prepare for a class and complete a writing assignment. Why didn't we have such professors in college?) Brettler also made use of roundtable sessions in which students helped each other, and of ongoing feedback reports in which the students evaluated their own progress.

Objective evaluation of the effectiveness of an academic course is notoriously difficult. Still, the signs suggest that Brettler's foray into reengineering was well received. He himself feels that the course was his most successful ever. "The papers were superior to the usual graduate student efforts," he says. "They were more polished and original and much less confused or simply wrong." The students themselves were extremely positive about their experience, in both their formal and informal evaluations. Brettler was given the highest ratings he had ever received.

Despite this happy outcome, Brettler's experience illustrates two dilemmas inherent in virtually every mission-driven reengineering. The first is how to determine success. One of the great virtues of business is its relatively unambiguous way of judging results: the bottom line. Obviously, there are some subtleties even here, most having to do with the right way to express the bottom line—for example, profit, return on equity, economic value added, NPV of future dividends, price/earnings ratio, or any of the multitude of financial measures constantly being cooked up. Still, there *is* a bottom line that provides a clarity and precision that is almost always missing in a mission-driven environment.

How does the Museum of Modern Art or Brandeis University or the Salvation Army or the Baptist Church know if it is doing a *better* job? Volume—more students, museum visits, church attendances, meals served—is one indicator, but an insufficient one. Answering how well an organization is achieving its mission takes one into dimensions of effectiveness and quality, where quantification is very difficult. This complicates any organization's decision to reengineer. While mission-driven organizations' costs are measured in dollars, their benefits are not. What's the *financial* value of a better course on the Bible? How much would it be worth to spend on its reengineering? Who can say for certain?

A second problem facing mission-driven organizations contemplating reengineering involves identifying their customers. Before long, such organizations will almost inevitably find themselves involved in an agonizing debate about who, in fact, their customers are. Once again, most companies find this question relatively easy to answer: Follow the money trail, as they say. But who is Marc Brettler's customer? The student attending the class? The student's parents, who are footing the bill? The employer who will eventually hire the student? The worldwide community of biblical scholars or humankind as a whole? An argument can be made in support of any of these alternatives. This ambiguity exists in virtually all mission-driven environments.

Since reengineering must begin by identifying one's customers, determining their needs, and deciding the best way to satisfy them, this is no (forgive the pun) "academic" question. It must be resolved, and it isn't easy.

Given these considerations, it's not surprising that the first mission-driven organizations to reengineer have been the most "businesslike" in the sense of having well-defined customers and performance measures expressible in financial terms. Across North America, the first governmental agencies to reengineer have mostly been (wouldn't you know it?) the tax collectors, from the Ontario Ministry of Revenue to the IRS. Having defined the taxpayers as their customers—never mind that they are captive ones—they are trying to make their processes customer and service oriented. A belief that making it easier to pay the right amount of tax will increase tax compliance and tax revenues underlies this effort. Since revenue departments have an "income" line—the amount of tax collected—as well as a cost line, it is possible to compute their "profit" and the financial improvements wrought by reengineering.

Another challenge of mission-driven reengineering is illustrated by the experience of the Jet Propulsion Laboratory (JPL), which is operated by the California Institute of Technology in Pasadena. The JPL designs and operates—develops and flies—unmanned planetary exploration spacecraft. Its decision to reengineer was prompted by pressure from NASA, its client organization, to operate faster, better, and at lower cost. As budgets shrank, NASA charged the JPL to increase the number of its missions without increasing overall expenditures. (Here, "mission" has a specific meaning: a spacecraft flight.) In other words, the cost per JPL mission—which could exceed a billion dollars—had to be significantly reduced. To accomplish this, JPL realized that a redesign of its entire operation would be necessary: no mean task, considering its past.

Throughout its history, the JPL's primary focus has been on spacecraft design. In its early days, merely designing any spacecraft at all was a major challenge. Later, when destinations moved from the moon to the inner planets of Mercury and Venus, long-term reliability became a key concern, since flights could last for months rather than days. When the goal shifted to exploration of the outer planets, flight duration began to be measured in years, which in turn made diagnostics a central design issue. Since messages to and from a craft took hours, controllers might not learn of a failure until it was too late to take corrective action. Onboard intelligence for detecting failure and switching to back-up systems became essential.

This emphasis on spacecraft design often obscured the rest of JPL's activities. In particular, spacecraft design has enormous implications for operations, the process by which a spacecraft is managed from launch to mission completion. Operations is a massive undertaking. Hundreds of scientists and technicians are usually needed to manage the complex task of tracking and navigating a craft through space: to analyze and correct the trajectory, orient the craft in space, decide when and for how long to fire the engines, aim the cameras, decide how many photos to take of each astronomical phenomenon. Every decision about spacecraft design has a major impact on operations design. For example, the spacecraft designers may decide to use a radically new antenna system with relay capability to a satellite. But the wonderful new technology could require a substantial increase in the size of the operations staff, an unexpected cost not covered by the mission's budget.

JPL's old processes were responsible for such disconnects. The designs—first of the overall mission, then of the spacecraft, finally of the operations—were developed almost as if they had nothing to do with one another. It was only at the end that costly consequences of the spacecraft design for operations were discovered. By then, it was usually too late to make significant changes, since the specs had been frozen and construction was already under way. (In essence, the JPL was experiencing an analog of the "design for manufacturability" issue that has confronted industries from electronics to automobiles.) As a result, operations costs kept rising—from under 10 percent to over 40 percent of total mission cost—as the spacecraft became more sophisticated.

JPL's senior management had to resolve a basic question at the beginning of their reengineering effort: "What business are we in? What's our real purpose?" Their answer was a revelation. The JPL had generally acted as if its mission were to build spacecraft. Now leadership recognized that its real mission was to visit planets, take photographs, and collect data to send back home. They were no longer in the spaceship business. Their mission, so to speak, was missions.

JPL's reengineering has caused its three major processes—mission design, spacecraft design, operations design—to be conducted concurrently rather than sequentially. Previously, its work could be seen as a string of twenty-five to thirty functional activities divided into those three processes. Now the three processes effectively operate as one, with all work being performed by seven thematic groups—such as avionics, telecommunications, and experiments—that address their given theme across the entire spectrum of mission, spacecraft, and operations design. The seven groups, all housed at a new facility called the Project Design Center (PDC) specially constructed to facilitate teamwork, are integrated by a coordinating mission team.

In many respects, JPL's redesign is similar to a process structure increasingly being used by corporations for product development. But JPL had to cope with a factor far more common in mission-driven organizations than in commercial ones: resistance based on idealism. Self-interest is the root cause of most resistance to reengineering. Mission-driven organizations, however, are full of people with principled commitments to causes that may be threatened, or seem threatened, by reengineering. When government agencies try to streamline their work, for example, they often run into a hail of criticism prompted by the government's commitment to maintaining the fairest and most open processes—which, as in the case of procurement, are rarely the most cost-effective. Hospitals conducting reengineering often encounter the wrath of those who fear it will compromise the quality of care. This conflict can grip profit-oriented companies too. At Hallmark, some 700 artists, designers, poets, and letterers fashion thousands of greeting cards every year. This creative community's name for their more business-oriented brethren reveals dissonance beneath the banter: They call them "suits." At newspapers, there is constant tension between those who run the business side of things—chiefly the advertising and circulation departments—and the "tweeds" working in the editorial departments. But the conflict is far more prevalent and intense in the mission-driven world.

At JPL, the ideals were science, knowledge, and design elegance, against which financial considerations could seem petty. Many designers, scientists, and engineers come to JPL determined to expand the boundaries of science in general and of their discipline in particular. In the past, they'd been encouraged to seek the most elegant solutions to space flight problems; their dream was to design the most innovative spacecraft, to go beyond all previously known limits of knowledge to create a perfect fusion of form and function. They had visions, and they'd be damned if they'd let them be dimmed by paper pushers.

The "paper pushers," however, were responsible for staying within budget and knew that the cost of building and maintaining overengineered spacecraft pushed JPL far beyond *its* financial limits. In a sense, this was a conflict—as is so often the case in mission-driven organizations—between dream and reality; between following the star of science, art, or scripture and submitting to budgetary seat belts. Pulled on the one hand by engineers who want to build the best craft and mission designers who want to learn the most from the flights, and on the other by managers who want to fly the largest number of missions, JPL has been forced to rethink its purpose and how it achieves it.

So far, the results at JPL are promising. The first team is up and running a prototype for the Pluto Fast Flyby Mission, and the demand from other planned missions for space at the new PDC is much greater than can be currently accommodated. Reengineering may not be rocket science, but it can apparently be applied to rocket science.

Businesses, too, can be mission-driven. Some companies have goals and transcendent values that override financial concerns; these goals and values often become the primary foci of their reengineering efforts. This was the case at a major electric power utility, which we shall call EPU. EPU operates a number of power plants, one of which had suffered serious safety problems. After one troubling incident, safety became an overarching concern at EPU. The company motto is now "Safety above everything."

In the aftermath of the incident, EPU instituted exhaustive documentation and safety procedures. The company wrote excruciatingly meticulous descriptions of all routine maintenance activities, spelled out in such detail that almost anyone could walk in off the street and tackle the work. Its procedures and guidelines read like satires of themselves, almost like the following: First pick up a pencil. Examine the pencil to determine if it is new. If it is indeed a new pencil, then sharpen it. For best results, the sharpener should be 5.98 inches from the edge of the table or desk onto which it is secured—or 46.723 inches from sea level if it is attached to a wall. If the sharpener fails to meet these safety standards, please consult page 1056 of Manual A, Vol. 4, paragraph 3 for appropriate modifications. Moreover, in the company's zeal to achieve absolute safety, each piece of equipment, each activity, was checked and monitored by a large number of people from several functional departments.

Mae West once said, "Too much of a good thing is wonderful," but she did not have safety procedures in mind. EPU's intense procedures were unable to achieve its expectations for safety performance. The reasons, unsurprisingly, sprang from the complexity and fragmentation of the maintenance processes. On the one hand, the job descriptions for plant personnel and the guidelines for equipment procedures were so overdocumented that they were well-nigh unintelligible and unusable. On the other, the proliferation of safety responsibility across so many different people meant that, in effect, no one was really in charge and accountable.

EPU's reengineering solution broke the long-standing assumption that workers were unintelligent and had to be programmed by documentation. Now all employees are assumed to be intelligent and capable individuals—an expectation that is reinforced by careful recruiting, extensive training, and rigorous testing. The documentation has been rewritten in a streamlined way that focuses attention on crucial operations and the truly critical steps that must be taken in case of emergency. Energy is now channeled to the important work; the amount of time spent on low-value activities has been dramatically reduced. Accountabilities have been simplified and clarified; instead of having to get ten to fifteen signatures for a routine activity, one often suffices. The reported safety errors have declined by more than 50 percent.

On its way to ultimate success, EPU experienced a special difficulty often present in mission-driven reengineering projects. Those who object to such projects frequently cite the mission's inviolable nature in an attempt to derail efforts that are in fact dedicated to enhancing it. EPU encountered this challenge from the Safety Review Board (SRB).

The SRB was a high-level oversight committee composed of a mixture of industry consultants, government regulators, and plant managers. The committee was very powerful, had a broad mandate, and reported directly to EPU's executive committee. Its job was to evaluate plant safety and to recommend actions to improve it.

When the new process design was presented to them, the SRB refused to support it and demanded several months of additional analysis before they would consider the matter again. The strong rebuff was led by a senior member who had been instrumental in designing the old process many years earlier. His protest that the design was too complex to be safe was surely disingenuous, since it was demonstrably far *less* complex than the process it would replace. But waving the safety flag allowed him to stall the project. Merely by raising the issue, the objector was able to marshal the support of the SRB, which demanded a management review.

At that management review before the executive committee, the design team was compelled to present a line-by-line justification of all their proposed changes. Even though the CEO was the reengineering leader and many senior executives were reengineering advocates and sponsors, this further review consumed three months. The end result was total validation for the design team, but the victory cost much time, effort, and money.

Reengineering Mission-Driven Organizations

Carefully identify and understand customers
Clearly specify performance measures
Be sensitive to the concerns of idealists in the organization
Deflect those who use the mission as a smokescreen for resistance

---

In summary, noncommercial entities that opt to reengineer face some special challenges. They include identifying the mission and the customers, finding ways to measure performance, and coping with resisters who, from idealism or cynicism, ground their opposition in the "higher" purpose of the mission-driven organization. But the principles and techniques are otherwise the same, the ingredients for success identical, and the benefits equally compelling. Reengineering works wherever work is done.

CHAPTER 17

Six Crises

"The course of true love never did run smooth," wrote Shakespeare in *A Midsummer Night's Dream*. The same can be said of reengineering. No matter how skilled the practitioners, how extensive the preparation, how diligent the execution, the fact of the matter is—strange things happen.

Given the raw complexity of reengineering and the sheer magnitude of the change it generates, it is impossible to anticipate everything that can go wrong. Crises are by their nature unexpected; improvisational skill, in addition to disciplined planning, is needed to save the day. Reengineering is more like jazz, with its constantly shifting melodies, than classical music, where the entire score is played exactly as written. The best definition of improvisation we've heard is that it is "the art of getting yourself out of a situation you got yourself into." And so too with reengineering: It's how you cope with surprises that counts.

DILBERT reprinted by permission of UFS, INC.

So with apologies to the late President Richard Nixon (who wrote a book of the same name), we present Six Crises. The stories are true, but the identities of these companies have been disguised to protect the innocent, the guilty, and the occasionally wicked. This chapter does not present an exhaustive list of possible crises; you are likely to run into some of them, but there'll be many others as well. Expect the unexpected. So you need to listen to the music of this chapter, not just the words.

1. The Crisis of Sudden Scale

The reengineering czar at a large insurance company was facing a wonderful but nonetheless very difficult problem. He had just gotten the go-ahead from his senior sponsors, including the CEO, for the next phase of reengineering—implementation of two new process designs. That was the good news. The bad news was that this meant he needed seventy-five more people. He also had to acquire a resource even harder to come by: space—in this case, ten conference rooms and seventy-five cubicles. And he had to do it fast.

Two process redesign teams—claims processing and customer service—had been hard at work for the past three months with the goal of achieving exactly this green light. They had compressed the design phase to the bare minimum so that they could begin the "real work" of implementation as soon as possible. This meant that they had spent just one month mapping and diagnosing the existing processes, one month developing breakthrough ideas, and one month fashioning a project plan.

It was while creating the project plan (also called the road map) that the teams began to realize just how many people they would need. They had identified $75 million in expected annual savings from staff reduction and the consolidation of field service locations; in other words, $6.25 million per *month*. Not surprisingly, the CEO wanted these benefits fast. He had insisted that the teams develop an implementation plan that would deliver these benefits in less than two years.

As the teams wrestled with creating the road map, they realized that the only way to achieve this rapid pace of implementation was to break their design solutions into a set of small projects so that many of the pieces could be worked on at the same time. Moreover, smaller projects are easier to execute. Therefore, the team's road map targeted ten implementation teams to begin work immediately: two to develop fully detailed versions of the new high-level process designs; three to identify and implement "quick hits," meaning ad hoc projects that would generate payback almost immediately; two to begin building the information system infrastructure the new processes would require; one to work through the human resource implications of the new processes; one to begin identifying pilot sites for initial implementations; and one (the "core team") to coordinate all these activities. In addition, the design teams had identified the basic composition of each of these implementation teams in terms of skills and roles, even specifying certain individuals to fulfill them. Beyond these ten, more teams would be needed three months later. The czar's urgent need was to staff the first ten teams.

The czar quickly realized that he actually had a number of interrelated problems. First, he had to get his sponsors to ensure these teams would be staffed with the organization's very best people—which would be a true test of the sponsors' commitment. Second, he had to address the mechanics and paperwork of such a large-scale personnel transfer. Third, he had to work with the facilities staff to get the needed space. And finally, he had to do this all very quickly because until these logistics were finished, no real reengineering work could be done, threatening the momentum that had been so diligently achieved.

The czar was facing a moment of truth—he was about to

find out if the company was truly serious about reengineering. It had been easy to staff the two initial design teams, but that wouldn't be the case now. The company was already stretched to the limit from earlier downsizings, and taking so many people out of daily operations would cause real pain and possibly even jeopardize current operations. The czar knew that thus far it had been easy for his senior managers to support reengineering. Their words were "politically correct" and cost them nothing. But from now on support would mean sacrifice, and he wondered if they would rise to the challenge.

In earlier chapters we have discussed the critical importance of reengineering leadership. This company had reached the crunch point at which leadership earns its wings—or crashes to earth. When reengineering transcends words and paper to become a reality, leadership must act forcefully. Fortunately for this czar—and for his company—the leadership came through.

The following week, the czar, the two process owners, and their design team leaders met with the CEO and four other key sponsors, including the vice presidents of information systems and human resources. Over the course of an intense two-day meeting, they crafted a detailed staffing and transition plan. Working team by team, they identified specific people for each position and fallbacks if they couldn't get their first choices. They decided who would call each candidate's boss (in some cases, the candidate's boss's boss). They refined the sales pitch they would use to persuade managers to relinquish their best performers. Finally, they committed to an organization-wide communication effort that would provide a context for their reengineering and staffing initiatives.

One area that would need special attention was the MIS organization. The MIS vice president was concerned because she realized that reengineering would take nearly 40 percent of her total resources and almost all of her best people. She demanded that the CEO support her when she had to inform various functional executives that reengineering was going to cause a delay in their projects. He agreed.

At the end of the meeting, the VP of human resources committed to assigning one of his direct reports to the czar for a two-month period to assist in processing the transition of the new team members. Pragmatic details like relocation budgets, compensation adjustments, supplemental bonuses, and tactical strategies for new backfill hiring had to be addressed. In effect, the czar would soon have his own mini-HR organization.

It's good to be smart, but it's better to be lucky, and the czar got lucky with space planning. The facilities group identified a recently vacated office building five miles from headquarters that could be modified to suit the reengineering team's needs. The price was right too. This was a very fortuitous turn of events, since, as the manager of facilities put it, "There are no internal options. We have no spare conference rooms: in fact all of our current meeting rooms are overbooked already."

But there was one fly in this ointment—the new facility would not be available for three months. Since there were no feasible alternatives, reengineering in effect ground to a near halt for ninety days. Its momentum was dissipated—there was no news, no work, no benefits. They were able to revive the effort later, but only after much frenzy and anxiety. If for the want of a nail, a kingdom was lost, then for the want of some conference rooms, reengineering was almost lost. Afterwards the czar realized that he had learned a valuable lesson. He should have anticipated his staffing and facilities problems before they became acute, beginning to work on them even before they were fully defined. Never again would he try to manage reengineering in the traditional way by planning the first step then the next and the next. Henceforth, he would

work "from right to left"—he would start at the end, anticipate what would eventually be needed, and work backwards
to the present. Not only was the company being reengineered,
so was his mentality.

2. The Crisis of Transition

How do you quickly and effectively train and orient 120
new reengineers? This was the dilemma faced by the reengineering leadership at a large West Coast high-tech firm as it
prepared to begin implementation. For four months, three
design teams—order fulfillment, procurement, and customer
acquisition—had developed new process concepts. Their recommendations had been accepted; implementation teams
had been staffed and were now ready to begin. But they
faced two problems. First, none of these newcomers knew
much about reengineering in general or the new process
redesigns in particular. Second, they would have to work
together, as teams. This company did not have a successful
track record with teamwork; its style was one of heroic solo
efforts.

The solution that was devised centered on a three-day off-
site meeting to be attended by the 120 new reengineers and
the 15 veterans of the redesign efforts. This program had
three primary goals: to teach everyone the basic methodology and techniques of reengineering implementation; to
share the redesign solutions with the new arrivals; and to
begin the process of turning this collection of individuals
into cohesive teams.

Of the three, this last objective was seen as the most difficult. The company had a long history of encouraging internal competition. Cross-functional cooperation was viewed
as collaborating with the enemy. The culture was one of "up
or out," as those who couldn't master the cutthroat politics
swiftly found other, safer employment. Not surprisingly,

positive team experiences were rare in this atmosphere.

Nonetheless, reengineering success was going to require high levels of teamwork. The large volume of work could only be accomplished if the teams minimized wasteful squabbling and allowed for simultaneous work by subteams. Most of all, each team needed to focus on a clear and common objective, a goal that would be understood and shared by all the members. Building such teams would take time and had to be started as soon as possible.

After two weeks of intensive preparation, the process owners and the design team leaders had crafted an agenda for the three-day off-site meeting that would satisfy all three of their primary objectives.

The first day would focus on the process redesigns themselves. Because there were so many interconnections and interdependencies, the czar had decided that everyone needed to understand all of the redesigns, not just the piece of the project on which they would be directly working. To that end, the members of each design team took ninety minutes to communicate their ideas and to describe how the future process would differ from the present one. In addition, information technology, human resource, and change management groups outlined the implications of the designs and their initial implementation plans.

Interspersed among these design presentations was the first round of team-building activities. Each of the twelve new teams was seated at a round table throughout the day; each table also had a designated facilitator/team builder. Since many of the team members had never even met each other before, the facilitators conducted a number of introductory games to break the ice. For example, each person shared four statements about himself or herself with the group—except that two of them were true and two were lies. Based on perception, intuition, and conversation, the rest of the group had to separate the truth from the lies.

Day one concluded with a stirring after-dinner presentation by the company's CEO. He spent an hour describing the competitive context that had led the company to launch reengineering, expressing his gratitude to all for their participation in such an important project, and communicating his enthusiasm for swift results.

The second day was devoted to understanding the road map and to initial training on the implementation methodology.

However, the highlight of the day, and probably of the entire meeting, was the evening's activity: the glider-building contest. A week later, when the planning group met to critique the off-site, they all agreed that this team-building exercise had surpassed their wildest expectations.

Picture this. It's 9:00 P.M. at the San Francisco hotel where the off-site was held. Nearly 120 people in twelve teams are clustered around tables in a crowded ballroom.

Electronics engineers, computer programmers, and marketing executives are all working feverishly—at building gliders. They are cutting balsa wood, testing flight patterns, stealing each other's good ideas, and drinking copious amounts of beer. Music from the movie *Top Gun* is blasting from a number of strategically placed loudspeakers. The environment is one of energy, excitement, and near chaos— just like reengineering itself.

Each team's assignment is to construct a glider for tomorrow morning's distance contest. The competition has two objectives: to help build teams and to encourage the teams to solve problems in innovative ways. Each team is given the same kit; the challenge lies in how they use it. The teams are permitted several test flights. Cheers fill the room whenever a group's creation flies successfully; sympathetic sighs greet the failures. The test flight session lasts well past midnight.

The next morning energy and excitement is still running

high. The variety of the entries (and of their airworthiness) is amazing, with sleek gliders followed by hollow, huge-winged crafts. What must have been the world's largest and heaviest Frisbee, thrown like a discus, narrowly misses beheading several people. Everybody is declared a winner, although the longest flight—over fifty yards—receives a special award.

In the afternoon, after the awards ceremony, the czar led an active discussion of the relationship between the glider exercise and reengineering. The assembly discussed what they had learned about working together, how it had felt to cooperate with "enemies," how building a working glider had seemed like an impossible challenge, how they had to use the unique skills of each team member, how frustrating it was to be given an unstructured assignment, and much, much more.

In retrospect, the czar and his staff felt that they had done a pretty fair job in realizing their objectives. The education on the process redesigns and methodology had helped set the context for reengineering. More important, the focus on team building, which at first had seemed so countercultural, had succeeded in laying the foundation for effective teamwork. Much more would be required to institutionalize this ethos, but a key step had been taken. A glider in the air had proven good medicine for a company accustomed to using a knife in the back.

3. The Crisis of Tangibility and Testing

After six weeks the implementation team leader was still unsure of two vital questions. Would the new process design really work? And if it did, would the field accept it? A lot was riding on the answers at this snack food company. Strong pressure from its top customers had stimulated the reengineering of its customer management (sales and service) process. In the past, the company had organized its sales force by product group, such as adult cookies, children's cookies, and crackers. As a result, a retailer might be visited by three or four sales reps during the same week, none of whom knew what had transpired with the others. In addition, the company's field service organization, which supported the sales force with cooperative advertising, merchandising, and promotion expertise, was a fragmented set of functional units, with no strong links to any particular account or salesperson.

The new process design featured an Integrated Sales and Service (ISS) team, in which sales reps had as partners a dedicated field support team drawn from merchandising, advertising, and promotion. Each ISS team would focus on a particular geographical market and handle all of the company's products for the retailers in that market. This would simplify life tremendously for the retailers by giving them a fixed set of people with whom they could develop a long-term relationship.

After receiving the design team's specifics, the implementation team spent six weeks busily fleshing out the details not included in the initial design. Concurrently, the team developed the specifications for the new pricing software that the ISS teams would need, and created the materials for training the first pilot group. The pilot project was scheduled to begin in three months, but the implementation team was still uncertain about the viability of the new process. The design looked great on paper, but the team knew that the real world always posed unforeseen complications—like personal vacation schedules; exceptions—like important retailers who insist on doing things their way; and human errors—like mistyped prices; none of which can be completely anticipated. Moreover, it is almost impossible to get meaningful reactions to an abstract design described on paper. The only way to decide if the process would really work was to make it tangible. The team decided to battle-test their solution by staging a major simulation of the new process in action. They would develop a realistic role-play of the new process in order to test the critical interactions among customers, the ISS team, and other parts of the company. To assess the field's acceptance, they would stage this drama in front of an "audience" of field personnel.

This was a critical juncture for the team. The next major steps were developing the information systems and getting the pilot site up to speed. If there were problems with the process design, the team needed to discover them *now* to avoid both systems rework and creating a bad rap on the design among those who would be expected to adopt it.

To stage the simulation, they partitioned a large conference room. One corner would represent the retail store manager's office, another the local sales office. A small filing cabinet became the warehouse and a table the factory. A spot near the wall was designated as the salesperson's home, from which the day's sales activities would be entered into the computer. To ensure the rigor of the role-play, the sales veterans on the team created a set of guidelines; these identified the sequence of events to be simulated and the topics to be raised in the interactions. Finally, the team selected the audience for the simulation. They needed a good cross-section of the field, with special emphasis on geographic representation. This way, if the simulation went well, the audience could be converted into a companywide wave of advocates. The team also felt it would be wise to have one or two "doubters" in the room, folks who had been loudly critical of the proposed design. The simulation represented a chance to convert these skeptics or, failing that, to neutralize them. At the very least, potential resisters would have accurate information about the new process so that they would understand what they were opposing rather than flailing at phantasms of their own imaginations. In addition to getting reactions, the team was also anxious to hear ideas for improvements. The test would not only supply that feedback but also inculcate the audience with a sense of ownership.

All told, twelve field reps were invited to the test. It was critical to set the right expectations. The audience was told that what they would see was *not* a completed system but a work in progress. The simulation began with a salesperson in a customer's office and ran through a typical interaction, including a review of prior sales, upcoming promotions, and new product introductions. The team needed to see whether the ISS sales rep could successfully cover the increased breadth of products, how long this new kind of meeting would last (store managers often have little time for sales reps), and whether the salesperson's handheld computer could cope with the speed and data requirements of the new sales call.

The role-play also included a salesperson calling the local sales office for permission to allow the retailer to apply one product's discount to another. Since there would be fewer levels of sales management in the new redesign, the team needed to see how, and if, this would work. Would the salesperson be able to find the boss? How many of these calls could one local manager handle?

The team also modeled a sales rep meeting with his extended ISS team to evaluate how they could cooperate and to determine if the compensation changes (team-based pay derived from account profitability) would lessen traditional cross-functional animosity. Other aspects of the simulation covered requests to the warehouse to meet a customer's unique delivery requirements and to the plant to commit production time for a high-selling item. The final portion of the role-play took place at the sales rep's "house" and tested his ability to "upload" data from his handheld computer to the company's computer by telephone. It was necessary to see whether the computer could withstand the vicissitudes of the rep's family. The communications test went well, but the computer did fail the dreaded peanut-butter-in-the-disk-drive test as conducted by the salesperson's two-year-old daughter.

Throughout the simulation the audience actively partici-pated by asking questions and providing feedback about what really happens in the field. Until now, all that they had really known about reengineering was what they had heard in management presentations or through the grapevine, or had read in the company magazine. Much to their surprise, many of them liked the new approach. They could see how it eliminated many of the complexities from which they and their customers had suffered. They also liked the new pay system and the new focus on geographical accounts. One pleasant by-product perceived by the audience was that most ISS members would have to travel less than before and could do work at home that previously needed to be completed at the local sales office; everyone appreciated the opportunity for more time with the family. While the audience did raise many tough questions and challenged the assumptions of the team at every turn, the meeting was not adversarial. In fact, as the day went on, the mood of the group became increas-ingly cordial and cooperative. Each time a field rep's sugges-tion was noted and accepted, their personal investment in, and sponsorship of, the design increased. The day ended when the team loaded up their guests with ISS sweatshirts for themselves and buttons and coffee mugs for their col-leagues.

In their debrief the next day, the team realized that they had succeeded beyond their expectations. Not only was their design stronger for having been tested, but it now possessed a new legion of advocates. The experience they had gained in modeling the field would prove to be invaluable in ensur-ing that the pilot project succeeded. In retrospect, they felt that they had made one mistake: They should have warned the field reps that the dress code for the event was adamantly casual. The reps had turned up in suits. As for the reengineering team—well, they had at least worn shoes.

4. The Crisis of Integration

At a large industrial products company, the czar and his reengineering staff were facing a significant, unexpected problem. They had started down the reengineering road six months earlier with a focus on improving the complex set of interfaces the company maintained with its customers. With over 100,000 products in two major product groups, multiple distribution channels, and a large number of people communicating, supporting, and contacting their customers, their field operations were frankly a mess. To rectify this, the company launched two major process reengineering initiatives. The first, and the more important, was targeted at integrating all their disparate customer service processes. The second, which was begun four months later, focused on sales support. Each effort was conducted by an interrelated set of design and implementation teams.

The problem confronting them was that of internal inconsistency. Unbeknownst to each other, the two reengineering teams had each redesigned the same job, that of the field engineer, and each had done it differently. One team had enhanced the field engineer's required technical skills and increased the scope of the position's responsibility. The other had done the opposite by placing more emphasis on a centralized sales support unit. Members of the two teams had gone out for a beer after playing tennis one evening, and in the midst of discussing their designs had become aware of these inconsistencies.

Two days later the problem was brought to the attention of the czar and his staff. At a meeting attended by both teams, the issue was hashed out and quickly resolved, but a larger and more alarming question was now on the table: How many other such inconsistencies might be lurking in their many reengineering activities? Until then, the czar and his staff had been furiously involved in implementation planning, business case presentations, and communication activities. But they had neglected the larger perspective. No one could really say how many other potential problems might be brewing.

Galvanized by the situation, the czar's staff set out to identify every potential inconsistency, overlap, or gap between the two processes. They quickly discovered over fifty possible integration problems. For example, they found that the teams were designing totally incompatible information systems, both to be used by the same people. One of the systems would require so much of a PC's memory that the other system would be unable to operate. Each of these programs would have a dramatically different user interface, one based on pull-down menus, the other using standard commands.

Similarly, the two teams had hired two different training vendors when they could just as easily have hired a single vendor at a lower cost. They had also made radically different assumptions about the required degree of job empowerment. Once the czar became aware of these discords, the source was obvious: The two reengineering teams and their many subteams weren't talking with each other.

Each of the teams had been chartered with a clear, self-contained objective, such as "produce a radical redesign within four months" and "be prepared to pilot by mid-September." Operating under tight deadlines and constant pressure, the teams had kept to themselves, narrowly focused. It was not that they were oblivious to larger issues; it was simply that they didn't have time for any more meetings. This lack of communication was exacerbated by the fact that the teams were often located in different buildings, some even in different cities. There was no formal mechanism in place to facilitate information sharing.

The czar's staff had two different problems. First, to resolve the fifty or more integration issues; second, in order to prevent future inconsistencies, to develop a mechanism by which the teams could communicate and resolve issues quickly.

To solve the first problem, the czar initiated a frenzy of emergency meetings. The initial round focused on the human aspects of reengineering. Each facet of the business system was addressed in turn: job design, career paths, reward and compensation, personal autonomy, and so forth. In each case, the impacts of the two reengineering efforts on all affected constituencies were brought to the surface and reexamined. Any conflicts were resolved by the two teams with the czar's "facilitation" (which sometimes entailed forceful intervention). The second round addressed information systems, the third timetables, and the fourth change management. These meetings were held over a two-week period, by the end of which most of the short-term problems had been resolved.

To prevent a recurrence of such problems, the czar also instituted a variety of mechanisms to force the teams to communicate and resolve issues in a disciplined manner. The most important new tool was the daily issue log—essentially, an electronic mail system with a standardized message format. At 4:00 P.M. every day, each team, regardless of what else they were doing, would perform two tasks. First, they had to enter into the log any issues resolved or decisions made that day, as well as any newly identified questions. Second, they had to respond to any questions submitted by other teams. Some teams initially resisted this new mode of operation, calling it time-wasting overhead; however, they were soon "convinced of the error of their ways," as the czar put it.

The czar also instituted on-line archives of each team's deliverables, so that these materials were accessible to all the other teams. Groupware conferences were arranged. Teams were required to file weekly summaries on the status of their projects, to be distributed to everyone, so that schedules could be synchronized.

The czar's intervention did slow the reengineering effort for a while, but it served the cause of speed in the end. Less rework would be necessary during implementation and roll-out of the new processes. By dramatically confronting the problem, the czar significantly reduced the number of integration snafus that could have damaged, if not destroyed, the reengineering program.

5. The Crisis of Loss

As the CFO of a large pharmaceutical company listened to the report from the pilot-planning team, she experienced a variety of emotions. On the one hand, she was delighted to hear that the technical issues surrounding the reengineering of their financial closing process had been resolved. On the other, she realized that this consolidation of field finance operations would inevitably lead to a significant loss of jobs.

In a sense this was unavoidable. The closing process had employed over 450 people in their twenty-five districts, four divisions, and at headquarters. Early on, the finance reengineering team had diagnosed the process as inefficient, even unnecessary. If the company could separate its statutory close—required by the government once a quarter—from its monthly close, and do all its financial consolidation at headquarters, it could consolidate many of its field offices and still satisfy both the regulators and internal reporting requirements.

The CFO realized it was time to move from speculation to

planning. Her concerns were both human, since she knew many of the field employees personally, and technical—how to manage this difficult transition in the most humane and effective way possible.

Because of reengineering's high visibility, she knew that before long everyone would learn of the new design and its implications. What exactly could she do to avoid hysteria among the rank and file? Soon, she and the CEO would have to issue a formal companywide announcement of the plan. There was no way this could be kept a secret; the grapevine would have the whole story before long.

She decided on a three-pronged attack. First, she needed to inform the entire finance organization about the redesign, the timetable, and the rationale behind it. Toward that end, she designed a tightly choreographed set of "cascaded" communications. With the help of the reengineering team, she wrote and delivered a speech to the company's senior finance managers at their quarterly meeting. She also provided her audience with materials they could present to their own staffs upon returning home, including a version of her presentation, a guide to delivering it, and answers to the questions most likely to be asked. The senior finance managers would then train their direct reports in how to deliver the news one level down the hierarchy. This way, everyone in finance would hear about the plan rapidly and, very important, from someone they knew.

The second prong consisted of a set of staffing contingencies. Possibly her most significant decision was that the planned layoffs would not begin until one year from the day the memo was issued. That would allow everyone plenty of time to make personal plans. She asked all the senior finance managers to identify their high performers, those whom they most wanted to retain. She then developed a schedule for personally contacting these "keepers" and informally letting them know that they would have a job, no matter what, and not to panic. She also contacted several temporary agencies that specialized in financial work in case people resigned suddenly.

Third, she and the CEO developed a traditional "blue memo," the companywide communication that informed all employees of important events. She wanted to time this letter so that it would arrive as soon as possible after the first two activities had been completed.

When the blue memo was distributed, almost everyone in the field reacted calmly to it. Although people naturally gathered around the water cooler to discuss the changes, there was none of the panic and rage that characterize firings and downsizings in other companies. Why not? Because this news was actually not news at all. Most of the key personnel knew exactly what was going to happen; they were only waiting for the official announcement.

The CFO had made a vital decision: She would tell no lies, nor even any falsely reassuring half-truths. She simply explained the situation as it was: The company's finance organization was bogged down in an overly expensive and complicated process; the money consumed by that process had to be deployed to support more value-adding activities. This honesty paid off. Although the situation was painful and difficult for many people, the open and truthful communications built an atmosphere of trust throughout the company.

People learned that the company was starting to tell the truth and that it cared about their future. In a sense, this experience marked the beginning of a new contract between employees and management; in the past, the truth, especially bitter truth, had rarely been shared in an open and timely fashion. Now those who were to lose their jobs were offered very fair terms and were able to leave the company without anger and resentment. They understood that in the new operation there simply could not be a place for everyone.

The CFO had succeeded triply—not only had she solved both the "hard" and the human dimensions of the problem, she had endowed the company with a legacy of trust that would, if not squandered, pay dividends for a long time to come.

6. The Crisis of Triage

The bank had run into business trouble, and its year-old reengineering program was experiencing some of the fallout. Over time, this money-center bank had become less of a lender and more of a trader. For several years, this strategy had sent profits soaring; but those who live by the sword die by it as well. A combination of a sudden change in interest rates and bad choices by a (now departed) star trader had cost the bank a lot of money. Everyone would have to tighten their belts, including the reengineering teams. The fact that reengineering managed to retain any funding at all was a testament to its successful track record. All three active pilots had met their target performance measures, and the prognosis for rollout was positive. But there was simply not enough cash to see all projects through to completion.

One week after being informed of a major reduction in funding, the czar convened a two-day meeting with her staff and the leaders of the three reengineering teams. The objective was to determine how to eliminate at least a third of their planned activities while still achieving the majority of their projected benefits. Also participating in the meeting were representatives of the finance organization, who had been working with the team leaders to develop financial projections.

Those attending the meeting quickly explored a variety of ad hoc cost-cutting solutions, such as combining rollouts, reducing the use of consultants, and employing less expensive technologies. However, these did not produce enough savings; radical surgery was needed. At the start of the meeting, the czar ranked the fifteen projects by their business value on a white board. She then drew a red line across the list, with nine projects above it and six below. She explained that they were dealing with a fixed sum of money and some things would have to be cut. The red line represented the starting point for a collective deliberation.

Needless to say, everyone in the room felt that "their" project was the most important one. So the czar began by reviewing the methodology that had been used to develop the projected benefits, explaining how each case had been adjusted for risk, how possible exaggeration had been discounted, and how all projects had been considered in an evenhanded way. The group then launched into an active discussion, which went well beyond financial considerations; the participants were encouraged to look at each project's strategic and customer impact, as well as its relationship with other projects and processes. Matrices were produced that correlated these independent variables. Over the course of the day, the red line moved all over the board. More than one person commented that this conference was just like many of the budget meetings they had attended over the years, except now the business under consideration was reengineering. Combinations were offered, compromises negotiated, and at the end of the day, many hard decisions were reached.

The czar was relentless in her push to get closure. She resisted emotional appeals, ignored spurious arguments about the sunk cost of work already begun, and forced the group to accept the fact that the cutback was irrevocable. She was determined not to let pity or history prevent the best combination of projects from surviving. Her rigor and discipline were remarkable. For the team leaders, this meeting was, in a strange way, their finest hour. The czar's style had rubbed off on them. Rather than persisting in fighting for their own projects, they focused their debates on what would be best for the program as a whole. They had realized that personal success and collective success were inextricably linked.

At the end of the dialogue, one entire process effort was shut down. Four teams that had been at work on postpilot design revisions, information systems development, training, and rollout planning would be disbanded. In addition, the rollouts for the remaining two processes would be consolidated. This solution maximized return while meeting the mandated expense reductions.

Everyone in the room agreed that they had made the best of a bad situation. Still, they felt devastated. So much hard work had apparently been in vain. How would they tell the teams that their projects would be terminated? Some of these team members had worked for an entire year, a long hard year, trying to bring their vision to reality. The news would break their hearts. Some of them had moved, or had forsaken promotions, in order to join the reengineering program. These people could not just be left hanging. In the final session of the meeting, the attendees began to discuss career paths for some of the soon-to-be ex-reengineers. The czar would spend much of the next month securing satisfactory placements for them, ensuring that they were reintegrated into the organization without having been disadvantaged by their reengineering assignment.

A communications plan was devised with meticulous care, specifying who would break the news to whom. All reengineering staff had to be informed within twenty-four hours, because after that the secret was sure to be out. The czar asked people for their ideas on what the memo should say. She wanted her message to reflect the spirit of their own meeting: shared and collective concern; a focus on the survival of the program as a whole rather than the disposition of the specific projects; the finding of strength and commonality in adversity. The group decided that the memo should be as positive as possible, stressing that although the reengineering program was being scaled back significantly, the business benefits were not being reduced proportionally (the drop was only from $175 million to $135 million). The memo would also praise the selflessness of the team members and assure them of the care and attention each would receive as they adjusted to the scaled-down effort and/or sought out new positions.

At the end of the two days, the participants left the meeting chastened but hopeful. They had learned firsthand a lesson, one usually confined to senior managers—that achieving the greater good is neither simple nor pleasant. As the Lovin' Spoonful put it, "It's not often easy, and not often kind. Did you ever have to make up your mind?"

Among other things, leaders get paid because of their minds and their ability to make them up quickly; to square off with problems that aren't easy and that demand decisions that are inescapably unkind. The qualities of mind and character that make a person a leader can only be tested in the crucible of crisis. But there's never any shortage of such testings in reengineering, which could be described as a series of self-generated and self-conquered crises.

What Next?

What comes after reengineering? This is a question we are often asked, and one that can have many meanings. Accordingly, we have many answers to it, depending on our assessment of what the questioner really has in mind.

Sometimes, especially if our questioner is a cynical journalist, the question really seeks to identify the next "hot" management concept or fad. In this case, our response is a quick dismissal. The implicit assumption—that reengineering is yet another flash in the pan whose day is dwindling—is one that we utterly reject. The reengineering revolution is, at the latest, only entering its adolescence; it has enormous growth and many years of vigor ahead of it. To be sure, there are some industries—insurance, telecommunications, automotive— where reengineering is firmly established and is being extensively implemented by virtually all major companies. But there are others—such as health care, banking, and retailing— where most companies are no further along than early feasibility studies and experimental pilots. Moreover, even the companies that helped to pioneer reengineering are discovering that the road is longer and slower than they had at first anticipated. While we have stressed repeatedly that the reengineering of an individual process must be done at breakneck speed, full implementation across all the processes of all the business units of a corporation can take many years. Most companies have neither the resources nor the tolerance for chaos needed to conduct the simultaneous reengineering of many processes. In addition, for a new project to begin, an old one must wind down. Thus, the entire reengineering journey can easily last five to seven years, or even longer. Reengineering is a marathon run at a sprinter's pace.

Outside the United States, reengineering is still in its childhood. In some cases, this simply reflects the time it takes for any concept to migrate from the land of its birth and to be adapted to the culture of another country. In others, however, it reflects the fact that some of the world's leading economic powers do not find reengineering entirely congenial. Managerial cultures that revere centralized control and meticulous planning have difficulty accommodating a devolution of responsibility to frontline workers and the idea of learning by making mistakes. Where gradual improvement is the reigning dogma and consensus the preferred decision-making style, the radicalism and top-down nature of reengineering may also be hard to swallow. However, even in such environments, reengineering is starting to take hold. It is an inexorable law of the global marketplace that when your competitors, wherever they are, reengineer, you have little choice but to follow. Being the best quickly becomes the benchmark, excellence the ticket of admission. In the world's newly emerging economies, of course, reengineering is still on the horizon.

In other words, to imply that reengineering is an idea with a very bright past would be like proclaiming the Industrial Revolution over after a few English pin factories had begun practicing the division of labor.

Sometimes people who ask us "What comes after reengineering?" are in fact inquiring about the next wave of the revolution. In response, we point out some new trends. Initially, reengineering was primarily used to reduce the costs of routine back-office processes (such as order fulfillment) in large corporations facing financial difficulties. Each of the conditions in that sentence is now in the process of being relaxed, thereby opening up new vistas for reengineering.

First, as we discussed in chapter 15, reengineering is by no means limited to large companies. As more and more reports of success filter through the small business community, we will witness a further democratization of what has thus far been primarily a big-company experience.

Second, reengineering is coming out of the back office and is being applied to both creative and selling processes. By the former, we mean processes that include a substantial amount of inventive and imaginative work, whether product invention, strategy formulation, or developing a marketing program. Some have argued that reengineering has nothing to say to such kind of work. They imply that trying to encompass creative work in a process framework puts a straitjacket on it. They are wrong, and their error flows from a misunderstanding of the nature of process. "Process" does not mean "routine." All work is describable in terms of a process: a set of tasks that achieve the desired result. In some cases, these tasks may be relatively straightforward (checking a customer's credit rating). In others, they may require great talent and imagination (creating a theme for a marketing campaign). Reengineering does not seek to routinize, automate, or constrain the performance of such tasks. It does not attempt to restrict the sometimes nebulous workings of the creative mind, whether they occur in scientists, marketers, or strategists. Reengineering is focused at the process level, at how a set of tasks is organized into a whole. Reengineering techniques can be applied as readily to the process of developing an advertising campaign as to the process of equipment maintenance. Similarly, some salespeople bridle at the notion that they perform processes. It does not diminish the importance of their personal charisma to insist they do in fact work in a process context, and that reengineering can leverage their abilities by revamping the process. Indeed, we saw an illustration of this at Engelhard Chemical in chapter 13.

Organizations are also starting to pay more attention to some of their enabling processes. Value-adding processes—those that directly create the value delivered to external customers—have been the subject of most of this book. Enabling processes, by contrast, have a more internal focus; their customers are within the organization. The links between the two processes are, however, direct and significant. Value-adding processes can achieve their highest potential only if the enabling processes perform at their maximum capability. For instance, the process of developing and deploying computer-based information systems supports virtually all the operating processes of an organization. Similarly, the process of employee recruitment and development creates no customer value; but no other process can operate without well-trained employees.

Many companies are now reengineering enabling processes because they realize their critical importance to the development and operation of new value-creating processes. In other cases, their enabling processes are so costly or poorly performing that they place a drag on the organization as a whole. (This was the case with Amoco's budgeting process in chapter 13.) Moreover, as reengineering becomes more widespread, world-class value-creating processes become a competitive requirement rather than a competitive advantage. In such an environment, enabling processes are left as the chief area for performance differentiation. A world-class customer service process can be given added oomph by improving the process for recruiting and developing superior people to perform it.

Third, reengineering is no longer the last refuge of the desperate. It is not surprising that in its early, relatively unproven days, only companies near the edge of disaster were bold enough to take the radical step of reengineering. After all, what did they have to lose? But now that reengineering is well established, and its practice substantially less hit-or-miss, even companies in good health are employing this tonic, sometimes as a preventative medicine and sometimes as a growth elixir.

Indeed, today many of the world's most prosperous and admired companies, whose recent histories have been hailed as models of success, have embarked on reengineering; their goal is to ensure that they continue to receive such rave reviews. This, too, is a trend that we expect will accelerate.

Fourth, reengineering is beginning to leave the domain of individual companies and is entering the world of entire industries. Many processes neither begin nor end at the doors of individual companies, but rather extend into customers, suppliers, and other external parties. For example, consider the order fulfillment process at a component supplier to a manufacturer. This process really begins in the customer's operations, where production schedules are set. The process extends back from there, through the component maker, and into its raw material suppliers, whose own production facilities and shipping capabilities must be in sync with both the manufacturer's and the component maker's. Treating this process as three processes rather than one inevitably introduces unnecessary interfaces and handoffs, resulting in duplication of effort, delay, and error.

More and more companies have begun to work with suppliers, customers, and others to reengineer total processes. In some cases, these processes are being tackled on a virtually industrywide basis. A striking example is the current effort to rethink the entire process by which consumer goods are delivered from manufacturers' plants to retailers' shelves, a process involving hundreds of manufacturers and thousands of retail stores, and dozens of trucking firms, wholesalers, and distributors in between. Reengineering will transform all these companies by transforming their entire industry. Similar efforts have been launched in areas ranging from the processing of insurance claims to the provision of medical care.

For all these reasons, asking what comes "after" reengineering is a little like asking what comes after the computer. At this point, it's a very premature question. The challenges and opportunities facing reengineering dwarf those that have been surmounted and achieved.

There is another, more benign way of interpreting the original question, one that focuses it on an individual company rather than on the reengineering revolution as a whole. Some people are actually asking, "What will we have to do after we have concluded our reengineering effort?" The answer to this is simple: What comes after reengineering is more reengineering.

Many companies mistakenly see reengineering as a once-in-a-lifetime activity, a unique response to a singular change in their operating environment. They hope that reengineering's successful implementation will take them to a new and permanently high plateau of performance. The very notion of a "permanently high plateau" should set off alarm bells. The phrase was first used by Professor Irving Fisher of Yale, who asserted that such a plateau had been reached for stock prices—in September 1929!

There are no plateaus anymore, only a mountain with no summit. Reengineering will not be one-time or short-term. While in a sense it did arise in response to a combination of intense competition, margin pressures, and customer demands, its underlying driving force can be summarized in one word: change. Compelling changes in technology, geopolitical realities, social values, and customer expectations created a new world arena of competition, in which the old modes of operation revealed themselves as grossly unsatisfactory.

The belief that reengineering can be done once and then be done with is predicated on the notion that change has run its course. But far from slowing down, the pace of change appears to be accelerating. Product life cycles are growing ever shorter. The rate of technological innovation is becoming even faster. Customer characteristics and expectations have less and less stability.

What was unimaginable yesterday has become routine today. Just witness the sudden evolution of the term "information highway" from neologism to cliché. Future shock is our permanent condition. A company can expect its reengineering to be permanent and durable only if it can also expect that its competition and its marketplace will remain constant, that next year will be much like this one. But of how many industries can that be prophesied with any confidence? Even companies that used to pride themselves on their twenty- to thirty-year planning horizons now define long-term planning in terms of Friday's luncheon menu. As the horizon draws in closer and our vision is more foreshortened, the unpredictable future starts tomorrow. Our motto for the age of change must be "Reengineering, now and forever."

As Niels Bohr, the Nobel prize–winning physicist, once observed, "Prediction is very difficult—especially about the future." The variables are so many, our uncertainties are so great, our predictive capacities so limited, that it would be foolhardy to pretend that we can design processes today with high confidence that they will last far into the future. Changes in geopolitical realities can unhinge the finest distribution process; sudden shifts in consumer preference may require a reinvention of customer service; new technologies may make obsolete formerly world-class production processes. In order to keep up with constant change, companies will be forced to abandon processes only recently redesigned. Reengineering must become a *core competence* of the twenty-first-century corporation, one of its defining strengths. In the long run, the hallmark of the truly successful organization will be its ongoing ability to abandon what had previously been successful and replace it with something completely different.

There is one final interpretation of the original question, "What comes after reengineering?" It is, "What is the aftermath of reengineering? What does reengineering lead us to?"

There are two answers to this question; the first is "an entirely new company." As we have stressed throughout this book, reengineering begins with process redesign but does not end there. The tenor and implications of new processes inevitably ripple into a company's every aspect: its structure, the nature of its jobs, the way work is measured and rewarded—even the bedrock of company culture is transformed.

It should hardly be surprising that a company that has been changed so dramatically and in so many ways will essentially be unrecognizable, and the ways in which it will need to be managed bear little resemblance to what is conventionally taught in business schools. One manages empowered professionals very differently from industrial-era workers; entirely new measurement systems, centered on processes rather than tasks, are called for; the concepts of strategy and planning take on new meanings. We are burning the old rule books of management, and new ones are waiting to be written.

Indeed, the consequences of reengineering will spread far beyond the boundaries of the corporation. And that leads us to the second historic aftermath of reengineering.

It would be naive to expect that something as profound as the transformation of human labor will be confined to the nine-to-five day. If we look back at the Industrial Revolution and the Industrial Age to which it gave rise, it is clear that much of life was reshaped by the new ways in which work was done. Cities were built around train stations, not cathedrals. New mentalities were created—from the very idea of progress to the notion of participatory democracy. A new world grew out of a revolution in the way man earned his bread. Perhaps it has always been thus. The Bible tells us that the penalty for disobedience in the Garden of Eden was that human beings had to earn their bread by the sweat of their brow. Ever since, human history can be described in terms of our efforts to sweat less in our laboring, to find ever better ways of doing our work. And this saga has not ended.

Just as the Industrial Revolution drew peasants into the urban factories and created the new social classes of workers and managers, so will the Reengineering Revolution profoundly rearrange the way people conceive of themselves, their work, their place in society.

It is already becoming possible to discern the outline of the world reengineering is leaving in its wake. It is a world in which people have careers rather than jobs, in which they grow rather than get promoted, in which income is based on results rather than position. It is a world of fulfilling, exciting work, but of work that can be stressful and all-consuming. It is a world of individual responsibility and autonomy, in which people have the opportunity to exhibit and profit from their individual talents, but also a world in which an individual's shortcomings and inadequacies are mercilessly exposed. This new world will not be a perfect one; it will possess many wonderful features but many others that give us pause. Like it or not, however, this new world will fast be upon us. We cannot hold it back any more than King Canute could hold back the tide. So our final answer to "What comes after reengineering?" is, "A new world."

This new world is not the product of our imagination nor of our desire, just as reengineering itself was not. Reengineering was happening before we happened across it and coined a term to describe it. Similarly, its consequences are about to appear, whether or not we have the right words to express them.

Just as it is difficult and painful for a company to go through reengineering, the transition from the world before reengineering to the world after it will not be simple or easy. Much that we take for granted will have to be abandoned; while our society and our economy as a whole, and many of us as individuals, will prosper and have better lives, some of us will not. Most will be winners, but not all. Yet we cannot imagine a more exciting time to live nor a more exciting change of which to be part. The Reengineering Revolution is a rare phenomenon in human events: a disjunction from the past. We are being given the opportunity to start again, to inscribe our visions on a clean sheet of paper, rather than merely to make some small modifications to what we have inherited from those who preceded us. We are being offered a unique privilege: to help create a new and better world, to shape the future for decades or even centuries to come. The future will not remember our age for our technological achievements or the political developments that so occupy our attention. Rather, the historians of tomorrow will point to some date in the late twentieth century and say that was when the work of the past gave way to its future. Ours will be remembered as the age of the Reengineering Revolution.

Index

Do you want to learn more about reengineering?

The Center for Reengineering Leadership, led by Dr. Michael Hammer, offers courses and publications that help individuals and organizations succeed at reengineering.

☐ **Yes, please send me information about the Center for Reengineering Leadership.**

_____
Name

_____
Title

_____
Organization Name

Organization Size: _____   _____
                   annual revenue   *number of employees*

_____
Telephone / Fax Numbers

_____
Street Address

_____
City, State, Zip Code, Country

To help us provide you with the right information, please tell us more about your needs:

What is your organization's stage of reengineering?

☐ learning and planning   ☐ in implementation

☐ just beginning   ☐ completed initial program

What is your role in reengineering?

☐ executive leader   ☐ team member

☐ coordinator (czar)   ☐ other (please specify)

In which of these areas are you facing your greatest challenges? (check all that apply)

☐ building executive understanding and sponsorship

☐ learning reengineering technique and methodology

☐ overcoming resistance to change

☐ engaging all parts of the company in the effort

☐ understanding the experiences of other companies

☐ developing process management and coaching skills in managers and supervisors

☐ other (please specify)

Center for Reengineering Leadership
One Cambridge Center
Cambridge, Massachusetts
02142

First Class
Postage
Here